Dedication

To **Pascal** , the star that pierces the darkness of misinformation, for his unwavering love and unwavering support in the quest for truth.

To my daughter **Léa** , bright light in this world of shadows, who inspires me every day to remain vigilant in the face of manipulation.

To my mother **Michelle** , the pillar of my resistance against lies, for her wisdom and strength which armed me to face deception.

And to **my friends** , the sentinels of my critical spirit, for their sincere friendship, their humor and their constant presence in this fight for the truth.

This book is for you, valuable allies in this era of misinformation.

Cédric Balcon-Hermand

To understand and fight disinformation

Table of Contents

Chapter 1: Introduction to the History of Disinformation

1.1 Origins: From Antiquity to the Renaissance

Disinformation, or the intentional manipulation of information for the purposes of deception or influence, is a practice deeply rooted in human history. Since the earliest civilizations, leaders have used disinformation to consolidate their power, justify controversial actions, and control people's perceptions. This phenomenon is not new, but it has evolved over time, following technological advances and socio political changes.

Antiquity: The First Strategies of Manipulation

The first traces of disinformation date back to ancient civilizations, where narratives were often manipulated to enhance the power of elites. In ancient Egypt, for example, pharaohs used monumental inscriptions to proclaim their military victories, even when these were exaggerated or even completely invented. These inscriptions, engraved in stone, were intended to withstand time, thus transforming these stories into indisputable truths for future generations. Temples and monuments were not only places of worship or commemoration, but also propaganda tools intended to consolidate the power of the pharaohs by constructing an image of grandeur and invincibility.

The pharaohs were also masters at manipulating their divine image. By presenting themselves as living gods or as the direct representatives of the gods on Earth, they reinforced their legitimacy and authority. Mythological stories, often carved on temple walls, told how the gods themselves chose and blessed the pharaoh to rule. These stories, although ostensibly religious, served a clear political purpose: to reinforce the idea that the pharaoh's power was of divine origin and, therefore, incontestable. This manipulation of divine information made it possible to justify the absolute power of the pharaohs, silencing any potential opposition by directly linking their authority to the will of the gods.

Likewise, civilizations in Mesopotamia, such as the Sumerians, Akkadians, and Babylonians, used disinformation to maintain control over their populations. Mesopotamian rulers manipulated historical accounts to legitimize their conquests and strengthen their authority. For example, the Code of Hammurabi, one of the oldest known legal texts, was not only a set of laws, but also a propaganda instrument that reinforced the image of Hammurabi as a just and divine king. In reality, the laws included in the Code were often biased in favor of elites and served to consolidate power.

Clay tablets, which were used to record business transactions, historical accounts, and legal texts, were often written in ways that favorably reflected the actions of rulers. Accounts of military victories and conquests were sometimes exaggerated or altered to downplay defeats and magnify successes. These manipulations of information aimed to strengthen the authority of kings and maintain social order by projecting an image of power and stability. This perceived stability was essential to justify the regimes in place and avoid revolts or insurrections.

Ancient Greece and Myths as Tools of Disinformation

In ancient Greece, misinformation often took the form of myths and legends, which were used to influence beliefs and behaviors. Mythological stories, such as those of the exploits of Heracles or the adventures of Odysseus, served to reinforce the values of courage, loyalty and piety, while masking the less glorious truths of Greek political and military life. These stories were also used to justify the actions of rulers and to legitimize wars, presenting them as heroic battles against evil forces or divine enemies.

The Roman Empire, on the other hand, perfected the art of disinformation through political and military propaganda. Roman emperors used monuments, coins, and public inscriptions to spread messages that glorified their achievements and downplayed their failures. For example, triumphal arches, erected to commemorate military victories, were often decorated with reliefs showing idealized battle scenes, where enemies were depicted as weak and barbaric, while Roman soldiers appeared as invincible heroes.

The poet Virgil also played a key role in spreading imperial propaganda through his epic work, the Aeneid. This poem, commissioned by the Emperor Augustus, tells the story of the Trojan hero Aeneas, who, according to legend, was the ancestor of the Romans. The Aeneid was used to legitimize the reign of Augustus by presenting him as the descendant of Aeneas and the restorer of the Roman Golden Age. This mythological tale served to reinforce the idea that Augustus' power was divinely ordained and that his reign brought peace and prosperity to Rome. This approach made it possible to solidify the power of Augustus by giving it historical and divine legitimacy, thus making any opposition practically impossible.

Additionally, the Roman Empire also used disinformation to control conquered populations and to maintain order in its vast territories. Information about revolts or resistance movements was often downplayed or completely removed from official records, creating an illusion of peace and stability. This manipulation of information allowed the empire to project an image of unshakable strength, thus deterring any attempt at rebellion.

The Middle Ages: The Manipulation of Information by the Church

The Middle Ages is a period when religion dominated social, political and cultural life. Religious institutions, particularly the Catholic Church, exercised immense control over minds and hearts, and used disinformation as a tool to maintain their power and influence the masses.

The Crusades, which took place between the 11th and 13th centuries, are an iconic example of how disinformation was used to mobilize populations for religious and political ends. Before the Crusades launched, popes and preachers spread terrifying tales of the suffering of Christians in the Holy Land and the atrocities allegedly committed by Muslims. These stories, often grossly exaggerated or entirely invented, served to galvanize European knights and legitimize military expeditions to the Middle East.

Pope Urban II, during his famous speech at the Council of Clermont in 1095, dramatized the dangers facing Christians in the East, urging lords and knights to take up arms to defend Christendom. This speech, widely relayed by preachers across Europe, was a major catalyst for the outbreak of the First Crusade. Graphic descriptions of the suffering of pilgrims and the desecration of holy sites were used to arouse outrage and to justify holy war against Muslims.

Papal bulls, official decrees issued by the pope, were also used to strengthen the authority of the Church and to justify controversial actions. Bulls proclaiming crusades were written in language that glorified the spiritual goals of these expeditions, while downplaying or justifying the more violent and rapacious aspects. These documents served to legitimize the Crusades and encourage the participation of nobles and knights, promising spiritual rewards such as remission of sins and assurance of eternal salvation. Furthermore, the Church controlled the production and dissemination of religious texts, ensuring that only messages conforming to orthodoxy reached the faithful. Sermons, works of art, and religious ceremonies were all used to instill the teachings of the Church into the masses and to strengthen the legitimacy of its leaders. This control of information allowed the Church to maintain its power by eliminating all intellectual or theological opposition.

Hagiographies, or biographies of saints, were another propaganda tool used by the Church. These stories, often embellished or largely fictional, presented the saints as models of virtue and faith, capable of miracles and extraordinary sacrifices. By disseminating these stories, the Church sought to strengthen the piety of the faithful and promote a way of life consistent with Christian teachings.

These stories also aimed to strengthen the spiritual authority of the Church by showing that its representatives, the saints, were in direct contact with the divine and possessed supernatural powers.

The Church also used disinformation to justify its persecutions, particularly against heretics. The Cathars and Waldensians, for example, were Christian groups who advocated beliefs different from those of the dominant Catholic Church. To eradicate them, the Church often spread misinformation about their practices, portraying them as dangerous heretics who threatened the Christian faith. These exaggerated accounts, which described ungodly rituals and immoral behavior, were used to justify brutal persecutions and crusades against these groups.

Another notable example is the Inquisition, an institution set up by the Church to combat heresy. The Inquisition used disinformation to create a climate of fear and suspicion, encouraging denunciations and accusations often based on rumors or false information. The Inquisition's trials, although presented as searches for the truth, were in reality tools to eliminate dissidents and strengthen the authority of the Church. Acts of faith, public ceremonies where heretics were condemned, were orchestrated to serve as a lesson and to dissuade any opposition to ecclesiastical authority.

The Renaissance: The Emergence of Printing and the Spread of Ideas

The invention of the printing press by Johannes Gutenberg in the mid-15th century marked a turning point in the history of disinformation. Before the printing press, books were copied by hand, a time-consuming and expensive process that limited the spread of ideas. The printing press enabled mass production of books, pamphlets, and other written materials, making information more accessible to a wider audience. However, this same technology has also facilitated the rapid spread of misinformation and propaganda.

The Protestant Reformation, which began in the early 16th century, is a prominent example of how printing was used to propagate religious and political ideas. Martin Luther, a German monk, launched the Reformation by publishing his 95 Theses in 1517, in which he criticized the abuses of the Catholic Church, including the sale of indulgences. Thanks to the printing press, these theses were quickly reproduced and disseminated across Europe, reaching audiences far beyond academic circles.

Luther and his followers also used pamphlets, tracts, and printed sermons to spread reformist ideas. These publications were often written in an accessible style, aimed at a broad audience, and used simplified arguments that made it easier for the masses to buy into them. This approach not only allowed the Reformation to spread rapidly, but also contributed to religious polarization in Europe. Defamatory pamphlets, which violently attacked the doctrines and practices of the Catholic Church, were particularly effective in inflaming passions and sparking religious conflict. In response to the rise of Protestantism, the Catholic Church launched the Counter-Reformation, a movement intended to reaffirm Catholic doctrines and combat Protestant influence. The Church used the printing press to disseminate apologetic writings and decrees from the Council of Trent, which defined Catholic doctrines in opposition to Protestant theses. These texts were often accompanied by commentaries and sermons intended to strengthen the faith of Catholics and dissuade them from turning to Protestantism.

The Counter-Reformation was also marked by an intensification of censorship. The Church created the Index Librorum Prohibitorum, a list of banned books that included works deemed heretical or contrary to the Catholic faith. Church authorities closely monitored printers and booksellers, ensuring that Protestant texts or texts critical of the Church were not distributed. This rigorous censorship was an attempt to control public discourse and preserve the authority of the Church in the face of the growing threat of the Reformation.

The printing press was also used for political purposes. Renaissance rulers, aware of the power of print, commissioned writings that glorified their achievements and justified their actions. Princes and kings often used pamphlets and books to manipulate public opinion and to legitimize their power. These documents, often written by courtiers or court writers, presented rulers in a favorable light, exaggerating their successes and downplaying their failures.

A striking example of this manipulation is the dissemination of Machiavelli's writings, notably "The Prince", which was used by rulers to justify realistic and sometimes cynical power politics. Although "The Prince" was written to advise rulers on how to maintain power, it was also used to legitimize controversial actions, such as betrayal and manipulation of allies. Machiavelli's ideas have thus helped to shape a vision of political power where the end justifies the means, a notion that has often been exploited for disinformation purposes.

The Renaissance also saw the emergence of religious wars in Europe, where disinformation played a key role in fueling conflict. Catholics and Protestants used pamphlets to demonize their opponents, spreading exaggerated or fabricated accounts of persecution, massacres, and desecration. These stories, widely disseminated thanks to the printing press, helped fuel hatred and justify violence between religious communities. For example, the St. Bartholomew's Day massacre of 1572, where thousands of Protestant Huguenots were killed in Paris and other French cities, was followed by a wave of propaganda justifying the actions of Catholics and accusing Protestants of plots. against the State.

The Renaissance period, although marked by a renewed interest in knowledge and science, was therefore also a time when disinformation and the manipulation of information were used on a large scale to serve religious interests, political and social. These practices laid the foundation for modern disinformation techniques, showing that the manipulation of information is a constant in human history, simply evolving based on available technologies.

2. Disinformation in the Age of Industrial and Political Revolutions

The era of industrial and political revolutions, which stretched from the 18th century to the beginning of the 20th century, was marked by profound economic, social, and political upheavals that redefined modern societies. During this period, disinformation has become an essential tool for political and economic elites, allowing them to manipulate public opinion, control populations, and shape the future of nations. This period saw the rise of the mass press, the rise of modern political ideologies, and the systematic use of disinformation to influence events.

The Industrial Revolutions: From Mechanical Printing to the Mass Press

One of the most significant innovations of the first industrial revolution was the invention of the steam press by Friedrich Koenig in 1812. This technology transformed newspaper production, enabling fast and cheap printing that made news accessible to a much wider audience. Before this invention, newspapers were often limited to an educated elite, but with the steam press, publications could reach thousands of readers, including the working classes.

However, this increased accessibility of information has also paved the way for broader manipulation of public opinion. In France, the French Revolution illustrated how the press could be used to whip up popular passions and manipulate perceptions of events. Publications like Jean-Paul Marat's **L'Ami du Peuple** played a central role in spreading false news and rumors intended to incite violence against perceived enemies of the Revolution. These stories, often exaggerated or fabricated, helped create a climate of fear and suspicion that culminated in the violence of the Terror.

In Britain, the press was also used to manipulate public opinion, notably during the workers' revolts of the early 19th century. Conservative newspapers, such as **The Times** , often portrayed strikers as violent agitators, exaggerating incidents of violence to justify harsh repression by the state. This strategy aimed to discredit labor movements by presenting them as a threat to the social and economic order, thereby strengthening the position of the ruling elites.

The second industrial revolution, which began at the end of the 19th century, amplified these dynamics with the rise of new communication technologies. The invention of the telegraph revolutionized the way information traveled, allowing for almost instantaneous dissemination of news across continents. News agencies, such as Reuters and the Associated Press, have emerged as key players in the centralization and dissemination of information. However, this centralization has also made it easier to manipulate information, with governments and corporations exerting considerable influence over the narratives disseminated.

In the United States, the late 19th century saw the emergence of the yellow press, a sensationalist journalism that favored scandalous and emotional stories over verifiable facts. William Randolph Hearst and Joseph Pulitzer were the chief moguls of this press, using their newspapers to wage disinformation campaigns that served their business and political interests. The term "yellow press" became synonymous with media manipulation, where the main goal was to sell newspapers by stirring popular passions, often at the expense of the truth.

Disinformation during the Political Revolutions of the 19th Century

The 19th century was marked by a series of political revolutions that redefined the sociopolitical landscape of Europe and the Americas. Each revolution was accompanied by an information war where disinformation played a central role in manipulating perceptions and legitimizing the actions of the different actors involved.

The Revolution of 1830 in France, which led to the fall of Charles X and the establishment of the July Monarchy under Louis-Philippe, is a striking example of the use of the press to influence public opinion. Liberal newspapers used dramatic stories to exaggerate government abuses and incite the masses to revolt. Political caricatures, which depicted Charles X as an oppressive tyrant, circulated widely in Paris, fueling popular anger and precipitating the events of July 1830.

The Revolution of 1848, often called the People's Spring, was a period of revolutionary uprisings that shook Europe. In every country, disinformation has been used for political purposes. In Austria, authorities distributed pamphlets that accused Hungarian revolutionaries of plotting with foreign powers to destroy the empire. This strategy aimed to divide the different nationalities of the empire and isolate the Hungarian revolutionaries. Although these stories were greatly exaggerated, they succeeded in creating distrust between different communities, thus weakening the revolutionary movement.

In Germany, the Revolution of 1848 was also marked by the use of disinformation. Conservative newspapers, supported by German monarchs, spread alarmist stories about the dangers of socialism and democracy, aimed at frightening the middle classes and turning them away from revolutionary ideas. For their part, revolutionary newspapers used the press to mobilize workers and peasants, often by promising economic and social reforms that were not achievable in the short term.

In Italy, the Risorgimento, or movement for Italian unification, was also marked by an information war. Pro-unification newspapers, such as Cavour's **Il Risorgimento** , used the press to galvanize support for the Italian cause, often by exaggerating the atrocities committed by the Austrians in the occupied territories. These stories played a key role in mobilizing forces for the Italian War of Independence, creating an image of heroic struggle against a cruel oppressor. This manipulation of information not only helped rally Italians to the cause of unification, but also helped shape the emerging Italian national identity.

Propaganda and Disinformation during the Wars of the 19th Century

War has always been a breeding ground for disinformation, and the conflicts of the 19th century were no exception. The Crimean War (1853–1856) is an early example of the use of large-scale propaganda to shape public opinion. British newspapers, particularly **The Times** , played a crucial role in mobilizing support for the war, publishing sensationalist accounts of Russian atrocities and glorifying the exploits of British soldiers. This media coverage helped create a climate of opinion favorable to the war, despite the high human and financial costs.

Accounts disseminated by the British press were often biased, presenting the Russians as barbaric and dehumanized enemies, while downplaying British errors and failures. The famous war correspondent William Howard Russell, although he also denounced the deplorable conditions of British soldiers, helped shape a heroic image of the war that was widely echoed by the press and public. This manipulation of information not only influenced public opinion, but also impacted the way the war was fought and perceived by future generations.

During the American Civil War (1861-1865), disinformation was used by both sides to influence public opinion and maintain troop morale. The Union government censored Confederate-sympathizing newspapers and spread exaggerated accounts of Union victories to maintain popular support for the war effort. For their part, the Confederates used the press to portray the Northerners as barbaric invaders, seeking to rally the Southerners to the secessionist cause.

Newspapers on both sides also used caricatures and illustrations to dehumanize the enemy and justify military actions. For example, Northerners were often depicted as brutal oppressors in the Southern press, while Southerners were portrayed as traitors and slavers in the Northern press. These simplistic and often misleading representations have contributed to exacerbating divisions and prolonging the conflict by creating a climate of hatred and distrust between the two camps.

The Spanish-American War of 1898 is another example of how disinformation was used to justify conflict. The yellow press in the United States, led by figures like William Randolph Hearst, published sensationalist accounts of Spanish atrocities in Cuba, often without any evidence. These stories stoked public sentiment for war, and played a key role in the United States' decision to intervene in Cuba.

The famous incident of the USS Maine, an American warship that exploded in Havana harbor in 1898, is a classic example of disinformation leading to conflict. Although the causes of the explosion are still debated, the yellow press immediately accused Spain of deliberately attacking the ship, thus stoking the anger of the American public and precipitating the United States' entry into the war. This manipulation of information showed the power of the press in manufacturing reality and in influencing political decisions.

The Age of Empires: Disinformation as an Instrument of Colonial Control

European colonial expansion in the 19th and early 20th centuries was accompanied by a massive disinformation campaign, aimed at justifying colonial rule and manipulating the perceptions of colonized and colonizing populations. Colonial empires used the press, literature, and even science to propagate narratives that legitimized colonization by presenting it as a civilizing mission.

In Africa, for example, European colonial powers often portrayed African societies as barbaric and backward, thereby justifying the imposition of European control. Tales of savagery and cannibalism, often exaggerated or invented, were used to justify military interventions and economic exploitation of the colonies. Similarly, in Asia, the British used disinformation to portray revolts against colonial rule, such as the Sepoy Revolt in India in 1857, as acts of uncontrollable barbarity, thereby justifying the brutal repression that followed.

Colonial disinformation was not limited to justifications for violence. It was also used to create divisions among colonized populations, by exacerbating ethnic, religious or tribal differences. This strategy, known as "divide and rule", was employed in many colonies to prevent unity and resistance against colonial power. For example, in East Africa, British authorities often favored certain ethnic groups over others, creating tensions that persisted well after colonization ended.

Colonial powers also used science to justify their rule. Pseudo-scientific racial theories, such as those of Joseph Arthur de Gobineau, were used to legitimize the idea of European racial superiority. These theories claimed that Europeans were naturally superior to other races and had a duty to civilize "inferior" peoples. These ideas were disseminated through scientific publications, colonial exhibitions, and school textbooks, creating an ideological framework that justified the exploitation and oppression of colonized peoples.

World War I: The Golden Age of Propaganda and Disinformation

World War I marked a turning point in the use of disinformation and propaganda on an unprecedented scale. The governments of the warring nations understood that modern warfare was not only fought on the battlefields, but also in the minds of civilian populations. Propaganda became a central tool for maintaining troop and civilian morale, for justifying the enormous sacrifices demanded by war, and for dehumanizing the enemy.

In Britain, the War Propaganda Office was established to coordinate propaganda efforts nationally and internationally. This office produced films, posters, pamphlets, and newspaper articles intended to mobilize support for the war. One of the most famous propaganda campaigns of this period is the story of the "Belgian atrocities", which claimed that German troops had committed barbaric acts against civilians in Belgium. Although some of these stories were based on true events, many were exaggerated or invented to stir up hatred against the Germans.

War propaganda was not limited to the Allies. Germany, for its part, used narratives to justify its military actions and to mobilize popular support for the war effort. German authorities also censored the media to control the narratives that reached the public, seeking to downplay military defeats and glorify victories. German newspapers and cinemas broadcast images of courageous soldiers and loyal civilians, creating an image of national unity in the face of Allied aggression.

In the United States, the Creel Commission, created by the American government, played a central role in the dissemination of pro-war propaganda. The commission used every available means of communication, including newspapers, posters, cinema, and even religious sermons, to convince Americans to support entry into the war in 1917. This propaganda campaign presented the war as a crusade for democracy against autocracy, thus justifying American intervention.

The Lasting Impact of Disinformation in the Early 20th Century

The period of industrial and political revolutions established the basis for modern disinformation and propaganda techniques. These techniques not only shaped the events of the time, but they also left a lasting legacy that continues to influence the way information is used and manipulated today. The lessons learned from this period are essential for understanding the current dynamics of disinformation, particularly in a world where communication technologies are evolving rapidly and where access to information has become more democratized, but also more vulnerable to manipulation

The study of this period shows that disinformation is not a new phenomenon, but a constant in human history, which has evolved according to technological and socio-political changes. By understanding the historical roots of disinformation, we can better understand the challenges we face today and develop strategies to address them.

3. The Propaganda of the World Wars

The Origin and Evolution of War Propaganda

The First World War, often referred to as a "total war", marked a turning point in the systematic use of propaganda by states to influence not only national, but also international, public opinions. Before this conflict, propaganda certainly existed, but it was often limited to one-off campaigns and specific targets. With the unprecedented scale of the fighting and the mobilization of millions of soldiers, it has become crucial for the belligerents to maintain constant support from the civilian population, to justify the sacrifices required and to undermine the morale of the enemy. This historical turning point gave rise to propaganda techniques that are still studied today for their lasting impact on societies.

British Propaganda: The War Propaganda Bureau

In the United Kingdom, the government established the War Propaganda Bureau in 1914, which quickly became a central player in the dissemination of patriotic and anti-German narratives. One of the most notorious campaigns was the "Belgian atrocities". This myth, based on a few real incidents but greatly amplified, presented German soldiers as barbarians committing systematic atrocities against Belgian civilians. These stories were widely distributed in the British press and beyond, with the intention of sparking international outrage against Germany and justifying British involvement in the conflict.

The press played a key role in this strategy, with articles, editorials, and caricatures that reinforced the image of Germany as a dehumanized enemy. This form of propaganda had a dual objective: on the one hand, to maintain the British population in a state of psychological mobilization against the enemy, and on the other hand, to influence neutral public opinions, particularly in the United States, so that they take a stand against Germany. British propaganda campaigns were not limited to alleged atrocities, but also included narratives glorifying the sacrifices of British soldiers, often portrayed as heroes fighting for civilization against barbarism.

In addition to print media, British propaganda also used posters, which became one of the most powerful visual communication tools of the time. Posters such as the one depicting Lord Kitchener pointing and declaring "Your Country Needs YOU" became emblematic of the British war effort. These images were designed to be direct, emotional and inspiring, encouraging men to enlist in the army and civilians to support the war effort in any way possible. These posters had a profound psychological impact, not only recruiting soldiers, but also reinforcing the idea that every citizen had a crucial role to play in victory.

German Propaganda: Information Control and Censorship

In Germany, war propaganda was also omnipresent, although structured differently. The German government strictly controlled the information released to the public through censorship and media manipulation. Newspapers were encouraged, even required, to publish articles glorifying German military victories while downplaying defeats. Posters and films showed brave and loyal German soldiers, contrasting with dehumanized depictions of the enemies.

The main goal of German propaganda was to maintain national unity and convince the population that the war was just and necessary to defend the homeland. However, as the war dragged on and living conditions deteriorated, the propaganda became increasingly difficult to sustain, and the gap between official accounts and the reality experienced by civilians and soldiers became apparent. This dissonance between propaganda and reality began to erode public trust in the government, contributing to the rise of protest movements towards the end of the war.

One of the most notable aspects of German propaganda was the use of national and historical myths to justify the war effort. For example, propaganda celebrated the legacy of historic battles, such as those fought by Frederick the Great, to inspire a sense of continuity and national destiny. These stories were often accompanied by patriotic symbols, such as the imperial eagle, to reinforce national identity. However, as the war progressed, the ability of these stories to motivate the population and maintain social cohesion diminished, especially in the face of increasing casualties and economic hardship.

In addition, German propaganda faced internal challenges, including growing social tensions between classes and regions. The war exacerbated economic and social inequalities, and despite the government's efforts to use propaganda to mask these divisions, they became increasingly apparent. Strikes, mutinies, and demonstrations became more frequent as the war dragged on, revealing the limits of propaganda for maintaining social order in a context of protracted crisis.

American Propaganda: The Creel Commission

When the United States entered the war in 1917, it established the Creel Commission, officially known as the Committee on Public Information. Under the leadership of George Creel, this commission became a model of modern war propaganda, using every means of communication available to convince Americans of the merits of their involvement in the conflict.

The Creel Commission produced films, posters, pamphlets, and even public speeches intended to galvanize support for the war effort. The emphasis was placed on the notion of a "crusade for democracy", pitting the Allies, defenders of freedom and civilization, against the Central Powers, portrayed as militaristic and oppressive autocracies. This simplistic but effective dichotomy helped to rally a population initially reluctant to go to war.

The Four Minute Men, a network of volunteers, played a vital role in spreading propaganda. These amateur speakers delivered four-minute speeches at various public events, repeating key messages from the Creel Commission about the importance of supporting the war. This network effectively delivered government messages across the country, reaching millions of Americans in their local communities. This decentralized approach to propaganda made it possible to reach segments of the population who were not necessarily exposed to national media, thus strengthening the effectiveness of the campaign.

Additionally, the Creel Commission used movie stars and popular figures to promote war loans and other initiatives related to the war effort. Hollywood's film industry, booming at the time, became a key partner in the production of propaganda films that glorified the war effort and portrayed American soldiers as heroes. These films, shown in theaters across the country, helped create a wartime culture where patriotism and support for the war effort were seen as civic duties.

The Impact of Propaganda during the First World War

The impact of propaganda during the First World War was profound and lasting. Not only did it maintain popular support for protracted and deadly conflicts, but it also laid the foundations for modern propaganda techniques used by governments to manipulate public opinion in times of war. Lessons learned from this period were quickly applied and perfected during World War II, where propaganda reached new heights of sophistication and effectiveness.

War propaganda also changed the relationship between governments and citizens, setting a precedent for the use of large-scale manipulation of information to influence people's behavior. Techniques developed during the First World War were reused in various contexts, whether to support war efforts, legitimize political regimes, or control civilian populations in peacetime. These practices have had long-term impacts on the way governments communicate with their citizens, and on the perception of the role of information in modern societies.

The Second World War: The Propaganda of Totalitarian States

With the rise of totalitarian regimes in Europe, notably Nazi Germany and Fascist Italy, propaganda became a central instrument of state power. In Germany, Joseph Goebbels, Minister of Propaganda, established a massive propaganda apparatus that touched every aspect of public life. Cinema, radio, the press, and the arts were all put at the service of Nazi ideology, with the aim of creating an alternative reality where Hitler's regime appeared infallible and omnipotent.

Nazi propaganda was pervasive, seeping into every aspect of daily life. Newspapers, such as the **Völkischer Beobachter** , carried daily stories glorifying the regime and demonizing Germany's enemies. Radio, with broadcasts like those of the **Reichs-Rundfunk-Gesellschaft** , was used to broadcast the speeches of Hitler and Goebbels to a national audience. These speeches, often broadcast live, were designed to galvanize the masses, using emotional language and inflammatory rhetoric to generate loyalty and support for the regime.

Propaganda Cinema: A Tool of Social Control

Cinema became a favored tool of Nazi propaganda. Films like Leni Riefenstahl's "The Triumph of the Will," which glorified the Nazi Party rallies at Nuremberg, were designed to arouse strong emotions and reinforce support for the regime. These films used innovative editing techniques and striking images to create a sense of power and grandeur, while obscuring the reality of the regime's repressive and genocidal policies.

Nazi cinema propaganda was not limited to Riefenstahl's films. Other films, such as **Jud Süß** and **Der ewige Jude** , were explicitly anti-Semitic, designed to justify the persecution of Jews in Germany and the occupied territories. These films presented racist stereotypes and blatant lies as truth, seeking to create a climate of hatred and legitimize the regime's ethnic cleansing policies. These works of propaganda played a crucial role in creating consensus around Nazi policies, setting the stage for the atrocities of the Holocaust.

Cinema, as a propaganda tool, was particularly effective because of its ability to reach a wide audience and captivate viewers' attention. Propaganda films were often shown before mainstream films, ensuring maximum exposure of the regime's messages. Furthermore, the production of these films was supported by significant resources from the state, which saw cinema as a means of controlling not only information, but also the collective imagination.

Allied Propaganda: The Office of War Information

In response to Nazi propaganda, the Allies set up their own propaganda structures to counter enemy narratives and mobilize their populations. In the United States, the Office of War Information (OWI) was created to coordinate propaganda efforts, producing films, posters, and radio broadcasts to support the war effort.

One of the OWI's most famous campaigns was the use of movie stars to promote war loans. Famous actors like Humphrey Bogart and Rita Hayworth went on tours to encourage Americans to buy war bonds, emphasizing the importance of everyone's contribution to ultimate victory. This campaign skillfully combined Hollywood glamor with the patriotic message, making the propaganda more attractive and persuasive to the American public.

In addition to cinema, the OWI used radio to broadcast propaganda messages on a large scale. Radio shows, such as **This is War!** , were designed to inform, motivate, and sometimes manipulate public opinion. These broadcasts covered various aspects of war, from battle accounts to stories of individual sacrifice, with the aim of creating a sense of national solidarity and maintaining morale among troops and civilians. The OWI also collaborated with journalists and writers to produce articles and books that supported the war effort, often by exaggerating Allied victories and downplaying defeats.

The War of the Airwaves: Radio Propaganda during the Second World War

Radio became a crucial battlefield in the information war. Propaganda broadcasts were broadcast not only to inform and motivate the population, but also to demoralize the enemy. In Germany, Radio-Berlin broadcasts were notorious for their attempts to undermine the morale of Allied soldiers by broadcasting messages of defeatism and information about Allied losses, often exaggerated or invented.

On the other hand, the Allies used stations like Radio Londres to broadcast messages of resistance to the populations of countries occupied by Germany. These broadcasts, often introduced by the famous notes at the start of Beethoven's Fifth Symphony (symbolizing victory with the Morse code "V"), provided information on Allied operations and messages of support for local resistance fighters. They also played a crucial role in maintaining morale and hope among populations subject to Nazi occupation.

Radio, as a mass medium, possessed a unique power to reach large and diverse audiences. Radio broadcasts could be listened to by millions of people simultaneously, and their impact was immediate. This made it an extremely powerful propaganda tool, capable of shaping public opinion in real time. The messages broadcast by the radio were often repeated, to ensure that they were well assimilated by the audience, and efforts were made to adapt the content to the local contexts of the different occupied regions.

Soviet Propaganda: Stalin and the Myth of the Great Patriotic War

In the Soviet Union, war propaganda focused on the glorification of the "Great Patriotic War", a term used to describe the fight against Nazi Germany following the invasion of the Soviet Union in 1941. Soviet propaganda, orchestrated by the People's Commissariat for Political Education, used heroic historical stories to strengthen national unity and justify the massive sacrifices demanded by the war.

Newspapers, posters, and films portrayed Stalin as a wise and steadfast leader, guiding the nation through its darkest hours. Historical events, such as the Battle of Stalingrad, were glorified and transformed into national myths, intended to inspire pride and determination in soldiers and civilians. Soviet propaganda also emphasized the barbarity of German troops, not only to justify Soviet reprisals, but also to galvanize hatred and the desire for revenge among the population.

Soviet propaganda posters, often highly stylized and colorful, used heroic images of soldiers, workers, and peasants to symbolize the Soviet people's resistance to the invader. Slogans, simple but impactful, such as "Everything for the front, everything for victory!" were omnipresent, reinforcing the message of the need for national unity and personal sacrifice in defense of the homeland. These posters, plastered in towns, villages and factories, were a constant reminder of the total commitment required of every Soviet citizen.

Cinematographic propaganda also played a key role in mobilizing the population. Films such as Sergei Eisenstein's **Alexander Nevsky** (1938), although predating the German invasion, were re-released to highlight the parallels between the fight against the Teutonic Knights in the 13th century and the war against Nazi Germany. These historical accounts, revisited through the prism of propaganda, served to establish continuity between Russia's glorious past and the sacrifices of the present, thus justifying the hardships endured by the Soviet people.

The Impact of Propaganda on the Outcome of World War II

Propaganda played a crucial role in the outcome of the Second World War, not only by mobilizing the human and material resources of the belligerents, but also by shaping perceptions of the war among civilian populations and soldiers. The ability to control and manipulate information became a key strategic factor, influencing military and political decisions at all levels.

The war ended, but the lessons learned from the use of propaganda remained with leaders around the world. Techniques perfected during the war were quickly adapted to the new contexts of the Cold War, where the battle for hearts and minds continued in new forms. Governments, recognizing the power of information, continued to use the media to influence public opinion, not only in times of war, but also in times of peace, in domestic and foreign policy.

The post-war period also saw the emergence of new forms of propaganda, adapted to emerging media such as television. Information manipulation techniques, developed during the world wars, were adapted and perfected for the new media realities of the second half of the 20th century. Propaganda thus became an integrated component of governance, used to legitimize government actions, influence electorates, and manage international crises.

4. Manipulation Strategies during the Cold War

Historical context of the Cold War

The Cold War, lasting from the end of World War II in 1945 until the dissolution of the Soviet Union in 1991, was a period of intense tensions and geopolitical rivalries between the United States and the Union. Soviet. This confrontation, although it never degenerated into a direct military conflict between the two superpowers, was marked by a series of proxy wars, diplomatic crises, and above all by an unprecedented information war. The two ideological blocs have engaged in a fierce struggle to expand their influence across the globe, seeking to win the support of non-aligned nations, control international narratives, and destabilize the adversary by any means possible.

The nature of the Cold War, where the threat of annihilative nuclear war required restraint in the use of direct military force, gave new importance to strategies of information manipulation, propaganda and disinformation. Both camps have developed sophisticated techniques for influencing public opinions, not only in their own countries, but also abroad. This war of minds and perceptions was waged on all fronts: political, economic, cultural and technological.

Soviet Disinformation: "Active Measures"

The Soviet Union was one of the main players in using disinformation as a strategic tool during the Cold War. Under the direction of the KGB, the Soviet intelligence agency, "active measures" (aktivnyye meropriyatiya) referred to a series of covert operations aimed at influencing political events around the world. These operations included spreading false information, fabricating documents, orchestrating rumors, and even encouraging violence and political instability in opposing countries.

One of the most emblematic disinformation campaigns of this period is Operation **Infection** , carried out by the KGB in the 1980s. This campaign aimed to make people believe that the AIDS virus had been created by the United States in a military laboratory at Fort Detrick, Maryland, as part of research into biological weapons. This false information was disseminated through newspapers in India, before being picked up by media in several countries, particularly in Africa and Latin America, regions particularly sensitive to anti-American messages. The aim of this operation was multiple: to weaken the image of the United States on the international scene, to create tensions between the United States and developing countries, and to fuel global distrust of American intentions.

This disinformation operation was carefully orchestrated. The KGB used a technique known as **"skate throwing"** , where false information is first placed in a relatively obscure media outlet, often in a third country, before being picked up and amplified by other outlets more influential. This technique made it possible to give the appearance that the disinformation had a legitimate and independent origin, thus strengthening its credibility. Once the rumor started, it was difficult to stop, and even when the truth was established, the damage was often already done, with the rumor continuing to circulate in certain circles.

In addition to disinformation campaigns, the Soviets also used false documents to discredit political figures in Western countries. For example, in 1961, the KGB fabricated a letter falsely attributed to former US President Harry Truman, in which he harshly criticized his successor Dwight Eisenhower. This letter was widely distributed in an attempt to sow discord within the U.S. government and discredit U.S. foreign policy. Although this attempt was quickly unmasked, it illustrates the sophistication and audacity of Soviet disinformation operations.

"Active measures" were not limited to the dissemination of false information. They also included clandestine support for guerrilla movements, communist parties, and revolutionary groups around the world. These operations were intended to weaken U.S. allied governments and create favorable conditions for the expansion of Soviet influence. For example, in Latin America, the Soviets supported revolutionary groups such as the Sandinistas in Nicaragua and Marxist guerrillas in Colombia and El Salvador. This support was often accompanied by propaganda campaigns aimed at legitimizing these movements in the eyes of international public opinion.

Africa was also fertile ground for Soviet "active measures". In Angola, for example, the Soviets supported the MPLA (Popular Movement for the Liberation of Angola) against forces supported by the United States and South Africa. This proxy war, which lasted several decades, was marked by intense propaganda on both sides, with each side seeking to present its allies as the true representatives of the aspirations of the Angolan people. Soviet media portrayed the MPLA as a liberation movement fighting against imperialism, while Western media portrayed the rebels as Kremlin puppets.

Soviet "active measures" also targeted intellectuals and peace movements in Western Europe and the United States. The KGB infiltrated anti-nuclear groups and peace organizations, using these platforms to spread anti-US and anti-NATO messages. In 1983, during the Euromissile Crisis, the Soviets orchestrated massive protests against the deployment of Pershing II missiles in Europe, manipulating fears of nuclear war to weaken NATO's position. These operations were intended to divide Western allies and create internal pressure on governments to adopt more conciliatory policies toward the Soviet Union.

American Propaganda: The Voice of America and Radio Free Europe

In response to Soviet operations, the United States also developed information manipulation strategies to counter communist influence. One of the most famous American initiatives in this area was the creation of **Radio Free Europe** (RFE) and **Radio Liberty** (RL). These radio stations, funded by the CIA, broadcast broadcasts in local languages to Eastern Bloc countries. Their goal was to provide populations under communist rule with an alternative to state-controlled media, by broadcasting censored information, international news, and messages in favor of freedom and democracy.

The **Voice of America** (VOA), another major tool of American propaganda, has played a key role in spreading democratic values and American ideals throughout the world. Founded in 1942, VOA used radio, and later television and the Internet, to reach millions of people in countries where free speech was suppressed. During the Cold War, VOA broadcast programs in several languages, including Russian, Chinese, Arabic, and the languages of Eastern European countries. These broadcasts aimed not only to inform, but also to counter the messages of Soviet propaganda and to offer an alternative vision of the world.

Radio Free Europe and Radio Liberty broadcasts specifically targeted Eastern European countries, with programs tailored to local cultures and languages. They broadcast censored news, critical analyzes of Soviet policies, and messages of hope for dissidents. These broadcasts were often jammed by communist governments, but despite these attempts at interference, they managed to reach a wide audience. Many dissidents in Poland, Hungary, and Czechoslovakia testified to the importance of these broadcasts in their struggle for freedom.

American propaganda was not limited to broadcasting messages by radio. It also involved sophisticated public relations campaigns, print publications, and efforts to influence popular culture. For example, the U.S. State Department's **Cultural Presentations Program** has organized international tours for American artists, musicians, and writers. These events aimed to present a positive image of the United States abroad, emphasizing the values of artistic freedom and expression. Jazz, in particular, was used as a symbol of American freedom, contrasting with the perceived cultural rigidity of communist regimes.

The United States also used disinformation campaigns to weaken Soviet influence. For example, the CIA carried out covert operations to sow doubt about the legitimacy of communist regimes by disseminating information about corruption, repression, and economic failures in Eastern bloc countries. These efforts were often coordinated with military or diplomatic operations to maximize their impact. A notable example is Operation **Aedinium** , where falsified documents were planted to show that members of the Polish government had links to organized crime, thus creating internal tensions within the regime.

Television and film have also been important tools of American propaganda. Hollywood produced many films during the Cold War that portrayed the Soviets as ruthless enemies and Americans as defenders of freedom. Films like **"The Iron Curtain"** (1948), **"The Red Menace"** (1949), and **"Invasion of the Body Snatchers"** (1956) used the language of entertainment to convey political messages. These films were not only intended for American audiences, but also for foreign audiences, particularly in Europe and Latin America, where they were shown in cinemas and broadcast on television.

Clandestine Broadcasts and the War of the Waves

One of the most fascinating aspects of information warfare during the Cold War was the **war on the airwaves** , a clash over radio frequencies between the two blocs. The United States, the Soviet Union, and their respective allies invested heavily in radio transmitters to broadcast propaganda messages across borders. These clandestine broadcasts aimed to break the information monopoly held by totalitarian governments and to create a media alternative for populations under communist control.

Radio Free Europe and **Radio Liberty** broadcasts specifically targeted Eastern European countries, with programs tailored to local cultures and languages. They broadcast censored news, critical analyzes of Soviet policies, and messages of hope for dissidents. These broadcasts were often jammed by
communist governments, but despite these attempts at interference, they managed to reach a large audience. Many dissidents in Poland, Hungary, and Czechoslovakia testified to the importance of these broadcasts in their struggle for freedom.

For their part, the Soviets used stations like **Radio Moscow** to broadcast pro-communist messages in several languages, including English, French, Spanish, and Arabic. These broadcasts aimed to influence public opinions in the West and the Third World, by presenting the Soviet Union as the champion of peace, anti-imperialism, and social progress. Radio Moscow programs regularly criticized American policies, particularly on civil rights, the Vietnam War, and support for dictatorships in Latin America. This propaganda sought to exploit the flaws and contradictions in Western societies to weaken their cohesion and credibility.

The Soviets were not alone in using radio broadcasts to influence public opinion. The Eastern bloc also had allies in the Arab world, where stations like **Radio Cairo** broadcast anti-Western messages, often coordinated with Moscow's strategic goals. These broadcasts aimed to mobilize nationalist and anti-imperialist sentiments in Arab countries, by criticizing the policies of the United States and its allies, notably Israel. The Arab world's wave war illustrates how the Cold War extended far beyond the borders of Europe and North America, affecting regions where superpowers sought to expand their influence.

Using the Media to Manipulate Public Opinion

Beyond radio, television and print media have also played a crucial role in information warfare. The United States, for example, has used Hollywood to promote the image of America as the bastion of freedom and democracy. Films like **"The Iron Curtain"** (1948) and **"The Red Menace"** (1949) portrayed communist regimes as tyrannical and oppressive, while American heroes were presented as defenders of universal values. These films were not only aimed at American audiences, but also at foreign audiences, particularly in Europe and Latin America.

The written press, for its part, was often used to disseminate articles commissioned by the intelligence services. The CIA funded newspapers and magazines in Europe and Latin America to publish articles favorable to the United States and critical of communist regimes. These publications were often presented as independent, but in reality they were part of a broader strategy to manipulate public opinion. The **"Operation Mockingbird" program** , for example, involved the covert collaboration between the CIA and influential journalists to spread stories favorable to American interests.

In the Soviet Union, the media was completely controlled by the state, and the press was a tool of mass propaganda. Newspapers like **Pravda** and **Izvestia** published articles glorifying the achievements of communism and denouncing the "atrocities" of capitalism. Soviet television broadcast documentaries and shows that presented the West as a world in decline, riddled with crime, racism, and social injustice. These programs aimed to maintain support for the communist regime by cultivating a negative image of the capitalist enemy.

Disinformation Networks and Covert Diplomacy

Information warfare during the Cold War was not limited to media propaganda. It also included covert operations aimed at manipulating political elites, intellectuals, and international organizations. The Soviets, for example, financed communist parties and left-wing movements around the world, using these organizations as conduits for their propaganda. In Western Europe, intellectuals influenced by Marxism often served as conduits for Soviet ideas, helping to spread a worldview favorable to Moscow.

The United States, for its part, has used "covert diplomacy" operations to influence foreign governments. The CIA financed coups, revolutions, and assassinations to overthrow perceived hostile regimes and install pro-American governments.

These operations were often accompanied by disinformation campaigns aimed at discrediting the targeted leaders and justifying American intervention.

A prominent example is the coup d'état in Chile in 1973, where the democratically elected government of Salvador Allende was overthrown with the support of the CIA. The United States used disinformation to portray Allende as a danger to regional security and to justify the establishment of Augusto Pinochet's military dictatorship. This operation marked a turning point in the use of disinformation as a Cold War weapon in Latin America.

The Legacy of Cold War Disinformation

The legacy of disinformation during the Cold War is still present today. The techniques developed during this period were adapted to new information technologies, notably the Internet and social networks. The concepts of "fake news" and "post-truth" that dominate current discourse on information manipulation have their roots in disinformation strategies developed during the Cold War.

The Soviet Union, and then post-Soviet Russia, continued to use disinformation as a foreign policy tool. Russian disinformation campaigns during the 2016 US presidential elections are a recent example. Likewise, American operations in Iraq, marked by the dissemination of false information on weapons of mass destruction, show that the manipulation of information remains a central component of geopolitical strategy.

In conclusion, the Cold War was a period where information manipulation became a weapon of choice in superpower rivalry. The disinformation strategies developed by the United States and the Soviet Union left a lasting legacy that continues to influence international relations and current conflicts. Understanding these strategies is essential to navigating the complex and often misleading media landscape of the 21st century.

5. The Emergence of Digital Disinformation

Introduction to Digital Disinformation

The emergence of digital disinformation in the 21st century has marked a watershed in how information is created, disseminated and consumed. Unlike traditional forms of disinformation which relied on relatively centralized means of dissemination such as the press, radio and television, digital disinformation relies on the vast decentralized networks offered by the internet. This transformation has been made possible by the massive adoption of the Internet, social networks and new information technologies, which have allowed millions of users to instantly access an infinite amount of information, often without filter.

Digital disinformation, commonly known as "fake news," has transformed the global media landscape. Information, whether true or false, can spread at unprecedented speed and scale, influencing public opinions and political decisions across the world. This ability to spread quickly is facilitated by online platforms' algorithms, which are designed to maximize user engagement by presenting them with content likely to elicit strong emotional reactions. These algorithms, while effective at holding users' attention, have also allowed misinformation to proliferate, creating an environment where fake news can spread faster and more widely than verified information.

The Origins of Online Disinformation

The history of online misinformation dates back to the early years of the internet, when forums, blogs and early websites allowed individuals to post content without going through traditional editorial filters. These early platforms, while modest by today's standards, opened the door to the dissemination of false information on a scale previously only accessible to mainstream media outlets. At that time, misinformation often took the form of hoaxes or rumors intended to entertain or deceive in a harmless way. However, as the internet has expanded and more people have started using it as their primary source of information, online disinformation has evolved into a strategic tool, used by various actors to manipulate public opinions.

A notable example from the early era of online disinformation is the "Minitel hoax" in France, where users spread false information about the results of the 1981 presidential elections via Minitel, a videotext service that was a precursor of the internet in France. This hoax, although having had limited impact, showed the potential of technology to disseminate false information on a large scale. At the time, the dissemination of this information was primarily motivated by amusement, but it also revealed the ability of new technologies to influence public perception.

With the expansion of the internet in the 1990s and 2000s, online disinformation took on more sophisticated forms. Platforms like 4chan, Reddit, and other discussion forums have enabled the emergence of movements like "Anonymous," a collective of hacktivists that used disinformation campaigns to target institutions perceived as corrupt. These early manifestations of online disinformation laid the groundwork for the more modern and dangerous forms we see today. The virality of this content was often reinforced by the lack of regulation and the absence of effective mechanisms to verify the veracity of the information circulating on these platforms.

Social Networks: Accelerators of Disinformation

Social media has played a central role in the spread of misinformation in the digital age. Their business model, based on advertising and user engagement, creates an incentive to maximize the time users spend on the platform, often at the expense of the veracity of information. Content that provokes strong reactions, such as outrage, fear, or humor, is favored by recommendation algorithms, allowing fake news to spread quickly and widely.

A prominent example of the impact of social media on the spread of disinformation is the 2016 US presidential election. Foreign actors, notably Russians, used platforms like Facebook, Twitter, and YouTube to spread disinformation aimed at influence the outcome of the election. Hundreds of fake accounts were created to share polarizing content and falsely attributed to credible sources, creating massive confusion among voters. These efforts were often coordinated with targeted advertising campaigns intended to sow discord and influence undecided voters. This disinformation campaign not only disrupted the election, but it also raised questions about the vulnerability of democratic processes in the digital age.

Social media is not just a passive platform where misinformation can spread; they are actively used by malicious actors to manipulate public opinion. "Bots," automated programs that mimic human behavior, are often deployed to amplify the reach of disinformation. These bots can generate thousands of messages in seconds, creating the illusion of massive popular support for false information. This technique has been widely used during geopolitical conflicts, such as the crisis in Ukraine, where pro-Russian actors used bots to spread disinformation about the situation on the ground. Bots also play a role in commercial disinformation campaigns, where companies or interest groups can manipulate markets or public opinion to gain economic advantage.

Deepfakes: A New Frontier of Disinformation

With advances in artificial intelligence, a new form of disinformation has emerged: "deepfakes". These manipulated videos or images use machine learning algorithms to superimpose people's faces or voices onto other bodies or audio, creating content that appears authentic but is actually entirely fabricated. Deepfakes represent a major challenge for fact-checking, as they can be used to create false evidence of crimes, false statements by politicians, or compromising images of public figures.

One of the most well-known examples of deepfake is the doctored video of former US President Barack Obama, in which he appeared to deliver a speech containing controversial statements. This video, although quickly unmasked as a deepfake, illustrated the potential of this technology to manipulate public opinion and sow confusion. Since then, many other deepfake videos have circulated online, some of them having real impacts on the perception of events. For example, deepfakes have been used to spread false statements attributed to political leaders during critical election periods, creating crises of confidence and political upheaval.

Deepfakes aren't just a threat to public figures; they can also be used to harm ordinary individuals. In cases of "revenge porn," pornographic images are created using the faces of real people without their consent. This malicious use of deepfakes raises ethical and legal questions about the protection of privacy and the integrity of visual evidence. The legal implications of deepfakes are still poorly understood, and there is a regulatory void that allows this content to spread without consequences for creators. This has led to calls for stricter legislation and more advanced detection technologies to counter the threat of deepfakes.

Information Warfare in the Digital Age

Digital disinformation is not just a domestic problem; it has become a tool in international conflicts. States and non-state actors use disinformation to destabilize their adversaries, influence foreign elections, and undermine trust in democratic institutions. These "information wars" are being waged on multiple fronts, including social media, fake news sites, and online forums, creating a media environment where it is increasingly difficult to distinguish fact from fiction.

Russia, for example, has been repeatedly accused of waging disinformation campaigns to weaken the West. The annexation of Crimea in 2014 was accompanied by a massive disinformation campaign, where Russian media and social media spread misleading narratives about the legitimacy of the annexation and the intentions of Russian forces. These efforts were complemented by cyberattacks and psychological operations aimed at dividing public opinion in Europe and the United States. Russian disinformation campaigns have often used sophisticated techniques to disguise their origin, creating the illusion that the information came from credible and independent sources.

The United States, for its part, has also been involved in disinformation operations, notably during the Iraq War, where false information about weapons of mass destruction was used to justify the invasion. Although these operations were carried out primarily by governments, they demonstrate how digital disinformation can be used as a weapon in modern conflicts. The war in Iraq has shown that disinformation can have catastrophic consequences, not only in terms of human lives lost, but also in terms of eroded trust in democratic institutions and the media.

Information wars in the digital age are also waged by non-state actors, such as terrorist groups or extremist movements, who use disinformation to recruit members, radicalize individuals, and spread their ideology. These groups exploit loopholes in online platforms to reach large audiences with messages of hatred and violence. Authorities struggle to counter these threats because the decentralized and often anonymous nature of social media makes it difficult to identify and remove extremist content.

Fact-Checking Platforms and Responses to Disinformation

Faced with the growing threat of digital disinformation, numerous initiatives have emerged to counter this threat. Fact-checking platforms, such as "Les Décoders" in France or "PolitiFact" in the United States, specialize in fact-checking and correcting false information. These organizations work closely with traditional media and social networks to identify, analyze, and correct fake news before it spreads too widely.

Governments and tech companies have also started taking steps to combat misinformation. In Europe, the European Union has adopted regulations aimed at making online platforms responsible in the fight against disinformation, by requiring them to quickly remove manifestly false or misleading content. In the United States, similar initiatives have been launched, although the issue of censorship and freedom of expression remains a matter of debate. The difficulty lies in the balance between combating disinformation and protecting individual freedoms, a challenge that remains at the heart of political discussions.

Social networks have started using fact-checking algorithms and warning labels to alert users when they encounter potentially false information. However, these measures are far from perfect, and much misinformation continues to circulate undetected or corrected. Algorithms, while effective to a certain extent, are often circumvented by users determined to spread misinformation. Additionally, automatically detecting misinformation remains a technical challenge, as algorithms must constantly adapt to new forms of misleading content.

In response to these challenges, some technology companies have begun collaborating with artificial intelligence experts to develop more sophisticated tools for detecting misinformation. For example, Google has invested in initiatives to use artificial intelligence to detect deepfakes and other forms of visual manipulation. These efforts, while promising, are still developing and require close collaboration between governments, technology companies, and civil society to be truly effective.

The Impact of Digital Disinformation on Society

Digital disinformation has profound consequences on society. It undermines confidence in democratic institutions, polarizes public opinion, and creates a climate of generalized distrust. Fake news can influence election results, exacerbate social conflict, and even endanger public health, as seen with the spread of misinformation about vaccines during the COVID-19 pandemic.

Younger generations, who increasingly consume information via social media, are particularly vulnerable to misinformation. Studies show that young people are more likely to believe and share fake news, in part because they often lack the skills to critically evaluate information sources. This highlights the importance of media and information literacy, which must be strengthened to prepare citizens to navigate today's complex media environment.

The long-term effects of misinformation on society are still poorly understood, but it is clear that they can be devastating. Loss of trust in the media and public institutions can lead to a fragmentation of society, where individuals increasingly turn to alternative sources of information that confirm their prejudices. This polarization can in turn fuel social and political conflict, making democratic governance more difficult and less effective.

Towards a Global Strategy to Combat Disinformation

To effectively combat digital disinformation, it is essential to develop a comprehensive approach that involves governments, technology companies, media, and civil society. This includes establishing clear regulations for online platforms, supporting fact-checking initiatives, and promoting media literacy.

Governments must play an active role in imposing sanctions on actors who deliberately spread disinformation, while respecting freedom of expression. Tech companies, for their part, need to improve their algorithms to detect and remove misleading content more quickly. Finally, civil society must be mobilized to promote a culture of fact-checking and critical thinking.

The future of digital disinformation will depend on our collective ability to recognize the dangers it poses and take action to respond. If we fail to meet this challenge, we risk seeing our public space become even more fragmented, to the detriment of democracy and social cohesion.

The fight against digital disinformation cannot be won by a single entity; it requires international cooperation and coordination between the different actors. Initiatives like the Global Partnership for Information and Democracy, launched by Reporters Without Borders, are examples of how countries can work together to combat disinformation while protecting human rights and freedom of speech. 'expression. These efforts must be supported by investments in research and development of technologies that can proactively detect and counter disinformation.

In conclusion, the emergence of digital disinformation has transformed the way we perceive and interact with information. It has created unprecedented challenges for society, governments, and technology companies, requiring a collective and coordinated response. Digital disinformation is not a passing problem; it has become an enduring feature of our media landscape, and it is crucial that we develop the tools, policies and skills to deal with it effectively.

Chapter 2: The Mechanisms of Disinformation

1. How Misinformation Spreads

Introduction to the Spread of Disinformation

The spread of disinformation is a phenomenon that has always existed, but which has taken on an unprecedented scale with the advent of digital technologies. Disinformation, which is in essence erroneous information disseminated intentionally to mislead, has found a rapid and massive vector of diffusion in new technologies. Understanding the mechanisms by which disinformation spreads is crucial to being able to deal with it effectively. This chapter explores in depth the various pathways by which disinformation spreads, the factors that facilitate this spread, and the social, political, and economic consequences it creates.

Disinformation Propagation Channels

The channels for spreading disinformation are varied and include traditional media, digital platforms and interpersonal interactions. Each of these channels plays a specific role in the spread of misinformation, often with distinct dynamics and impacts.

Traditional Media: Historically, print media, radio, and television have been the primary means of disseminating information. Although these media now compete with digital platforms, they continue to play a significant role in the spread of disinformation, particularly through biased reporting, inaccurate or deliberately distorted information. These media can also serve as a sounding board for false information initially disseminated online, giving it additional legitimacy.

Digital Platforms: Social media, blogs, and online forums have become the primary vectors of misinformation in the modern era. Platforms like Facebook, Twitter, YouTube, and Instagram allow millions of users to instantly share content, making the viral spread of misinformation possible. The algorithms of these platforms, designed to maximize user engagement, often favor sensational content, which generates strong emotional reactions, whether true or false. This content is more likely to be shared, commented on, and distributed, which contributes to its rapid spread.

Interpersonal interactions: Misinformation doesn't just spread online. Face-to-face interactions, telephone conversations, and exchanges within small social networks, such as family or friend groups, also play a crucial role. In these contexts, rumors and false information are often perceived as more credible because they are shared by people you trust. This interpersonal spread of misinformation is particularly difficult to counter because it relies on established relationships of trust, where information is rarely questioned.

Factors That Promote the Spread of Disinformation

Several factors contribute to the speed and extent of the spread of disinformation. These factors include cognitive biases, group dynamics, and economic and political motivations, each playing a crucial role in how misinformation is created, disseminated, and accepted by the public.

Cognitive biases: Cognitive biases are systematic biases or thinking errors that affect the way individuals process information. Among the cognitive biases most relevant to the spread of misinformation is confirmation bias, which leads people to seek out, interpret and remember information that confirms their pre-existing beliefs. Anchoring bias, where early information received has a disproportionate impact on subsequent decisions, and availability bias, where recent or dramatic events influence risk perception, also play a major role. These biases make individuals more likely to believe and share false information that confirms their personal beliefs or resonates with their lived experiences. **Group dynamics:** The spread of misinformation is often facilitated by group dynamics, where individuals are influenced by the opinions and behaviors of those around them. Online environments, where social networks create "filter bubbles," exacerbate these dynamics. In these bubbles, users are primarily exposed to content that reinforces their existing views, leading to increased polarization and faster spread of misinformation. Social conformity, where individuals adopt the dominant views of their group to avoid cognitive dissonance or exclusion, is also a key factor.

Economic and political motivations: Disinformation is often spread by actors who derive economic or political advantages from it. Companies may disseminate misleading information to protect their business interests, such as greenwashing, where companies exaggerate their green initiatives to attract environmentally conscious consumers. Governments and political parties can use disinformation to influence public opinions and manipulate elections, as has been observed in numerous cases of electoral manipulation around the world. Disinformation can also be used as a weapon in geopolitical conflicts, where states or interest groups seek to destabilize their adversaries by sowing confusion and discord.

Stages of Disinformation Spread

The spread of misinformation can be broken down into several key stages, each of which plays a crucial role in how false information is created, disseminated, and ultimately accepted by the public.

Creation: The first step in the spread of disinformation is its creation. Disinformation can be fabricated or based on real facts that are distorted or taken out of context to serve a specific agenda. This creation can be the work of isolated individuals, organized groups, or even States, each with their own motivations and objectives.

Initial Dissemination: Once created, disinformation is disseminated through specific channels, often chosen for their ability to reach a large audience quickly. Social media and blogs are common channels for initial outreach because they allow for quick and inexpensive distribution. Disinformation creators often use manipulative techniques, such as creating fake accounts or using bots, to make the information appear widely supported or accepted.

Amplification: After initial distribution, misinformation is often amplified by users who share it, often without verifying its veracity. This amplification is facilitated by the algorithms of digital platforms, which favor content likely to generate strong emotional reactions, such as indignation, fear or shock. Bots also play a key role in this phase, artificially increasing the visibility of misinformation.

Viral Spread: If misinformation resonates with a large audience, it can go viral. At this stage, it is often picked up by traditional media or influential figures, which gives it an appearance of legitimacy. Viral spread is often accompanied by a process of "mutability," where misinformation is modified and adapted over time to reach new audiences or to evade fact-checking.

Institutionalization: In some cases, disinformation can become institutionalized, meaning it is adopted by institutions or organizations that present it as established truth. This can happen when powerful actors, such as governments or large corporations, support or promote disinformation to serve their interests. Once institutionalized, misinformation becomes extremely difficult to correct because it is embedded in existing belief systems and power structures.

The Consequences of the Spread of Disinformation

The spread of disinformation has profound consequences for individuals, societies and political systems. At the individual level, misinformation can mislead people about crucial issues, such as health or safety, leading to poorly informed decisions that can have serious consequences. For example, the spread of misinformation about vaccines has led to falling vaccination rates in some countries, which in turn has contributed to the re-emergence of preventable diseases.

At the societal level, disinformation can weaken social cohesion by exacerbating divisions and creating a climate of widespread mistrust. In political systems, it can undermine democracy by manipulating voters and distorting electoral processes. Disinformation can also be used to justify policies or actions contrary to human rights, distorting reality to legitimize abuses or attacks. For example, in some authoritarian regimes, disinformation is used to create an internal or external enemy, thus justifying repression or military intervention.

Strategies to Counter the Spread of Disinformation

Countering the spread of disinformation requires a multifaceted approach that includes education, media regulation, and the development of fact-checking technologies.

Media and Information Literacy: One of the most effective strategies to combat disinformation is to strengthen media and information literacy. This includes teaching critical thinking skills, fact-checking training, and awareness of cognitive biases. By training citizens to recognize and critically evaluate the information they encounter, it is possible to reduce vulnerability to misinformation.

Platform Regulation and Accountability: Governments and international organizations can play a key role in regulating digital platforms to be more accountable for the content distributed on their sites. This could include requirements for algorithm transparency, moderation of misleading content, and sanctions for platforms that fail to prevent the spread of misinformation. Regulation could also include measures to protect freedom of expression while preventing the spread of harmful content.

Fact-Checking Technologies: The development of advanced fact-checking technologies can also help limit the spread of misinformation. AI-powered tools can be used to quickly detect misleading content and alert users before they share false information. These technologies can also help journalists and researchers analyze large amounts of data to identify trends and sources of misinformation. For example, natural language processing algorithms can be used to detect language patterns typical of fake news and flag them for further review.

International Collaboration: Finally, it is essential to promote international collaboration to combat disinformation, especially when it is used as a weapon in geopolitical conflicts. Countries can share information, coordinate responses and adopt common standards to regulate disinformation globally. International organizations like UNESCO have already started working on these issues, but further efforts are needed to create an effective global framework.

Building Media Capacity: The media plays a crucial role in combating disinformation, providing verified information and exposing fake news. It is therefore important to strengthen the capacities of the media, notably by supporting investigative journalism and encouraging ethical practices. Journalists need to be trained in fact-checking techniques and digital tools that can help them identify and expose misinformation. Additionally, it is essential to support independent media in countries where press freedom is under threat, as these outlets often play a key role in disseminating truthful information.

Involvement of Civil Society: Civil society must also be involved in the fight against disinformation. Non-governmental organizations, community groups and citizens can all play a role in raising public awareness, promoting media literacy and exposing fake news. Citizen fact-checking initiatives, where individuals verify information and share it with their networks, can be particularly effective in countering grassroots disinformation.

Historical and Contemporary Examples of the Spread of Disinformation

History is replete with examples of the spread of misinformation, each offering valuable lessons about how false information can spread and how to counter it.

The Case of the Protocols of the Elders of Zion: One of the most infamous examples of disinformation is that of the "Protocols of the Elders of Zion", a fabricated document that purported to reveal a global Jewish plot to dominate the world. Although this document was proven false in the early years of the 20th century, it was widely distributed, notably by the Nazis, and helped fuel anti-Semitism and justify persecution. This example shows how disinformation can be used to legitimize extremist ideologies and repressive policies.

Nazi Propaganda: The Nazi propaganda machine, led by Joseph Goebbels, is another example of how disinformation can be used to manipulate the masses. Using sophisticated mass communications techniques, the Nazi regime spread false narratives about Jews, political opponents, and enemy countries, thereby justifying criminal actions like the Holocaust. Nazi propaganda demonstrates how disinformation, when supported by a powerful state, can have devastating consequences.

The 2016 United States Elections: More recently, the 2016 US presidential elections highlighted the role of social media in the spread of misinformation. Foreign actors, including Russians, used platforms like Facebook and Twitter to spread fake news and conspiracy theories in an attempt to influence the outcome of the election. This disinformation campaign was particularly effective due to the use of "bots" to amplify messages and targeted ads to reach specific voters. This example shows how digital disinformation can be used as a weapon to destabilize democratic processes.

The COVID-19 Pandemic: The COVID-19 pandemic has also been marked by an unprecedented wave of misinformation. Conspiracy theories about the origin of the virus, misinformation about treatments and unfounded rumors about vaccines have circulated massively on social media, sowing confusion and mistrust. This misinformation has had serious consequences, delaying vaccination efforts and exacerbating the health crisis. The pandemic has shown how dangerous misinformation can be in emergency situations, where accurate and reliable information is crucial for making informed decisions.

Conclusion: Understanding and Combating the Spread of Disinformation

The spread of disinformation is a complex phenomenon that requires a deep understanding of the underlying mechanisms and strategies to combat it. By analyzing the channels through which disinformation spreads, the factors that facilitate its dissemination, and the consequences it generates, it is possible to develop effective responses to counter this threat. However, the fight against disinformation cannot be carried out in isolation. It requires close cooperation between governments, technology companies, media and civil society, as well as constant vigilance to adapt to new forms of disinformation that emerge.

Media and information education, the regulation of digital platforms, the development of fact-checking technologies and the promotion of international collaboration are all avenues to explore to stem the spread of disinformation. In the long term, it is essential to strengthen the resilience of societies to disinformation, by cultivating a culture of fact-checking, supporting independent media and raising awareness of the dangers of fake news. Only by adopting a comprehensive and proactive approach can we hope to reduce the impact of disinformation and preserve the integrity of our information systems.

2. Techniques Used by Disinformation Actors

Introduction

Disinformation is a complex phenomenon that encompasses a multitude of strategies deliberately designed to deceive, manipulate and influence. Disinformation actors, whether they are states, interest groups, businesses or individuals, employ sophisticated techniques to achieve their objectives. These techniques are constantly evolving, adapting to new technologies and changes in information consumption habits. In this section, we will explore these methods in detail, highlighting the underlying mechanisms and the impacts they have on contemporary societies.

1. The Creation of Manipulated Content

The creation of manipulated content is one of the cornerstones of modern disinformation. This content can take many forms, including falsified documents, edited images, altered videos or deepfakes. Deepfakes, in particular, represent a technological advancement that makes it possible to create videos where people appear saying or doing things they have never done. This technology, while fascinating, raises many ethical and legal concerns because it can be used to create false evidence that can have serious consequences.

Deepfakes: Deepfakes are generated by deep learning algorithms that analyze hundreds of hours of video to realistically recreate someone else's face and voice. This technology has the potential to destabilize elections, damage the reputations of innocent people, and create widespread confusion. For example, a deepfake video showing a political leader making controversial statements could be used to influence public opinion or incite violence.

Example: In 2020, a deepfake video of the Speaker of the United States House of Representatives, Nancy Pelosi, was distributed on social media. In that video, Pelosi appeared to be under the influence of alcohol, stumbling over her words and appearing disoriented. Although the video was quickly identified as a deepfake, it was widely shared before the truth was revealed, sowing doubt about Pelosi's sanity and ability to lead.

2. The Spread of Misleading Information through Social Networks

Social networks have become favored vectors for the rapid spread of disinformation. Their algorithms, designed to maximize user engagement, often favor sensational content, whether true or false. Disinformation actors exploit this dynamic by creating content that elicits strong emotional reactions, making that information more likely to be shared and go viral.

Use of fake accounts and bots: Fake accounts and bots are key tools used to amplify the reach of disinformation. Bots, in particular, can generate thousands of posts in a matter of minutes, creating the illusion of massive popular support for a specific idea or cause. These techniques are often used to flood platforms with content, making it difficult for users to discern fact from fiction.

Example: During the COVID-19 pandemic, thousands of fake accounts and bots were used to spread misleading information about vaccines, treatments, and the origin of the virus. These accounts shared articles, videos and memes that questioned the effectiveness of vaccines, promoted unproven treatments and fueled conspiracy theories about the origins of the virus. As a result, this misinformation has contributed to public distrust of health authorities and increased resistance to vaccination.

3. The Exploitation of Cognitive Bias

Cognitive biases are flaws in the way humans process information. They are exploited by disinformation actors to make their stories more convincing and harder to challenge. These biases include confirmation bias, where individuals are inclined to believe information that confirms their pre-existing beliefs, and anchoring bias, where the first information received disproportionately influences subsequent judgments.

Confirmation bias: This bias causes people to seek out, interpret, and remember information that confirms their beliefs. For example, a person who already believes that vaccines are dangerous will be more likely to accept and share negative information about vaccines, even if that information is false or misleading.

Example: Conspiracy theories about the 2020 United States presidential elections, which claimed the election was "stolen" from Donald Trump, largely exploited confirmation bias. Proponents of this theory were exposed to an avalanche of misinformation and fabricated "evidence" that seemed to confirm their pre-existing beliefs. Even when these claims were refuted by official investigations, many individuals continued to believe in the legitimacy of these theories because of their initial anchoring in their beliefs.

4. The Use of Simple and Emotional Narratives

Simple, emotional stories are easier to understand and remember than complex analyses. Disinformation actors use this technique to make their messages more accessible and more likely to be shared.

Exploitation of emotions: By playing on emotions such as fear, anger or outrage, misinformation spreaders can cause people to react impulsively, often by sharing information without taking the time to verify it. Stories that elicit strong emotional reactions are more likely to go viral because they exploit human nature to react instinctively to perceived threats.

Example: During the 2019 European elections, simplified and emotional narratives about the migration crisis were used to polarize voters. Shocking images of migrant boats in distress, often accompanied by alarmist comments, have been shared thousands of times on social media. These stories, although often based on distorted facts or taken out of context, have managed to provoke strong emotional reactions, thus influencing public debate and electoral results.

5. Distraction by Information Overload

Information overload is a technique deliberately used to inundate the public with so much information that it becomes difficult to discern the truth. This strategy aims to fatigue news consumers, making them more likely to accept simplified narratives or fall back on sources that confirm their biases.

Flooding the information space: Disinformation actors spread massive volumes of content, including facts, opinions, rumors and lies, to drown out critical voices and make it difficult to distinguish between truth and falsehood. This tactic is particularly effective in digital environments, where the speed and volume of information shared make real-time verification nearly impossible.

Example: During the war in Syria, an avalanche of conflicting information about the actors involved, events on the ground and allegations of atrocities was released. This overabundance of information, often deliberately fueled by the conflicting parties, has created widespread confusion, making it difficult for outside observers to understand the reality of events and take an informed position.

6. Media Control and Censorship

In some cases, disinformation actors seek to control or censor the media to ensure that only their versions of the facts are disseminated. This may include shutting down independent media outlets, implementing restrictive press freedom laws, or using state propaganda to spread specific messages while preventing access to alternative information.

Monopolization of information: By controlling distribution channels, disinformation actors can ensure that their version of events is the only one heard. In authoritarian regimes, this control is often reinforced by censorship of foreign media and the imprisonment of journalists who attempt to report facts contrary to the official version.

Example: In Russia, Vladimir Putin's government has consolidated its control over the media over the years, including closing or restricting independent media and increasing state propaganda. During the 2014 annexation of Crimea, Russian state media spread narratives that justified the annexation while demonizing Ukraine and the West. Dissenting voices were silenced, and the Russian public was given access to only a tightly controlled version of events.

7. Destabilization through the Spread of Rumors

Rumors are unverified information that spread quickly, often due to their sensational or alarming nature. Disinformation actors exploit this dynamic to sow doubt, destabilize political adversaries, or simply create confusion. Rumors are particularly effective in crisis contexts, where uncertainty is already high and people are desperate for answers.

Deliberate Spread: Rumors can be spread deliberately by disinformation actors to manipulate public opinion. They are often launched in a subtle way, using innuendo or "leaks", and amplified by complicit media or social networks. Once a rumor spreads, it becomes extremely difficult to counter, because it continues to circulate even after it has been debunked.

Example: During the Iraq War, rumors about the existence of weapons of mass destruction were deliberately spread by international actors to justify the 2003 invasion. Although these allegations turned out to be unfounded, they played a role crucial in supporting the military intervention and had devastating consequences for the region.

8. Amplification through the Use of Bots and Trolls

Bots and trolls are essential tools in the arsenal of modern disinformation. Bots are automated programs that can post and share content widely, while trolls are individuals or groups paid to provoke conflict online and amplify misinformation. These actors often work in tandem to maximize the impact of disinformation.

Artificial amplification: Bots are used to create the illusion of mass support for an idea or misinformation. By generating thousands of messages in seconds, they can influence social media algorithms, pushing platforms to promote this content to a wider audience. Trolls, on the other hand, attack dissenting voices and spread misleading narratives to destabilize online discussions.

Example: During the Brexit referendum in 2016, trolls and bots were used to massively spread misinformation and fear-mongering narratives, thereby influencing public opinion. These actions have contributed to polarizing the debate and making informed dialogue on the consequences of Brexit more difficult. False information about the economic and social impacts of Brexit has been amplified by these bots, making it almost impossible for citizens to make an informed choice.

Conclusion

The techniques used by disinformation actors are numerous and varied, and they are constantly evolving to adapt to new technological and social realities. Whether it is the creation of manipulated content, the propagation of misleading information via social media, or the exploitation of cognitive biases, these techniques are designed to manipulate public opinion and influence political events. Understanding these techniques is essential to developing effective strategies to combat disinformation and to protect the integrity of information systems.

By examining these techniques in detail, we can better understand how misinformation spreads and how it can be countered. However, the fight against disinformation cannot be led solely by governments or technology platforms. It requires collective awareness and concerted effort from society as a whole, including citizens, media, educators and regulators. Together, we can develop the tools and skills needed to resist information manipulation and maintain an informed and democratic society. **3. The Role of Social Media and Algorithms**

Introduction

In the digital age, social media has revolutionized the way information is distributed and consumed. Platforms such as Facebook, Twitter, Instagram, and YouTube have not only accelerated the flow of information, but have also changed the dynamics of information sharing on a global level. At the same time, the algorithms underlying these platforms play a crucial role in the selection and prioritization of content visible to users. This section explores in depth how social media and its algorithms contribute to the spread of misinformation, examining their mechanisms, effects and the challenges they pose.

1. The Algorithm: An Invisible Filter

Social media algorithms are designed to maximize user engagement by showing them content that will capture their attention. These algorithms analyze a wealth of data, including a user's past interactions, interests, and even their social network, to personalize the flow of information they receive.

Personalization of news feeds: One of the main problems with this personalization is the creation of "filter bubbles", where users are exposed primarily to content that reinforces their existing beliefs, while being less exposed to divergent points of view. This dynamic reinforces confirmation bias, making individuals more likely to believe false or misleading information that confirms their pre-existing beliefs.

Example: A study conducted by the Pew Research Center found that users who frequently engage with political content on Facebook are more likely to be exposed to polarizing content. Facebook's algorithms, in seeking to maximize engagement, amplify content that elicits strong emotional reactions, often at the expense of nuance and truth.

Online behavior monitoring: Social media algorithms not only filter content, they also monitor users' online behaviors to further refine the personalization of feeds. This constant monitoring allows platforms to better understand the consumption habits of their users, but it also raises privacy concerns. This massive data collection is then used to predict what type of content is most likely to capture the user's attention, leading to even further personalization of information feeds.

Implications for democracy: The personalization of information flows has profound implications for democracy. By enclosing users in filter bubbles, algorithms can contribute to the fragmentation of public space, where citizens no longer share the same information base. This fragmentation can lead to increased polarization, making democratic dialogue more difficult and reinforcing divisions within society.

2. The Virality of Disinformation

The structure of social media favors the virality of information, that is to say its ability to spread quickly and widely. Content that arouses strong emotions, such as fear, anger or indignation, is particularly likely to go viral, even if it is false or misleading.

The mechanisms of virality: Social media allow instant and large-scale sharing of information. Features like "share" and "retweet" buttons allow users to broadcast information to their networks with one click. Algorithms reward these interactions by increasing the visibility of the most shared content, creating a vicious cycle where misinformation can reach millions of people in a very short time.

Example: During the COVID-19 pandemic, conspiracy theories regarding the origins of the virus and treatments have circulated widely on social media. Posts containing false information, such as the idea that the virus was made in a laboratory, were shared millions of times before platforms acted to moderate them. The speed with which these theories reached a global audience shows the potential for misinformation to go viral on social media.

Emotions as drivers of virality: Content that provokes strong emotional reactions is more likely to go viral. Emotions such as fear, anger, or outrage increase the likelihood that users will share information, even if that information is unverified. This dynamic is exploited by disinformation actors, who create content specifically designed to arouse these emotions and thus maximize their reach.

Speed of Spread: The speed at which information can spread on social media is unprecedented. In a matter of hours, false information can reach millions of people, long before fact-checking efforts can be made to counter it. This speed of diffusion is amplified by the use of bots and fake accounts which can increase sharing and interactions, making disinformation all the more difficult to contain.

3. The Effects of Disinformation on Social Media

The consequences of disinformation on social media are numerous and affect various aspects of social and political life. Among the most notable effects are political polarization, diminishing trust in institutions, and the spread of widespread distrust.

Polarization and radicalization: Social media can exacerbate political polarization by exposing users to content that reinforces their existing beliefs while isolating them from opposing viewpoints. This dynamic can lead to radicalization, where individuals become increasingly extreme in their opinions and less open to dialogue.

Example: Studies have shown that social media users who primarily engage with content of a single political orientation are more likely to develop radical views. For example, in the United States, heavy use of Twitter by political activists has been associated with an increase in polarization between Democrats and Republicans, with each side increasingly convinced of the wrongdoing of the other.

Decreased trust in institutions: The spread of misinformation on social media can also undermine public trust in traditional institutions, such as the media, government, and science. When false or misleading information is widely shared, it can erode the credibility of reliable sources of information and sow doubt about the veracity of information disseminated by authorities.

Example: The spread of misinformation about vaccines has led to increased distrust of health authorities and contributed to declining vaccination rates in several countries. This distrust has been fueled by disinformation campaigns on social media, where misleading information about vaccine side effects has been shared thousands of times.

The spread of distrust: In addition to undermining trust in institutions, disinformation on social media can also create a climate of widespread distrust. Users are becoming increasingly skeptical of all sources of information, including those traditionally considered reliable. This distrust can lead to political disillusionment and a withdrawal from civic participation, thereby weakening democracy.

Example: In France, the spread of false information on social networks concerning the Yellow Vest demonstrations contributed to creating a climate of distrust towards traditional media and public authorities. Many Yellow Vest protesters and supporters expressed their belief that the media was being manipulated to discredit their movement, which fueled distrust and exacerbated social tensions.

4. Techniques Used by Disinformation Spreaders

Disinformation actors use a variety of techniques to exploit the characteristics of social media and maximize the dissemination of their messages.

Use of fake accounts and bots: Fake accounts and bots are often used to amplify the reach of disinformation. These accounts, sometimes automated, can generate thousands of posts in a very short time, creating the illusion of popular support for an idea or theory.

Example: During the 2016 US presidential election, Russian bots were used to spread false and polarizing information. These bots amplified extreme political messages, contributing to the polarization of the electorate and the spread of misinformation about candidates.

Astroturfing: Astroturfing is a technique where disinformation campaigns are disguised as spontaneous popular movements. Disinformation actors create fake groups or use fake accounts to simulate grassroots support for a cause or idea.

Example: During the Ukraine crisis in 2014, astroturfing campaigns were used to create the illusion of popular support in Crimea for annexation by Russia. Fake accounts and bots have flooded social media with pro-Russian messages, giving the impression of a grassroots movement in favor of annexation.

Microtargeting audiences: Another technique used by disinformation spreaders is microtargeting, where specific messages are sent to targeted groups of users based on their personal data and online behaviors. This technique helps deliver messages tailored to specific subgroups, thereby increasing the effectiveness of disinformation.

Example: During the Brexit campaign, companies like Cambridge Analytica used microtargeting to deliver pro-Brexit messages to specific segments of the British population, based on psychographic data. These messages were designed to exploit the fears and concerns of these groups, thereby helping to influence the outcome of the referendum.

The use of misleading visual content: Images and videos play a crucial role in the spread of misinformation because they have a powerful emotional impact and are often perceived as more credible than text alone. Disinformation spreaders use manipulated images, out-of-context videos or deepfakes to spread misleading messages.

Example: During the 2017 French presidential elections, a fake image of Emmanuel Macron, supposedly burning a French flag, circulated on social media. Although quickly denied, this image was widely shared and fueled heated debates online, illustrating the effectiveness of misleading visual content in disinformation.

5. Algorithms: Amplifiers of Disinformation

Social media algorithms don't just disseminate information; they filter it and prioritize it according to criteria that do not take into account veracity. By optimizing content to maximize engagement, these algorithms can unintentionally promote the spread of misinformation.

Engagement Optimization: Platform algorithms are designed to maximize the time users spend on the platform by showing them content likely to spark interactions. However, emotionally charged content, such as misinformation, often generates more engagement than informative or nuanced content.

Example: A Princeton University study found that fake news spreads faster and wider than truths on Twitter. Posts containing misinformation were 70% more likely to be retweeted than those containing truth. This amplification of disinformation is largely due to the platform's algorithms, which prioritize viral content.

The filter bubble: News feed personalization algorithms contribute to the creation of filter bubbles, where users are exposed primarily to content that reinforces their existing beliefs. This dynamic can lead to increased polarization and reduced exposure to divergent viewpoints, thereby exacerbating divisions within society.

Example: A study conducted by the University of Oxford showed that Twitter users in the United States were increasingly likely to follow accounts that shared their political views, creating isolated information ecosystems. This fragmentation of public space has contributed to political polarization and the spread of disinformation.

Recommendation algorithms: Recommendation algorithms, which suggest content based on users' past interactions, also play a key role in the spread of misinformation. These algorithms, by seeking to maximize time spent on the platform, can direct users towards increasingly extreme content, contributing to radicalization and polarization.

Example: YouTube has been criticized for its recommendation algorithm, which has been accused of pushing users toward conspiracy videos after watching more neutral content. Surveys have shown that users who watch videos on controversial topics are often directed to increasingly extreme content, contributing to the spread of misinformation.

6. Moderation Efforts and Their Limits

Faced with the rise of disinformation, social media platforms have taken steps to moderate content, but these efforts are often limited by the complexity of the task and by economic interests.

Content moderation: Platforms have implemented fact-checking systems, teams of moderators, and algorithms to detect misleading content.
However, these systems are often overwhelmed by the massive amount of information to process and the speed with which misinformation can spread.

Example: Facebook was criticized for its failure to effectively moderate misinformation during the 2020 US election. Despite introducing new rules and partnerships with fact-checkers, millions of posts containing misinformation continued to circulate on the platform.

Economic Interests: Social media platforms have an economic interest in maintaining a high level of user engagement, which may conflict with moderation efforts. Viral content, even if misleading, often generates more advertising revenue, creating a dilemma for platforms.

Example: YouTube has been accused of favoring sensationalist and misleading content to maximize views and advertising revenue. Investigations found that YouTube's recommendation algorithm pushed users toward conspiracy videos after viewing more neutral content, increasing exposure to misinformation.

Challenges of automated moderation: Although platforms have invested in automated moderation algorithms, these systems have their limitations. Algorithms may have difficulty distinguishing between satire, parody content, and actual misinformation, which can lead to moderation errors.

Example: Twitter was criticized for suspending satirical accounts that mocked conspiracy theories, confusing them with accounts that actually spread misinformation. These errors highlight the challenges platforms face in moderating content at scale.

7. User Response and Awareness Initiatives

Social media users play a key role in spreading or combating misinformation. Their reaction to the content they see and share can either amplify misinformation or help contain it.

The importance of media literacy: One of the most effective responses to misinformation is media literacy. By teaching users how to check facts, recognize reliable sources, and identify cognitive biases, it is possible to reduce the spread of misinformation.

Example: Initiatives like "Media Literacy Now" in the United States or "Les Clés des Médias" in France were set up to raise awareness among young people of the dangers of disinformation and teach them to critically navigate the media environment .

The role of fact-checking initiatives: Fact-checking organizations play a vital role in combating misinformation by verifying facts and exposing falsehoods. However, their effectiveness depends largely on their ability to reach a wide audience and influence opinions.

Example: Platforms like "PolitiFact" in the United States or "Les Décoders" of the newspaper Le Monde in France actively work to verify information circulating on social networks. Their work has helped correct many misinformation, although the real impact on public opinion is sometimes limited by polarization.

Limitations of fact-checking initiatives: Although fact-checking initiatives are crucial, they often face obstacles. The rapid spread of disinformation, coupled with some groups' distrust of traditional news sources, limits the effectiveness of fact-checking.

Example: Even after being debunked, some conspiracy theories continue to circulate widely. For example, despite fact-checking efforts, the conspiracy theory that the COVID-19 vaccine contains microchips to monitor the population has persisted in some online communities.

The "Streisand" effect: In some cases, attempts to remove or correct misinformation can have the opposite effect, drawing more attention to the original content. This effect, known as the "Streisand" effect, can complicate moderation efforts.

Example: When Facebook tried to remove posts containing false information about the US elections, it led to an increase in the spread of this information on other platforms and in private groups, thus amplifying its reach.

8. Towards a Global Strategy to Combat Disinformation

Combating disinformation requires a comprehensive and coordinated approach, involving governments, technology companies, media and civil society. This fight must focus on regulating platforms, raising user awareness and improving moderation tools.

Platform regulation: Governments must take an active role in regulating social media platforms to ensure they take effective action against misinformation. This may include requiring transparency about algorithms, sanctions for spreading false information and measures to protect freedom of expression.

Example: The European Union passed the Digital Services Act, which requires major social media platforms to take steps to combat misinformation and report on their algorithms. This regulatory framework aims to hold platforms accountable and protect users from harmful content.

International collaboration: Disinformation is a global problem that requires an internationally coordinated response. Countries must work together to share information, coordinate responses and adopt common standards to combat disinformation.

Example: The "Global Partnership for Information and Democracy", launched by Reporters Without Borders, is an initiative aimed at promoting international information governance and combating disinformation on a global scale. This partnership brings together countries, civil society organizations and technology companies to work together on these issues.

The role of tech companies: Tech companies, especially social media platforms, must take responsibility in combating misinformation. This includes developing more sophisticated detection tools, providing transparency on algorithms, and working with independent experts to improve content moderation.

Example: Facebook has invested in artificial intelligence technologies to automatically detect and remove misleading content. Additionally, the platform works with fact-checking organizations to label questionable content and notify users when they are exposed to potentially false information.

The importance of transparency: Transparency is essential to regain user trust. Platforms must be transparent about how their algorithms work, moderation decisions, and partnerships with fact-checking organizations.

Example: Twitter introduced a transparency policy that allows users to see why certain content is recommended to them and details the criteria used for moderation decisions. This transparency is an important step towards a better understanding of the dynamics of online information.

Conclusion

Social media and the algorithms behind it play a central role in the spread of misinformation in the digital age. While these platforms offer unprecedented opportunities for the dissemination of information, they also pose major challenges in terms of truth and transparency. The fight against disinformation on social networks requires a multidimensional approach, involving both increased moderation efforts, adapted regulation, and reinforced information education for users. Without these concerted efforts, disinformation will continue to undermine public trust and polarize societies.

4. Case Studies: Elections, Pandemics and International Crises

Introduction

In the context of the digital age, disinformation has taken on increasing importance, influencing public opinions and political decisions on an unprecedented scale. Elections, pandemics and international crises are critical situations where the manipulation of information can have serious and lasting repercussions. This section takes an in-depth look at how disinformation was used and influenced these major events, exploring the techniques employed, the motivations of the actors involved, and the short- and long-term consequences.

1. Elections: Manipulation of Opinions and Foreign Interference

Elections are times when democratic societies determine their political future, making them prime targets for disinformation. Manipulating public opinion during elections can alter outcomes, undermine trust in democratic institutions, and polarize societies in lasting ways. Electoral disinformation takes many forms, from fake news about candidates to disinformation campaigns orchestrated by foreign powers.

Example from the 2016 US presidential election:

The 2016 US presidential election is an emblematic case of foreign interference through disinformation. US intelligence agencies have confirmed that Russian actors, including the Internet Research Agency (IRA), carried out a massive disinformation campaign aimed at sowing discord and influencing the outcome of the election. This campaign included the use of fake accounts on social networks, the distribution of targeted advertisements, and the spread of fake news.

Disinformation techniques used:

1. **Creation of fake accounts:** Thousands of fake accounts have been created on platforms like Facebook, Twitter, and Instagram. These accounts, which posed as Americans, spread polarizing messages, promoting division and exacerbating racial and political tensions.

2. **Targeted Ads:** Russian actors have used targeted ads to reach specific segments of the population, particularly undecided voters or groups likely to abstain from voting. These advertisements often conveyed misleading information about candidates, encouraging voters not to vote or to change their voting preference.

3. **Manipulation of social media algorithms:** By generating highly viral content, disinformation actors have exploited social media algorithms to maximize the reach of their messages. Algorithms, which favor content that generates engagement (likes, shares, comments), have unintentionally amplified the spread of disinformation.

Short and long term consequences:

The 2016 disinformation campaign had profound and lasting consequences. In the short term, it has contributed to the polarization of American society and eroded trust in democratic institutions. In the long term, it has led to increased distrust of the media and information circulating on social networks. Additionally, it has pushed digital platforms and election authorities to review their security protocols for subsequent elections, although the threat of foreign interference remains high.

Example of the 2017 French presidential election:

In France, the 2017 presidential election was also marked by disinformation attempts, although these did not reach the same scale as those observed in the United States. Candidate Emmanuel Macron was the target of a disinformation campaign, notably with "MacronLeaks", a massive leak of internal emails a few days before the second round of the election. The emails contained authentic information mixed with falsified documents, intended to sow doubt and confusion.

Reactions and mitigation strategies:

1. **Responsiveness of the media and authorities:** Unlike the United States, where the disinformation of 2016 took many actors by surprise, France reacted quickly.
   The media were alerted to the possibility of manipulation and treated the leaks with caution, avoiding giving too much credit to unverified documents.

2. **Public Education:** Raising public awareness of misinformation has also played a crucial role. Ahead of the elections, awareness campaigns were carried out to educate voters about the risks of information manipulation.

3. **Collaboration with platforms:** French authorities have worked with social media platforms to quickly identify and remove misleading content.
   This collaboration made it possible to limit the impact of the disinformation campaign.

Long-term impact:

The long-term impact of disinformation attempts during the 2017 election was limited in France, largely thanks to the responsiveness of the media and authorities. However, the MacronLeaks incident highlighted the vulnerability of electoral processes to information manipulation, prompting increased vigilance for future elections.

2. Pandemics: Misinformation in Times of Health Crisis

Pandemics, by their nature, create an environment conducive to the spread of misinformation. Widespread uncertainty, combined with high demand for information, makes populations more vulnerable to false information. Misinformation during health crises can have serious consequences, including delaying the response of authorities, sowing panic, and undermining public health efforts.

Example of the COVID-19 pandemic:

The COVID-19 pandemic was accompanied by an "infodemic," an overabundance of information – much of which was false or misleading. This infodemic has been characterized by the spread of conspiracy theories about the origin of the virus, rumors about treatments, and misinformation about public health measures.

Different forms of disinformation:

1. **Conspiracy theories:** One of the most popular theories was that the virus was made in a laboratory in Wuhan and deliberately released. Although this theory has been disproven by the scientific community, it has persisted largely due to its spread on social media and its adoption by influential public figures.

2. **Vaccine Misinformation:** COVID-19 vaccines have been the target of much misinformation. Unsubstantiated claims about the dangers of vaccines, such as the idea that they cause infertility or contain microchips, have circulated widely. This misinformation has contributed to vaccine hesitancy, complicating efforts to achieve herd immunity.

3. **Unproven remedies:** Various unproven remedies have been promoted as effective treatments for COVID-19, despite a lack of scientific evidence. For example, hydroxychloroquine was touted as a silver bullet by some public figures, leading to a run on the drug and shortages for patients who actually needed it.

Response from authorities and challenges encountered:

Health authorities and governments have tried to counter this wave of misinformation by strengthening public communication and working with digital platforms to limit the spread of false information. The World Health Organization (WHO) has played a central role in providing evidence-based information and working with social media to promote this information.

Ongoing challenges:

1. **Speed of spread of disinformation:** The speed at which disinformation spreads on social media has made it difficult for authorities to effectively counter it. In many cases, the false information reached millions of people before corrections could be published.

2. **Distrust of authorities:** In some segments of the population, distrust of authorities and experts has made awareness-raising efforts ineffective. Conspiracy theories and fake news have found fertile ground among already skeptical individuals, exacerbating divisions and complicating the response to the pandemic.

3. **Impact on public health:** Misinformation has had a direct impact on public health, by delaying the adoption of protective measures, contributing to vaccine hesitancy, and inciting some people to adopt dangerous behaviors.

Historical example: The Spanish flu of 1918:

Although modern disinformation is amplified by digital technologies, the phenomenon is not new. During the 1918 Spanish Flu pandemic, rumors and misinformation also circulated. For example, unfounded theories about the origin of the flu, such as the idea that it was caused by chemical weapons used during World War I, fueled fear and confusion.

Lessons learned:

Pandemics show that misinformation can exacerbate health crises by creating confusion and delaying effective responses. To combat disinformation in these contexts, it is essential to strengthen public communication, educate the public on reliable sources of information, and work closely with communications platforms to limit the spread of false information.

3. International Crises: Disinformation and Geopolitics

International crises, whether military, diplomatic or humanitarian in nature, are often marked by the use of disinformation as a weapon of war or political manipulation. Disinformation in these contexts aims to influence public opinion, destabilize governments, or justify military actions.

Example of the crisis in Ukraine (2014-present):

Since Russia's annexation of Crimea in 2014, disinformation has been a central element of the conflict in Ukraine. Russian media have spread misleading narratives to justify the annexation and discredit the Ukrainian government. In response, Ukraine and its allies have mounted counterpropaganda efforts to expose fake news and raise international awareness of the realities of the conflict.

Disinformation techniques used:

1. **Misleading Narratives:** Russia has used simplified and emotional narratives to justify its actions in Ukraine. For example, she presented the annexation of Crimea as a necessary response to the threat posed by Ukrainian "fascists," a term deliberately chosen to evoke strong negative images.

2. **Manipulation of local media:** Russian and pro-Russian media in Ukraine have spread misleading information, ranging from exaggerated reports of the persecution of Russian speakers to baseless claims about NATO involvement in the conflict.

3. **Cyberattacks and fake documents:** In addition to media disinformation campaigns, Russia has also carried out cyberattacks to steal and distribute falsified documents, adding an additional layer of complexity to the crisis.

Impact of misinformation:

Disinformation has had a profound impact on international perceptions of the conflict in Ukraine. It helped polarize global public opinion, complicating diplomatic efforts to resolve the conflict. Additionally, it sowed confusion among local populations, making it difficult for citizens to discern the reality of events.

Example from the Syrian Civil War:

The civil war in Syria is another example of the use of disinformation in an international crisis. The actors involved, including the Syrian government, rebel groups, and foreign powers, have all used disinformation to influence public opinion, both domestically and internationally.

Disinformation techniques:

1. **State Propaganda:** The Syrian government has used propaganda campaigns to portray rebels as terrorists and to justify brutal military actions. Syrian state media broadcast stories that distorted or downplayed atrocities committed by government forces.

2. **Competing narratives:** Rebel groups and their international backers have also spread alternative narratives, accusing the Syrian government of war crimes and highlighting the suffering of civilians. This battle of narratives has created widespread confusion about the reality of the conflict.

3. **Use of social media:** Social media played a central role in the spread of disinformation during the Syrian civil war. Videos and images, often taken out of context or manipulated, have been shared to influence public opinion and mobilize international support.

Consequences of disinformation:

Disinformation has exacerbated the conflict in Syria by deepening divisions between different factions and complicating efforts to find a diplomatic solution. It has also contributed to the radicalization of certain segments of the population, both in Syria and abroad.

The importance of resilience in the face of misinformation:

These case studies show the importance of developing resilience in the face of misinformation, both at an individual and collective level. Elections, pandemics, and international crises will continue to be targets for disinformation actors, and it is essential to have strategies in place to deal with them.

Resilience strategies:

1. **Media and information literacy:** Education is one of the most effective weapons against disinformation. By teaching citizens how to check facts, recognize reliable sources, and understand manipulation techniques, it is possible to reduce vulnerability to disinformation.

2. **Strengthening democratic institutions:** Trust in institutions is crucial to countering disinformation. Strong, transparent and accountable institutions can better resist attempts to manipulate information.

3. **International collaboration:** Disinformation is a global problem that requires an internationally coordinated response. Countries must work together to share information, coordinate responses and adopt common standards to combat disinformation.

4. **Use of advanced technologies:** Technologies such as artificial intelligence can be used to detect and counter disinformation on a large scale. However, these technologies must be deployed ethically and transparently to avoid abuse.

Conclusion

Disinformation in elections, pandemics, and international crises highlights the scale of the impact that fake news can have on the contemporary world. Combating disinformation in these contexts requires a multifaceted approach, combining technological efforts, education campaigns, and international cooperation. By understanding the mechanisms by which disinformation spreads in these critical situations, we can better prepare societies to deal with it and preserve the integrity of our institutions. **5. Disinformation in the Age of Deepfakes**

Introduction

The digital age has brought a new dimension to disinformation with the emergence of deepfakes, videos and images artificially created using artificial intelligence (AI) to manipulate reality. Deepfakes have become a powerful tool for spreading disinformation, posing significant challenges for society, governments and technology companies. This section explores the impact of deepfakes on disinformation, the technological mechanisms behind these creations, known use cases, ethical implications, and strategies to combat this growing threat.

Origin and Development of Deepfakes

Deepfakes get their name from the combination of "deep learning" and "fake". Deep learning is a subdiscipline of artificial intelligence that uses neural networks to analyze and synthesize complex data, including images and videos. Deepfakes emerged in the late 2010s, when researchers began applying image generation techniques to video manipulation.

First experiments and distribution:

The first deepfakes were often created for entertainment or malicious purposes, notably to insert celebrity faces into pornographic videos. However, the technology quickly evolved and spread to other areas, including politics and media manipulation. The accessibility of the tools needed to create deepfakes, combined with the availability of vast amounts of personal data online, has made it possible for almost anyone to produce highly compelling content.

Examples of early deepfakes:

One notable early example of deepfake involved the creation of videos where celebrities' faces were realistically superimposed onto actors in adult films. While these early videos revealed the technical capabilities of deepfakes, they also highlighted the ethical and legal issues associated with the technology.

The evolution towards more sophisticated applications:

As the technology has improved, deepfakes have started to appear in more serious contexts, including politics. In 2018, a doctored video of US President Barack Obama circulated, showing a fictionalized version of him giving a speech he never gave. This video, although created for demonstration purposes to warn of the dangers of deepfakes, illustrated the disruptive potential of this technology.

Technology and Mechanisms of Deepfakes

Deepfakes rely on several key technologies, including generative adversarial networks (GANs), transfer learning, and 3D modeling. Understanding these mechanisms is essential to understanding how deepfakes are created and why they are so difficult to detect.

Generative adversarial networks (GAN):

GANs are at the heart of creating deepfakes. A GAN consists of two neural networks: a generator and a discriminator. The generator creates images or videos, while the discriminator attempts to distinguish these creations from actual images or videos. The two networks compete in a learning process, where the generator continually improves the quality of its creations to fool the discriminator. This process leads to the production of extremely realistic, but fake, videos and images.

Transfer of learning:

Transfer learning allows pre-trained models to be used on large amounts of data to speed up the process of creating deepfakes. By using existing models, deepfake creators can quickly adapt algorithms to new faces or contexts, making the manufacturing process faster and accessible.

3D modeling and face tracking:

3D modeling is often used to superimpose faces onto existing bodies in videos. This technique involves creating a three-dimensional model of the target's face, which can then be manipulated to match the expressions and body movements in the original video. Face tracking is another key component, which helps maintain consistency between facial and body movements, even in complex scenes.

Text-to-speech algorithms:

In addition to images and videos, deepfakes can also involve synthesized voices. Advanced speech synthesis algorithms can recreate a person's voice by analyzing existing recordings. Combined with deepfake videos, these synthesized voices can make fake videos even more convincing.

Impact of Deepfakes on Disinformation

Deepfakes represent a new frontier in disinformation, amplifying the abilities of malicious actors to manipulate public opinion, discredit public figures, and sow confusion.

Political manipulation:

The use of deepfakes in a political context is particularly worrying. Faked videos can be used to spread misleading messages, discredit candidates or leaders, or incite violence. For example, a deepfake video of a political leader making controversial or illegal statements could influence the results of an election or cause social unrest.

Example of electoral manipulation:

Let's imagine a scenario where a deepfake video shows a presidential candidate making a racist speech or making confessions of corruption. Even if the video is quickly denied, the damage could be irreparable, as public perception would have already been affected. This type of manipulation could be used by domestic political adversaries or by foreign powers seeking to destabilize a country.

Disinformation in times of crisis:

Deepfakes can also be used to sow confusion during crises, whether military, health, or economic. For example, a doctored video showing a leader announcing an imminent attack could trigger panic or a military response, escalating an already tense situation.

Impact on trust in the media:

One of the most insidious consequences of deepfakes is the potential to undermine public trust in media. If people can no longer trust what they see or hear, they may become cynical and reject not only false information, but also uncomfortable truths. This can lead to increased fragmentation of public opinion and social polarization.

Example of crisis of confidence:

In 2020, during the COVID-19 pandemic, doctored videos showing world leaders making erroneous statements about the virus or vaccines circulated on the internet. Although some of these videos were quickly debunked, their mere existence fueled distrust of authorities and the media, complicating public health efforts.

Deepfakes Use Cases

Deepfakes have been used in a variety of contexts, from politics to the entertainment industry to non-consensual pornography. This section examines some notable use cases of deepfakes.

Deepfakes and international politics:

Deepfakes have been used in state-orchestrated disinformation campaigns to influence public opinion in other countries. For example, state actors have been alleged to have created and distributed deepfakes to influence elections in rival countries or to discredit foreign leaders. These manipulations often aim to destabilize governments, exacerbate internal divisions, or weaken a country's position on the international stage.

Hypothetical example:

Suppose a doctored video shows a foreign president secretly admitting to cheating in the election. Although the video is fake, it could be used by political opponents to fuel conspiracy theories and mobilize protesters. Even after the video has been debunked, it could leave lasting marks on public perception.

Deepfakes and cyberharassment:

Deepfakes are also used to harass or discredit individuals, often women, by creating non-consensual pornographic videos. These videos are then shared online, causing immense harm to the reputations and personal lives of the victims. This form of cyberharassment raises serious questions about privacy and the legal remedies available to victims.

Example of online harassment:

A female politician could be the target of a pornographic deepfake, released shortly before an election to harm her campaign. Although the video is fake, it could lead to negative media coverage and attacks on social media, affecting its credibility and reputation.

Deepfakes in entertainment:

In the entertainment industry, deepfakes have been used for more benign purposes, such as recreating deceased actors for films or series. For example, iconic actors like Carrie Fisher have been brought back to the screen using deepfakes, allowing directors to complete scenes after their deaths. Although these uses are generally well accepted, they nevertheless raise questions about the ethics of posthumous use of a person's image.

Use cases in social media:

Deepfakes also circulate on social networks in the form of memes or humorous videos. While this content may seem harmless, it contributes to trivializing the use of deepfakes and reducing public vigilance in the face of this type of manipulation. The virality of this content increases its impact, even when its intention is not malicious.

Ethical and Legal Implications

Deepfakes raise complex questions about ethics, privacy, and legal liability. This section explores these challenges and discusses potential legal frameworks to regulate the use of deepfakes.

Ethics of deepfakes:

Deepfakes pose major ethical issues, particularly regarding identity falsification and consent. Using a person's image without their consent to create a deepfake can be considered a serious violation of privacy. Additionally, the ability to manipulate someone's appearance and voice raises questions about the authenticity and integrity of communications. **Consent and exploitation:**

Consent is a central aspect of ethical debates over deepfakes. For example, in the case of non-consensual pornographic deepfakes, the creation and distribution of these videos without the permission of the people involved constitutes clear exploitation. Even in non-pornographic contexts, using someone's image for political, advertising, or other purposes without their consent can be perceived as abusive.

Responsibility of creators and broadcasters:

The question of liability is complex. Who should be held responsible for the creation and distribution of deepfakes: the creator, the person who distributes them, or the platforms that host them? Existing laws on defamation, privacy, and copyright may offer some protections, but they are often inadequate to address the specific challenges posed by deepfakes.

Emerging legal frameworks:

Some countries have started to introduce laws to regulate the use of deepfakes. For example, in 2019, California passed a law banning the use of deepfakes for political purposes in the 60 days before an election. Other jurisdictions have followed with similar laws, but enforcement of these laws remains a challenge due to the transnational nature of the Internet and the difficulty of assigning responsibility for online content.

Law Enforcement Challenges:

Enforcement of laws against deepfakes is complicated by the ability of creators to remain anonymous and operate from jurisdictions with less strict regulations. Additionally, the speed with which deepfakes can be shared online makes it difficult to remove them before they cause harm. Law enforcement and judicial authorities must therefore develop new technical skills and collaborate internationally to combat this threat.

Strategies to Combat Deepfakes

Faced with the growing threat of deepfakes, several strategies have been proposed to detect, limit and counter their impact.

Deepfake detection:

Deepfake detection is a growing area of research. Researchers are developing algorithms that can identify telltale signs of deepfakes, such as visual artifacts, inconsistencies in lip movement, or anomalies in lighting. However, as techniques for creating deepfakes become more sophisticated, detection tools must constantly evolve to remain effective.

Development of verification tools:

Tech companies, in collaboration with academic researchers, are working on automated verification tools that can be integrated into social media platforms to alert users when they are exposed to potentially fake content. For example, real-time analytics tools can be used to analyze videos shared on social media and detect deepfakes before they go viral.

International collaboration:

The fight against deepfakes requires international collaboration. Governments, technology companies, and non-governmental organizations must work together to establish global standards and share best practices. This collaboration could include agreements on information exchange, development of shared databases for deepfake detection, and coordination of legislative efforts.

Education and awareness:

Educating the public about deepfakes is crucial to limiting their impact. Awareness campaigns can help people understand the dangers of deepfakes and learn to recognize the signs of a fake video. Additionally, integrating media education into school curricula can prepare younger generations to navigate an increasingly complex media landscape.

Responsibility of platforms:

Social media platforms have a key role to play in the fight against deepfakes. They must have clear policies in place to manage fake content, including reporting mechanisms and fact-checking processes. Some platforms have already started banning deepfakes in their terms of service, but the effectiveness of these measures depends on their rigorous enforcement.

Encouragement of research and innovation:

Finally, it is essential to support research and innovation in the field of deepfake detection and prevention. This can include funding research projects, organizing competitions to develop new detection technologies, and creating partnerships between the private sector and universities. Research must also focus on ethical and legal aspects, to ensure that the solutions developed respect individual rights and civil liberties.

Conclusion

Deepfakes represent a major challenge for modern society, as they call into question trust in media and the reality of information. As technology continues to evolve, it is imperative that governments, businesses, and citizens work together to develop effective strategies to detect, counter, and regulate deepfakes. By educating the public, improving detection tools, and establishing strong legal frameworks, we can hope to minimize the harm caused by this insidious form of disinformation. **1. Cognitive Bias and Misinformation**

Introduction

In a world where information is just a click away, misinformation proliferates at an alarming rate. To understand how and why it spreads so easily, it is essential to look at the cognitive mechanisms that underlie our perceptions and judgments. Cognitive biases, these systematic distortions in the way we perceive reality, play a central role in how we process information, especially when it comes to misinformation. These biases, often unconscious, are exploited by those who seek to manipulate public opinion, whether for political, economic or ideological reasons. This chapter explores in depth various cognitive biases and their relationship with misinformation, analyzing their impact on society and proposing strategies to mitigate them.

1.1 Confirmation Bias

Origin and nature of confirmation bias

Confirmation bias is one of the most studied cognitive biases in psychology. It reflects our tendency to seek out, interpret, and remember information in a way that confirms our pre-existing beliefs. This bias is deeply rooted in our need for internal consistency and psychological comfort. The idea that we might be wrong or that our worldview might be flawed is often too uncomfortable to accept, causing us to avoid or ignore information that contradicts our beliefs.

Manifestations in daily life

- **Politics and Ideologies:** Individuals who strongly identify with a political ideology or religious belief are particularly likely to succumb to confirmation bias. For example, loyal voters of a political party may reject criticism or scandals involving their leaders, even when the evidence is overwhelming. This phenomenon is visible in many political contexts around the world, where supporters of a leader or party continue to support them despite accusations of corruption or incompetence, downplaying the facts or dismissing them as "fake news".

- **Conspiracy Theories:** Confirmation bias also fuels belief in conspiracy theories. Individuals who believe that hidden forces control world events will seek evidence that supports this belief, while ignoring evidence that refutes it. For example, conspiracy theories about the 1969 moon landing, where some believe the moon landing was faked, continue to circulate despite overwhelming evidence to the contrary. Proponents of these theories ignore photographic evidence, astronaut testimonies, and scientific analysis, preferring to focus on minor anomalies or misinterpretations of the facts.

Impact of confirmation bias on the spread of misinformation

Confirmation bias reinforces the spread of misinformation by creating "information bubbles" where individuals are exposed only to information that reinforces their existing beliefs. These bubbles are exacerbated by social media algorithms, which favor content likely to generate high engagement, often by presenting polarizing information that elicits strong emotional reactions.

Real-world examples of disinformation reinforced through confirmation bias

- **Migration crisis in Europe:** During the migration crisis in Europe starting in 2015, confirmation bias played a key role in the spread of false information about migrants. For example, unsubstantiated rumors about violent acts by migrants were widely shared and believed by those already opposed to immigration, despite official denials and evidence to the contrary.

- **Vaccination and anti-vaccine movements:** Anti-vaccine movements exploit confirmation bias by spreading false or distorted information about the dangers of vaccines. Parents who are already concerned about vaccine safety are more likely to believe and share alarming stories, even when they are scientifically discredited.

Strategies to mitigate confirmation bias

- **Encourage exposure to diverse viewpoints:** One of the most effective ways to reduce confirmation bias is to encourage individuals to expose themselves to a variety of viewpoints. Social media platforms and search engines could be modified to promote a diversity of opinions, rather than reinforcing filter bubbles.

- **Promote critical thinking:** Critical thinking education can help individuals recognize their own cognitive biases and evaluate information more objectively. This could include specific courses in schools on how to recognize and correct confirmation bias, as well as awareness campaigns for the general public.

- **Fact-checking and transparency:** Media and fact-checking platforms play a crucial role in correcting misinformation. By providing transparent, evidence-based information, they can help counter the effects of confirmation bias.

1.2 Anchoring Bias

Origin and operation of anchoring bias

Anchoring bias occurs when individuals rely too heavily on the first information they receive (the anchor) when making decisions. This initial information serves as a reference point and disproportionately influences subsequent judgments. This bias is particularly problematic in the context of misinformation, because it means that first impressions, even if wrong, can have a lasting impact on individuals' beliefs and decisions.

Impact of anchoring bias on information perception

Anchoring bias is exploited in many forms of misinformation, including how news headlines are written or how events are initially reported. Early reports of an event, even if later corrected, can continue to influence public perceptions. For example, in the case of a false accusation of a political scandal, the mere fact that the accusation was made can entrench the idea that the politician in question is corrupt, even if the accusation is quickly refuted. **Historical examples of the anchoring effect in misinformation**

- **Iraq War (2003):** Before the 2003 invasion of Iraq, the US administration entrenched the idea that Saddam Hussein's regime possessed weapons of mass destruction (WMD). Even after these WMDs were never found, this initial belief continued to influence public perception of the war and justified intervention in the eyes of many Americans.

- **Financial Crises:** During economic crises, initial interpretations of the causes of the crisis, even if inaccurate, can lastingly influence public perceptions and policy responses. For example, the 2008 financial crisis was initially attributed to the failure of investment banks, and although other factors were subsequently identified, this initial impression has dominated public discourse. **Strategies to mitigate anchoring bias**

- **Rapid and corrective communication:** It is crucial to correct incorrect information quickly to prevent it from becoming lasting mental anchors. Media and public officials must be prepared to provide clarifications whenever incorrect information is disseminated.

- **Promoting In-Depth Analysis:** Encouraging individuals to seek out additional sources of information and deepen their understanding of topics before drawing conclusions can help mitigate the anchoring effect.

- **Debiasing Techniques Training:** Specific debiasing techniques, such as counter-anchoring, where individuals are exposed to information contrary to the initial anchor, can be taught in critical thinking training programs.

1.3 Availability Bias

Nature and origin of availability bias

Availability bias occurs when individuals evaluate the likelihood of an event based on how easily they can recall similar examples. This bias is particularly pronounced for recent or striking events, which are more easily recalled and therefore perceived as more likely or more representative than more common but less memorable events.

Exploitation of availability bias in disinformation

Disinformation creators exploit this bias by promoting stories or images that are emotionally striking, even if those stories are statistically rare or unrepresentative. For example, a viral video showing a violent incident involving a specific group may lead to an exaggerated perception of how dangerous that group is, even if aggregate data shows that such incidents are rare.

Contemporary Examples of Availability Bias

- **Terrorism and risk perception:** Acts of terrorism, although relatively rare, are often intensely publicized, leading the public to overestimate the threat of terrorism compared to other, more frequent dangers, such as car accidents or chronic diseases.

- **Urban Crime:** Media coverage of crimes in large cities can cause residents to perceive their environment as more dangerous than it actually is. This phenomenon is amplified by sensationalist reporting that highlights violent crime or vandalism, without providing context on overall crime trends.

Impact on public and personal decision-making

Availability bias can lead to political or personal decisions based on incorrect perceptions of reality. For example, politicians may be pushed to adopt "zero tolerance" policies in response to exaggerated perceptions of crime, when more nuanced, evidence-based approaches would be more effective.

Strategies to mitigate availability bias

- **Contextualizing Statistics:** Journalists and educators can help mitigate availability bias by providing statistical context to publicized events, allowing the public to understand the true frequency of these events relative to other risks.

- **Exposure to varied stories** : Diversifying the stories to which the public is exposed, particularly by highlighting positive or less sensational stories, can help balance perceptions.

- **Risk Perception Education Campaigns:** Raising public awareness of how media and cognitive biases can influence risk perception can help individuals develop a more balanced perspective on real-world dangers.

1.4 The Overconfidence Bias

Origin and functioning of the overconfidence bias

Overconfidence bias is the tendency of individuals to overestimate their own abilities, knowledge or judgments. This bias is particularly pernicious because it often leads individuals to reject expert opinions or ignore evidence that contradicts their views. Overconfidence is linked to the Dunning-Kruger effect, where people with little skill or knowledge in an area are most likely to overestimate their expertise.

Exploiting the overconfidence bias in disinformation

Misinformation creators exploit the overconfidence bias by presenting simplified information or fallacious arguments in a convincing manner, so that individuals feel capable of judging complex topics without having extensive training or knowledge. For example, in debates about climate change, climate deniers often use pseudo-scientific arguments that seem accessible and logical, even if they are fundamentally flawed.

Examples of the impact of overconfidence bias

- **Public health decisions:** During the COVID-19 pandemic, overconfidence bias has led some people to ignore public health advice or adopt unproven treatments, such as hydroxychloroquine, despite warnings from health authorities.

- **Financial investments:** In finance, overconfidence can lead investors to take excessive risks, overestimating their ability to predict market movements. This can result in significant financial losses when investments do not go as planned. **Strategies to Reduce Overconfidence Bias**

- **Promoting intellectual humility:** Encouraging an attitude of intellectual humility, where individuals recognize the limits of their own expertise and are open to learning, can help reduce overconfidence bias.

- **Valorization of specialized knowledge:** It is crucial to value and promote the opinions of experts in complex fields. This can be done through public information campaigns that highlight scientific evidence and expert analyses.

- **Continuing education and updating of knowledge:** In a constantly changing world, it is important that individuals continue to update their knowledge

  and to train in new information and technologies. This can help reduce overconfidence by exposing individuals to the complexity of topics and the need for expertise.

1.5 The Negativity Bias

Nature and origin of negativity bias

Negativity bias is the tendency to value negative experiences more than positive ones. This bias has an evolutionary basis, as it is more important for survival to pay attention to potential threats than to positive opportunities. However, in the modern context, this bias can lead to a distorted perception of reality, where the negative aspects of life are amplified while the positive aspects are downplayed.

Exploitation of negativity bias in the media

The media exploits the negativity bias by highlighting negative news because it captures more public attention. Reports of disasters, crimes, or political scandals often dominate the news, which can create a distorted and pessimistic worldview. For example, news about violent crimes is often overrepresented compared to their actual occurrence, which can lead to an exaggerated perception of insecurity.

Impact of negativity bias on society

Negativity bias can have corrosive effects on public morale and trust in institutions. When people are constantly exposed to negative news, they can develop a sense of hopelessness or distrust toward the government, the media, and even toward their fellow citizens. This phenomenon can also lead to social apathy, where individuals feel powerless in the face of world problems, which can reduce civic engagement and political participation.

Strategies to mitigate negativity bias

- **Balancing media stories:** It is important to balance negative stories with positive or constructive news. The media can play a key role in highlighting stories of success, resilience, or innovations that provide solutions to current challenges.

- **Emotional Resilience Education:** By teaching individuals how to deal with negative information in a healthy way, it is possible to reduce the impact of negativity bias. This may include techniques for stress management, mindfulness, and developing personal resilience.

- **Promoting critical thinking:** Encouraging individuals to analyze the information they receive critically, considering context and comparing sources, can help mitigate the effect of negativity bias.

Origin and nature of ingroup bias

Ingroup bias refers to the tendency of individuals to favor members of their own group (ingroup) over those of other groups (outgroup). This bias is rooted in the human need for belonging and social identity. In contexts of conflict or competition, this bias can lead to distrust, discrimination, and dehumanization of members of outgroups.

Exploitation of ingroup bias in disinformation

Disinformation often exploits ingroup bias to inflame tensions between different social, ethnic, or political groups. Disinformation narratives are often designed to strengthen ingroup cohesion by denigrating outgroups, which can lead to increased polarization and social conflict. For example, during political crises or ethnic conflicts, rumors or fake news may be spread to fuel hatred or distrust between conflicting groups.

Historical Examples of Ingroup Bias

- **War Propaganda:** During wars, governments often use propaganda to strengthen a sense of national cohesion and to portray the enemy as morally inferior or inhumane. For example, during World War II, the Allies and Axis powers both used caricatures and stereotypes to dehumanize the enemy, thereby reinforcing ingroup bias.

- **Ethnic conflicts:** In ethnic conflicts, ingroup bias is often exacerbated by narratives of victimization and revenge. For example, during the Rwandan genocide of 1994, Hutu propaganda portrayed Tutsis as an existential threat, thus justifying the atrocities committed.

Impact on social cohesion

Ingroup bias contributes to social division and fragmentation of society. When groups become increasingly isolated and distrustful of each other, it becomes difficult to build social consensus or work together to solve common problems. This dynamic can be exploited by malicious actors seeking to destabilize a society or manipulate public opinion for political purposes. **Strategies to mitigate ingroup bias**

- **Encouraging intergroup dialogue:** Promoting dialogue and interactions between different social, ethnic, or political groups can help reduce prejudice and mitigate ingroup bias. This may include mediation initiatives, cultural exchange programs, and collaborative community projects.

- **Empathy education:** Developing empathy toward members of outgroups can help reduce distrust and foster better mutual understanding. Empathy education can be integrated into school curricula, professional training, and public awareness campaigns.

- **Reducing stereotypes:** The media, educators, and opinion leaders can play a key role in reducing stereotypes by presenting diverse stories and highlighting positive examples of intergroup collaboration.

Conclusion

Cognitive biases are powerful mechanisms that shape how we perceive the world and interact with information. In the context of disinformation, these biases can be exploited to spread false information, reinforce erroneous beliefs, and polarize opinions. Understanding these biases and the underlying mechanisms is essential to developing effective strategies to counter misinformation and promote a better informed and more resilient society.

2. Group Effects and Social Dynamics

Introduction

Misinformation is not just an individual phenomenon; it is deeply rooted in social dynamics and group interactions. Social mechanisms, such as conformity, polarization, and crowding, greatly influence how misinformation is spread, accepted, and even defended. Understanding these dynamics is crucial to designing effective strategies to counter disinformation and promote a better informed and more resilient society. This chapter explores various aspects of group effects and social dynamics in relation to disinformation, drawing on historical examples, psychological and sociological analyses, as well as mitigation strategies.

2.1 Social Compliance and Disinformation

Origin and definition of social conformity

Social conformity is the tendency of individuals to change their opinions, attitudes, or behaviors to conform to the norms of the group to which they belong. This phenomenon is driven by the desire for social acceptance and the fear of marginalization or rejection. Conformity is a powerful mechanism that, although it can strengthen social cohesion, can also lead to the acceptance of false information when it is widely accepted by the group.

Historical and contemporary examples

- **Asch's experiment (1951)** : Solomon Asch demonstrated that individuals could deny obvious facts to conform to the majority. This classic experiment found that up to 37% of participants were willing to give an incorrect answer along the length of a line just to align with the majority of the group. This phenomenon is found in online group dynamics, where social pressure often encourages individuals to spread or accept false information.

- **Social Media and Filter Bubbles** : On social media platforms, algorithms are designed to show users content that is consistent with their interests and past opinions, creating "filter bubbles." These bubbles reinforce social conformity by limiting exposure to divergent viewpoints and encouraging the spread of misinformation that aligns with the group's beliefs.

Impact of social conformity on the spread of misinformation

Social conformity plays a central role in the spread of misinformation, especially in environments where groups are highly polarized. Individuals, out of a desire for belonging and acceptance, may share false information simply because it is accepted by their group, thereby reinforcing misinformation. **Contemporary examples**

- **COVID-19 Crisis** : During the COVID-19 pandemic, online groups have spread misinformation about the virus, treatments and vaccines. Social pressure within these groups has led some members to reject scientific information and embrace conspiracy theories, despite evidence to the contrary.

- **Political movements** : In polarized political movements, such as those surrounding the U.S. presidential elections, social conformity has reinforced the spread of misinformation. Supporters on both sides of the political spectrum have shared false or misleading information to support their cause, often in response to social pressure from their group.

Strategies to mitigate social conformity

- **Promoting diversity of opinion** : Encouraging a diversity of perspectives within groups can help reduce social conformity. Educators, thought leaders and the media must promote open discussions where differences of opinion are respected and encouraged.

- **Critical Thinking Education** : Critical thinking education is essential to help individuals recognize and resist the pressure of social conformity. This includes skills such as evaluating information sources, fact-checking, and being aware of cognitive biases.

- **Creating safe spaces for dialogue** : Creating spaces where individuals can express their opinions without fear of judgment or rejection can encourage more honest discussions and reduce the pressure of social conformity.

2.2 Crowd Effect and Misinformation

Definition and operation of the crowd effect

The crowd effect occurs when individual responsibility is diluted in a group, often leading to extreme or irrational behavior. This phenomenon is particularly relevant in the context of disinformation, where online crowds can quickly spread false information without consideration of consequences. **Examples and illustrations**

- **Riots and demonstrations** : The crowd effect is often observed during riots or demonstrations, where individuals, caught up in the collective energy, may participate in acts of violence or vandalism that they would not commit alone. For example, the U.S. Capitol riots in January 2021 showed how mob effect, coupled with misinformation on social media, can lead to collective actions based on erroneous beliefs.

- **Economic crises and bank panics** : Bank panics are often exacerbated by the crowd effect, where unfounded rumors about a bank's insolvency lead to mass withdrawals of funds by customers, thereby precipitating the crisis. These dynamics are amplified by the speed with which information (true or false) circulates in online crowds.

Psychological analysis of the crowd effect

The crowd effect is reinforced by several psychological factors, including anonymity, diffusion of responsibility, and social mimicry. Online, these dynamics are exacerbated by the relative anonymity of users and the speed with which information can go viral.

Consequences of the crowd effect on disinformation

Disinformation spread by the crowd effect can have serious consequences, in particular by amplifying social tensions, provoking irrational collective reactions, and leading to political or economic decisions based on incorrect information. **Strategies to mitigate crowding**

- **Promoting individual responsibility** : Encouraging individuals to think critically about their actions and decisions, even within a group, can help mitigate the crowd effect. This may include awareness campaigns about the potential consequences of spreading misinformation.

- **Moderation and regulation of online platforms** : Social media platforms can play a crucial role in establishing effective moderation mechanisms to limit the spread of misinformation and in promoting responsible behavior. This may include tools for reporting misinformation and sanctions for those who deliberately spread misinformation.

- **Crowd and crisis management training** : For authorities and organizations, specialized training on crowd and crisis management can help prevent and mitigate the effects of crowd effect in crisis situations, especially in online environments.

Definition and mechanisms of group polarization

Group polarization occurs when interactions within a group lead to positions more extreme than those initially held by its members. This phenomenon is often exacerbated by misinformation, which can radicalize opinions and create deep divisions within society.

Concrete examples of polarization

- **Political polarization** : Polarization around elections and public policies is often fueled by disinformation campaigns that reinforce divisions between different groups. For example, the United States presidential elections in 2016 and 2020 were marked by extreme polarization, where partisans on both sides of the political spectrum were exposed to polarizing and sometimes false information.

- **Religious and ethnic conflicts** : In many countries, disinformation is used to inflame tensions between different ethnic or religious groups, leading to violence and prolonged conflict. For example, in India, rumors and fake news shared on WhatsApp have led to lynchings and communal violence.

Analysis of the causes of polarization

Group polarization is fueled by several factors, including the homogenization of opinions within the group, the demonization of out-groups, and the selective dissemination of information that reinforces the group's beliefs. Online, this phenomenon is accentuated by social media algorithms that favor polarizing content.

Impact of polarization on society and democracy

Group polarization seriously harms democracy by making dialogue and compromise more difficult. It can also lead to a radicalization of positions, making governance and social cooperation more complicated. Polarized societies are also more vulnerable to foreign interference and political manipulation through disinformation. **Strategies to Reduce Group Polarization**

- **Promoting dialogue and mutual understanding** : To reduce polarization, it is essential to create spaces for dialogue where individuals from different backgrounds can exchange their views in a respectful manner. Mediation initiatives, civic education programs, and collaborative community projects can help reduce tensions and promote better mutual understanding.

- **Encouraging exposure to divergent opinions** : Media and social media platforms can play a key role in encouraging exposure to divergent opinions and promoting content that encourages dialogue and reflection rather than polarization.

  Education in Critical Thinking and Tolerance : Education in critical thinking and tolerance is essential to helping individuals navigate an increasingly polarized media landscape. This includes skills in evaluating sources, analyzing arguments, and understanding cognitive biases.

Role of emotions in the diffusion of information

Emotions play a crucial role in how information is perceived and disseminated. Content that arouses strong emotions, such as fear, anger, or outrage, is more likely to go viral, even if it is factually incorrect. Creators of misinformation often exploit these emotions to maximize the impact of their messages.

Examples and analyzes

- **Fear and anxiety** : Disinformation campaigns about health crises, like the COVID-19 pandemic, exploit fear to spread conspiracy theories and misinformation. For example, rumors about vaccine side effects have been widely shared, creating widespread anxiety and vaccine hesitancy.

- **Anger and outrage** : Fake news that provokes anger or outrage is often shared more widely because it resonates with individuals' strong emotions. For example, rumors about acts of corruption or social injustice are often amplified by the emotions they arouse.

Impact of emotions on the perception and diffusion of disinformation

Emotions can alter the perception of information and influence the way it is interpreted and disseminated. For example, studies show that individuals are more likely to believe and share information that confirms their emotions, even if that information is false. This can lead to the rapid spread of misinformation, particularly in contexts of crisis or social tension.

Strategies to mitigate the influence of emotions on misinformation

- **Emotion management education** : Raising individuals' awareness of the impact of emotions on their perception of information can help them develop a more critical and thoughtful approach. This may include training on stress management, mindfulness, and emotional regulation.

- **Promoting rational and balanced discourse** : Media and educators can help mitigate the influence of emotions by promoting rational and balanced discourse, which emphasizes facts and evidence rather than emotions.

- **Creating positive counter-narratives** : To counter emotional misinformation, it is important to create and disseminate counter-narratives that highlight positive stories, constructive solutions, and examples of resilience in the face of challenges.

2.5 The Impact of Opinion Leaders on the Spread of Disinformation

Role of opinion leaders in society

Opinion leaders, whether they are celebrities, influencers or political figures, play a crucial role in the dissemination of information. Their status and credibility with their audience can amplify the impact of the information they share, whether true or false.

Historical and contemporary examples

- **Political Propaganda** : Political figures have often used their influence to spread misleading narratives or biased information in order to manipulate public opinion. For example, during World War II, leaders on both sides used propaganda to justify their actions and mobilize popular support.

- **Social networks and influencers** : Today, influencers on social networks

    play a similar role, using their platform to share information, sometimes without verifying its veracity. For example, celebrities and influencers have spread conspiracy theories about COVID-19, amplifying misinformation and sowing confusion among their millions of followers.

-

Psychological analysis of the influence of opinion leaders

Individuals are more likely to believe information shared by figures they respect or admire, even if that information is false. This phenomenon is amplified by the halo effect, where a person's authority or charisma reflects on the perceived credibility of their messages. Opinion leaders therefore have disproportionate power in spreading misinformation, especially when they speak on controversial or emotionally charged topics.

Social consequences of the influence of opinion leaders

The influence of opinion leaders in spreading misinformation can reinforce social divisions, polarize opinions and make correcting misinformation more difficult. Their impact is particularly pronounced in online environments, where their messages can reach millions of people in minutes.

Strategies to mitigate the impact of opinion leaders on misinformation

- **Fact-checking and platform regulation** : Social media platforms should strengthen their fact-checking policies, particularly for thought leader accounts with large audiences. This can include warning labels on unverified or misleading information, as well as sanctions for opinion leaders who deliberately spread false information.

- **Promoting accountability among opinion leaders** : It is essential to promote a culture of accountability among opinion leaders, encouraging them to verify information before sharing it and to use their influence ethically.

- **Public education in critical thinking** : Raising public awareness of the influence of opinion leaders and the importance of verifying information, even when shared by respected figures, can help reduce the impact of misinformation.

2.6 The Echo Chamber Phenomenon and Radicalization

Definition of echo chambers

Echo chambers refer to environments, often online, where individuals are exposed primarily to opinions and information that confirm their pre-existing beliefs, thereby reinforcing those beliefs and isolating individuals from divergent viewpoints. This phenomenon is often exacerbated by social media algorithms, which favor content likely to generate high engagement. **Examples and analyzes**

- **Online echo chambers** : On platforms like Facebook, Twitter or YouTube, users are often locked in echo chambers where the information presented to them is filtered to match their interests and beliefs. This can lead to a radicalization of opinions, where users are increasingly exposed to extreme or polarizing content.

  Political and social radicalization : Echo chambers are fertile ground for radicalization, where individuals can be gradually led to adopt increasingly extreme positions. For example, online forums and private groups on social media have played a role in radicalizing some individuals, leading them to embrace violent or extremist ideologies.

Impact of echo chambers on society

Echo chambers contribute to social polarization and the fragmentation of society, by insulating individuals from any confrontation with opposing ideas. This reinforces the misinformation, because users are less likely to question the information they receive and more likely to share it with other members of their echo chamber. **Strategies for Breaking Down Echo Chambers**

- **Promoting content diversity** : Social media platforms can play a key role in modifying their algorithms to encourage exposure to a diversity of points of view. This may include recommendations for balanced content and suggestions for connections with users with differing opinions.

- **Encouraging intergroup dialogue** : Creating spaces where individuals from different backgrounds can constructively exchange views can help break down echo chambers. Mediation initiatives, public debates and civic education programs can all help to foster open and respectful dialogue.

- **Raising awareness about the dangers of echo chambers** : Raising public awareness of the harmful effects of echo chambers and the importance of seeking varied sources of information can encourage more balanced media consumption.

Conclusion

Social dynamics play a central role in how misinformation is spread and accepted within society. Understanding group effects, such as social conformity, crowd effect, polarization, and the influence of emotions, is essential to developing effective strategies to combat misinformation. By promoting media literacy, critical thinking, and open dialogue, it is possible to reduce the impact of these dynamics on society and build a more resilient and better informed community.

3. The Influence of Emotions on the Spread of Misinformation

Introduction

Emotions are powerful drivers of human behavior, and they play a central role in how we receive, interpret and disseminate information. In the context of disinformation, emotions can be exploited to manipulate public opinion, amplify erroneous beliefs, and propagate misleading narratives. This chapter explores in depth how emotions influence the spread of misinformation, examining the underlying psychological mechanisms, the strategies used by misinformation propagators, and the social and political consequences of these dynamics. We will also discuss strategies to mitigate the impact of emotions on misinformation, strengthening individual and collective resilience.

3.1 The Role of Emotions in Reception of Information

Understanding the impact of emotions on information processing

Emotions profoundly influence how we process information. They can alter our perception of facts, reinforce our pre-existing beliefs, and affect our judgment. Emotions such as fear, anger, hope or indignation can intensify our reaction to information, making us more likely to believe it and share it, even if it is false.

Examples of emotional influence on information perception

- **Fear and Anxiety** : Fear is one of the most powerful emotions that can alter our perception of reality. For example, during a health crisis, such as the COVID-19 pandemic, fear of the virus has led many people to believe and spread conspiracy theories about the origins of the virus or the effects of vaccines, even without solid scientific evidence.

- **Anger and indignation** : These emotions are often exploited to mobilize social or political groups. For example, political campaigns or social movements that use narratives of corruption or injustice

    -

to incite anger can lead to the rapid spread of misinformation, as individuals are more likely to share information that confirms their outrage.

- **Hope and Optimism** : Conversely, positive emotions like hope can also be manipulated to spread misinformation, particularly in health or personal finance contexts. For example, false promises of miracle treatments for serious illnesses often exploit the hope of desperate patients.

Psychological mechanisms of emotional influence

Emotions influence information processing through several psychological mechanisms:

- **Emotional confirmation bias** : Individuals are more likely to believe and share information that reinforces their current emotions. For example, someone who is angry with the government is more likely to believe rumors of corruption.

- **Emotional framing effect** : The way information is presented can reinforce its emotional impact. For example, the same fact can be framed in a way that arouses fear or hope, thereby influencing how it is perceived and shared.

- **Emotional memory** : Events or information that elicit a strong emotional response are more easily remembered and recalled, which can enhance their impact and spread, even long after they were first broadcast.

3.2 The Exploitation of Emotions through Disinformation

Common Emotional Exploitation Strategies in Disinformation

Disinformation spreaders deliberately use strategies that exploit emotions to maximize the impact of their messages. These strategies include creating content that elicits intense emotional reactions, manipulating narratives to play on fears or hopes, and using emotionally charged images and videos. **Historical and contemporary examples**

- **War propaganda** : During conflicts, propaganda has often used stories and images that arouse fear or hatred toward the enemy to mobilize popular support. For example, during World War II, propaganda posters depicting the enemy in a dehumanizing manner were widely used to justify military actions.

    Health crises and rumors : During health crises, such as influenza or COVID-19 epidemics, alarmist stories about the origins of illnesses or treatments have been used to sow panic and influence behavior. For example, misinformation about vaccine side effects has exploited fear to dissuade people from getting vaccinated.

- **Political disinformation** : Election campaigns are often marked by disinformation strategies that play on voters' emotions. Rumors about candidates, accusations of electoral fraud, or stories of corruption are often used to polarize the electorate and influence outcomes.

The role of social media in amplifying emotions

Social media plays a central role in amplifying emotions and spreading misinformation. Platforms like Facebook, Twitter, and YouTube use algorithms that favor content likely to generate high engagement, often based on emotional reactions. This creates an environment where the most viral information is often the one that arouses the strongest emotions, whether true or false. **Examples of Online Emotional Amplification**

- **Viral Rumors** : Rumors that spark fear or outrage are often among the most shared on social media. For example, misinformation about the dangers of 5G towers during the COVID-19 pandemic has been widely shared online, fueling conspiracy theories and acts of vandalism.

- **Social movements** : Online social movements, such as those around civil rights or environmental issues, often use emotional narratives to mobilize support. However, it can also lead to the spread of misinformation, where simplified or exaggerated narratives are used to amplify the message.

3.3 The Impact of Emotions on the Diffusion and Acceptance of Misinformation

How do emotions influence the spread of misinformation?

Emotions play a key role in how misinformation spreads. Information that arouses strong emotions is more likely to be shared because it creates a sense of urgency or solidarity. Additionally, individuals who are emotionally engaged with information are more likely to defend it, even in the face of contrary evidence. **Examples of emotional impact on the spread of misinformation**

- **Collective outrage** : Information that sparks outrage, such as accusations of corruption or social injustices, is often disseminated quickly because it resonates with individuals' feelings of justice. For example, political scandals, even when exaggerated or unfounded, can have a lasting impact on public opinion.

- **Fear and irrational behavior** : Fear can lead to irrational behavior, such as mass purchasing of goods or avoiding certain actions, in response to rumors. For example, false information about fuel shortages has led to panic buying, exacerbating supply problems.

The effect of emotions on resilience to misinformation

Emotions can also affect individuals' resilience in the face of misinformation. People who are emotionally engaged with a belief or narrative may be more resistant to corrections and conflicting information. For example, a person who strongly believes in a conspiracy theory out of fear or outrage may ignore or reject evidence that disproves that theory.

Examples of emotional resilience to misinformation

- **Online communities** : In some online communities, shared beliefs

-

are reinforced by collective emotions, creating environments where misinformation is protected from external correction. For example, conspiracy forums where members share emotions of distrust and suspicion are particularly resistant to debunking efforts.

- **Radical social movements** : Social movements that are based on strong emotions, such as anger or despair, may be particularly vulnerable to misinformation because their members are less likely to question the narratives that support their cause.

3.4 Social and Political Consequences of the Exploitation of Emotions

Impact on social cohesion

The exploitation of emotions through disinformation can have serious consequences for social cohesion. Stories that arouse fear, anger or hatred can divide communities, exacerbate social tensions, and lead to conflict. For example, rumors about minority groups can lead to intercommunal violence, while political misinformation can polarize voters and make democratic dialogue more difficult.

Examples of impact on social cohesion

- **Intercommunity violence** : In certain contexts, disinformation that plays on emotions can lead to intercommunity violence. For example, in India, fake news spread on WhatsApp has been linked to lynchings and violence against minority communities.

- **Political polarization** : Disinformation that exploits emotions can reinforce political polarization, making cooperation between different factions more difficult. For example, in the United States, conspiracy theories surrounding the 2020 presidential elections helped to further divide the electorate and weaken trust in democratic institutions.

Impact on political and economic decisions

Emotional misinformation can also influence political and economic decisions, creating a climate of fear or uncertainty that pushes decision-makers to take extreme or inappropriate actions. For example, rumors about the economic effects of certain policies can cause stock market panics or excessive reactions from governments.

Examples of impact on political decisions

- **Political reactions to health crises** : During the COVID-19 pandemic, some political decisions have been influenced by rumors and conspiracy theories, such as adhering to unproven treatments or implementing containment measures based on incorrect information.

- **Economic and social reforms** : In some countries, economic or social reforms have been delayed or canceled due to misinformation that has sparked fear or outrage among the population. For example, reforms to promote renewable energy have been thwarted by misinformation campaigns about the dangers of green energy.

3.5 Strategies for Mitigating the Impact of Emotions on Disinformation Media and Information Literacy

One of the most effective strategies for mitigating the impact of emotions on misinformation is media and information literacy. This includes learning the skills necessary to identify emotional biases in information, understand the mechanisms of emotional manipulation, and critically evaluate sources of information. **Examples of media literacy programs**

- **School curricula** : Many countries now integrate media literacy into their school curricula, teaching students how to critically analyze information and recognize manipulative emotional narratives.

- **Public awareness campaigns** : Governments and non-governmental organizations regularly launch campaigns to raise public awareness of the dangers of emotional disinformation, providing tools to check facts and evaluate sources.

Promoting emotional resilience

Building individuals' emotional resilience is also crucial to reducing the impact of misinformation. This includes learning stress management, emotional regulation, and critical thinking techniques that can help individuals respond more thoughtfully to emotionally charged information.

Examples of Emotional Resilience Programs

- **Stress management training** : Training and workshops on stress management and emotional regulation can help individuals better manage their emotional reactions to alarming or provocative information.

- **Online interventions** : Social media platforms can also play a role in providing resources to help users manage their emotions, for example by offering fact-checking tools or highlighting balanced and informative content.

Encouragement of dialogue and empathy

Promoting dialogue and empathy between different social groups can help mitigate the impact of emotions on misinformation. By encouraging mutual understanding and open communication, it is possible to reduce tensions and foster a more nuanced and rational approach to information. **Examples of dialogue strategies**

- **Mediation Initiatives** : Mediation initiatives between conflicting groups can help defuse tensions and promote mutual understanding. For example, interfaith or intercommunity dialogues can help reduce the effects of misinformation that plays on emotions.

- **Community projects** : Community projects that bring people from different backgrounds together around common goals can strengthen social cohesion and reduce susceptibility to emotional misinformation.

Conclusion

Emotions play a central role in the spread of misinformation, influencing how information is received, interpreted and disseminated. Understanding these dynamics is essential to developing effective strategies to combat disinformation. By promoting media literacy, building emotional resilience, and encouraging open dialogue, it is possible to reduce the impact of emotions on misinformation and build a more resilient and better informed society.

4. Social and Political Polarization

Introduction

Social and political polarization is one of the most significant phenomena of our time. It manifests itself in a growing division between different groups within society, with increasingly rigid and extreme positions. This phenomenon is exacerbated by disinformation, which fuels tensions by spreading partisan narratives, conspiracy theories and distorted information. This section explores in depth the mechanisms of polarization, its interaction with disinformation, and the resulting sociopolitical impacts, as well as strategies to counter these harmful effects.

Definition of social and political polarization

Social and political polarization refers to the division of a society into distinct and opposing groups, where individuals within these groups adopt increasingly extreme positions. This polarization often manifests itself as an "us versus them" mentality, where ideological, cultural, or ethnic differences are accentuated to the point of creating open tension and conflict.

Polarization mechanisms

Polarization is the result of several interconnected processes, including:

- **Ingroup homogenization** : Individuals tend to associate with those who share similar beliefs and values. This grouping reinforces shared points of view and excludes divergent perspectives, creating information bubbles where opinions are never contested.
- **Demonization of the out-group** : Polarization often leads to the dehumanization or demonization of the other group. Outgroup members are seen not only as having different opinions, but as inherently evil or threatening.
- **Echo chamber effect** : Social media and online algorithms amplify this phenomenon by presenting users with content that confirms their beliefs, while filtering out opposing opinions. This reinforces the belief that the opposing group is irredeemably incorrect or ill-intentioned.

Historical origins of polarization

Polarization is not a new phenomenon. Historically, societies have always experienced periods of intense division, often linked to economic crises, religious conflicts, or political struggles. However, the speed and extent of polarization in the contemporary context is largely due to the digital revolution and the way information is consumed and shared.

- **The French Revolution (1789-1799)** : Polarization between revolutionary factions (the Jacobins and the Girondins, for example) led to intense internal violence, illustrating how ideological divisions can destabilize an entire society.
- **The Spanish Civil War (1936-1939)** : The struggle between republican and nationalist forces in Spain is an example of political and social polarization exacerbated by economic and ideological factors, leading to a bloody conflict that left a lasting mark on the country.

The role of disinformation in worsening polarization

Disinformation plays a key role in deepening polarization. By spreading partisan narratives and conspiracy theories, disinformation reinforces existing divisions by providing "evidence" that justifies extreme beliefs and fuels distrust of the other group.

Concrete examples of disinformation in the context of polarization

- **The 2016 and 2020 US presidential elections** : These elections were marked by extreme polarization, largely fueled by misinformation spread on social media. Conspiracy theories, such as Pizzagate and QAnon, have not only divided voters, but also led to violent actions, such as the attack on the Capitol in January 2021.
- **The Brexit referendum** : The Brexit campaign was characterized by strong polarization, fueled by misleading narratives about the economic and social consequences of leaving the European Union. Leave campaigns have often used simplistic arguments and false claims to stoke fear of immigration and loss of sovereignty, while the Remain camp has been accused of downplaying economic risks.

Disinformation as a tool of political manipulation

Political actors and other opinion leaders often exploit misinformation to polarize public opinion to their advantage. By playing on emotions and prejudices, they can mobilize their electoral base while weakening social cohesion.

Psychological analysis of disinformation in the context of polarization

Cognitive biases, such as confirmation bias and ingroup bias, are particularly active in polarized environments. Individuals are more likely to believe and share information that confirms their pre-existing beliefs, especially when that information comes from sources perceived to be part of their ingroup. **Examples of psychological manipulation**

- **Election campaigns** : Political campaigns often use disinformation to manipulate perceptions. For example, fear messages about immigration or security are often used to mobilize voters, even when these messages are based on exaggerated or false information.
- **Partisan media** : Cable news channels in the United States, such as Fox News or MSNBC, are often accused of reinforcing polarization by presenting biased narratives that support their audience's beliefs while demonizing the opposing side.

4.3 Impact of Polarization on Society and Democracy

Social consequences of polarization

Social polarization has profound effects on social cohesion and the functioning of democratic institutions. When polarization reaches a certain level, it can lead to a fragmentation of society, where different groups no longer share common values or mutual understanding.

- **Weakening democracy** : A polarized society is often marked by political paralysis, where opposing groups refuse to cooperate, making effective governance almost impossible. This situation can lead to a crisis of legitimacy of democratic institutions, perceived as being controlled by one camp or the other.
- **Violence and social conflicts** : Polarization can also degenerate into violence, riots or even civil wars, as historical examples have shown. Social tensions exacerbated by misinformation can lead to direct clashes between groups, fueling a cycle of violence that is difficult to interrupt.
- **Social isolation** : Polarization can also lead to increased social isolation, where individuals avoid interactions with those who do not share their views. This can reinforce echo chambers, where people are only exposed to information that confirms their beliefs, thereby worsening polarization.

Historical and contemporary examples of the impact of polarization

- **The American Civil War** : Polarization around the issues of slavery and states' rights led to one of the most devastating periods in American history. Disinformation and misleading narratives have played a role in radicalizing each side's positions.
- **Ethnic conflicts in former Yugoslavia** : The 1990s saw the breakup of Yugoslavia due to ethnic tensions exacerbated by disinformation campaigns. The media, controlled by nationalist leaders, fueled hatred and contributed to polarization which resulted in civil wars and genocides.

Impact on democracy

Extreme polarization is particularly dangerous for democratic systems. When citizens are deeply divided, the ability of institutions to function effectively is compromised. Electoral processes may lose legitimacy, and political violence may become more common.

- **Political paralysis** : Polarization makes it difficult to form political coalitions and achieve the compromises necessary for governance. Polarized legislatures are often unable to pass laws, leading to legislative gridlock.

- **Legitimacy crisis** : Elections and democratic institutions may be perceived as illegitimate by part of the population, which can lead to contestations of electoral results and an erosion of confidence in the political system.

Contemporary examples of democratic crises linked to polarization

- **The political crisis in Brazil** : Brazil has experienced intense polarization around the impeachment of President Dilma Rousseff and the election of Jair Bolsonaro. Disinformation has played a crucial role in dividing public opinion, contributing to a crisis of legitimacy that has shaken Brazilian democracy.
- **Post-election unrest in Kenya** : Elections in Kenya have often been marked by ethnic violence, exacerbated by disinformation campaigns. Polarization between different ethnic groups has led to violent clashes and disputes over election results.

4.4 Online Polarization: The Role of Social Media

Social networks as catalysts of polarization

Social media plays a central role in amplifying polarization. Designed to maximize user engagement, these platforms' algorithms favor polarizing content because it generates more emotional reactions and interactions. This creates an environment where extreme opinions are amplified, while moderate perspectives are marginalized.

Case studies on online polarization

- **The 2020 American presidential election** : Social networks, especially Facebook

    and Twitter, have been key platforms where polarizing narratives have spread. Misinformation about voter fraud has been shared millions of times, contributing to dividing the electorate and calling into question the legitimacy of the electoral process.
- **Anti-vaccine movements** : Social networks have also played a role in polarizing opinions on vaccination. Anti-vaccine groups are using platforms like YouTube and Facebook to spread misinformation, exacerbating tensions between supporters and opponents of vaccination.

Impact of social networks on the perception of information

Social networks don't just disseminate information, they actively shape users' perceptions by filtering the content they see. This reinforces polarization by creating echo chambers where users are only exposed to opinions that confirm their existing beliefs.

Examples of the impact of online polarization

- **The rise of conspiracy theories** : Social media is fertile ground for conspiracy theories, which exploit polarization to spread. For example, COVID-19 conspiracy theories, such as those linking the virus to 5G towers, have flourished online, fueling distrust and division.
- **Polarized social movements** : Social movements that grow online, like Black Lives Matter or the Yellow Vests, can also be polarized by misinformation. Although these movements have legitimate goals, they can be infiltrated by polarizing narratives that exacerbate tensions and undermine constructive dialogue.

Solutions to reduce online polarization

To mitigate polarization on social media, several strategies can be implemented:

- **Overhauling Algorithms** : Platforms can adjust their algorithms to reduce the promotion of polarizing content and favor fact-checked and balanced information.
- **Media literacy** : Raising awareness about the dangers of misinformation and providing them with the tools to identify and reject misleading content can help mitigate polarization.

- **Promoting intercommunity dialogue** : Encouraging constructive exchanges between groups with divergent opinions can help reduce tensions and promote mutual understanding.

Promote education and critical thinking

Education is one of the most powerful tools to combat polarization. By teaching citizens to think critically and analyze information discerningly, it is possible to reduce the impact of misinformation.

- **Educational programs** : Schools and universities can integrate media literacy programs into their curricula, focusing on critical thinking and fact-checking.
- **Awareness campaigns** : Governments and non-governmental organizations can launch campaigns to raise public awareness of the dangers of polarization and misinformation.

Encourage dialogue and compromise

Promoting dialogue and compromise is essential to overcoming polarization. This involves creating spaces where individuals can exchange their views in a respectful and constructive manner.

- **Mediation Initiatives** : Mediation programs can help defuse conflicts between polarized groups, facilitating communication and encouraging mutual respect.
- **Public debates** : Organizing public debates where different perspectives are represented can promote a better understanding of issues and reduce misunderstandings.

Strengthening democratic institutions

Democratic institutions play a crucial role in managing polarization. By ensuring fairness, transparency and inclusiveness, they can help restore public trust.

- **Electoral reforms** : Electoral reforms that promote proportional representation and inclusion can help reduce polarization by giving voice to a greater diversity of perspectives.
- **Transparency and Accountability** : Institutions must be transparent and accountable in their actions to maintain public trust and avoid accusations of bias or corruption.

Role of traditional media in polarization

Traditional media, such as television, radio and newspapers, also have a significant impact on polarization. In many cases, these media outlets have polarized to attract specific audiences, adopting strong editorial positions that reinforce social divisions.

Examples of Polarization in Traditional Media

- **Cable news channels in the United States** : Fox News, for example, is often criticized for its pro-Republican coverage, while MSNBC is seen as being aligned with the Democrats. This media polarization reinforces political divisions and contributes to distrust of the media among those who do not share their political orientations.
- **The partisan press in Europe** : In several European countries, the press is highly polarized, with newspapers and magazines clearly aligned with specific political parties or ideologies. This limits the diversity of perspectives and reinforces divisions within society.

Impact on trust in the media

The polarization of traditional media has a direct impact on public trust in the media. Individuals tend to trust only sources that confirm their beliefs, which reinforces echo chambers and limits exposure to different perspectives. **Strategies to reduce polarization in the media**

- **Encouragement of impartiality** : Media should strive to maintain balanced and unbiased coverage, providing a diversity of viewpoints and avoiding aligning too closely with any one ideology.
- **Transparency of sources** : Media can build public trust by being transparent about their sources of information and clearly explaining their fact-checking process.

4.7 Polarization and Social Identities

The impact of social identities on polarization

Social identities, such as ethnicity, religion, or political affiliation, play a crucial role in polarization. When social identities are activated in a context of polarization, they can lead to a radicalization of opinions and a reduction in tolerance towards other groups.

Examples of polarization based on social identities

- **Ethnic conflicts** : In many countries, polarization is exacerbated by ethnic identities. For example, conflicts in East Africa, such as those in Rwanda and Burundi, have been amplified by the manipulation of ethnic identities.
- **Religions and sectarianism** : In societies where religion plays a central role, polarization can manifest itself in increased sectarianism, as seen in the Middle East with tensions between Sunnis and Shiites.

Strategies to mitigate identity polarization

- **Cross-community dialogue** : Promoting dialogues between different identity groups can help reduce tensions and foster mutual understanding.
- **Inclusive policies** : Governments can adopt inclusive policies that recognize and respect the diversity of social identities, while promoting common values.

4.8 The Psychological Consequences of Polarization

The impact of polarization on mental health

Polarization does not just divide societies; it also has negative effects on the mental health of individuals. Living in a polarized environment can lead to stress, anxiety, and feelings of isolation.

Examples of psychological consequences

- **Social anxiety** : Individuals may experience anxiety due to pressure to conform to the norms of their group or fear of being ostracized for their opinions.
- **Isolation** : Polarization can lead to social isolation, where individuals cut themselves off from friends or family who do not share their views, which can worsen loneliness and depression.

Strategies to mitigate the psychological effects of polarization

- **Psychological support** : Providing psychological support to people affected by polarization can help them manage their stress and rebuild positive relationships.
- **Promoting emotional resilience** : Teaching individuals emotional resilience techniques can help them navigate a polarized environment without sacrificing their mental well-being.

Conclusion

Social and political polarization is a complex and multidimensional phenomenon that has profound implications for society and democracy. Disinformation plays a central role in exacerbating polarization, fueling divisions and reinforcing extreme positions. Understanding the mechanisms of polarization and its interaction with disinformation is essential to developing effective strategies to counter this phenomenon. By promoting education, dialogue, and transparency, it is possible to build a more resilient society, capable of resisting forces that seek to divide and destabilize.

5. The Psychological and Social Consequences of Disinformation

Introduction

Disinformation, defined as the deliberate dissemination of false or misleading information, has far-reaching consequences that go far beyond simple distortion of facts. It affects not only the perception of reality but also the mental health of individuals, social cohesion, and even the functioning of democratic institutions. Understanding these impacts is essential to developing resilience strategies in the face of misinformation. This chapter explores in depth the psychological and social consequences of misinformation, analyzing its effects on the individual and society as a whole.

5.1 Psychological Impact of Misinformation on Individuals

Stress and anxiety related to exposure to misinformation

Constant exposure to misinformation can lead to significant psychological stress. Individuals who encounter false or alarming information may develop anxiety, especially when they are unable to discern fact from fiction. For example, conspiracy theories about the dangers of vaccines have created widespread anxiety among certain populations, leading them to refuse life-saving medical care.

Examples of anxiety caused by misinformation

- **COVID-19 pandemic** : During the pandemic, misinformation about the origins of the virus, treatments, and vaccines has caused massive public anxiety. Misinformation about vaccine side effects has been particularly stressful for individuals who were already hesitant to get vaccinated.
- **Economic Crises** : Misinformation about economic crises, such as rumors of stock market crashes or bank failures, can cause panic and financial anxiety among individuals, who fear for their savings and investments.

Effect of misinformation on perception of reality

Misinformation can alter perceptions of reality, creating a discrepancy between the truth and what individuals believe to be true. This phenomenon is known as **cognitive dissonance** , where individuals experience psychological discomfort when confronted with information contradictory to their beliefs. **Examples of reality distortion**

- **Conspiracy theories** : Conspiracy theories, such as those claiming that the Earth is flat or that the moon landings were falsified, illustrate how misinformation can lead people to adopt beliefs disconnected from scientific reality.
- **False political perceptions** : Political misinformation, such as false accusations of voter fraud, can lead individuals to doubt the integrity of democratic processes, even in the absence of evidence.

Long-term psychological consequences

Prolonged exposure to misinformation can have long-term psychological effects, including:

- **Paranoia** : Individuals may develop feelings of generalized distrust and paranoia, believing that hidden or malicious forces are manipulating world events.
- **Social isolation** : People who hold beliefs based on misinformation may cut themselves off from others, including friends and family, who do not share those beliefs. This can lead to social isolation and increased marginalization.

5.2 The Influence of Misinformation on Mental Health

Depression and feelings of helplessness

Misinformation can also contribute to feelings of depression and helplessness, especially when individuals feel overwhelmed by a constant stream of negative or contradictory information. This situation can be exacerbated by **information fatigue** , where individuals feel unable to process or judge the veracity of the information they receive. **Examples of depression linked to misinformation**

- **Environmental Crises** : Misinformation about the ineffectiveness of efforts to combat climate change can lead to a sense of hopelessness and fatalism among those who are already concerned about the state of the environment.
- **Apocalyptic theories** : End-of-the-world narratives, amplified by misinformation, can cause depression in individuals who believe impending disasters are inevitable.

Impact on self-confidence and decision-making

Misinformation can also erode individuals' self-confidence, making them uncertain about their own abilities to discern the truth. This can lead to erratic decision-making or abandonment of decision-making, for fear of making mistakes based on incorrect information.

Examples of loss of self-confidence

- **Financial Investments** : Market rumors and false information about companies' financial performance can discourage investors, leading them to make financial decisions based on fear rather than rational analysis.
- **Health decisions** : Misinformation about medical treatments can lead patients to avoid necessary interventions or adopt unproven therapies, thereby compromising their health.

Effect of misinformation on mental resilience

Mental resilience, the ability to overcome challenges and adapt to stress, can be seriously compromised by continued exposure to misinformation. Individuals may become more vulnerable to manipulation and more likely to fall into negative thought spirals.

Examples of Erosion of Mental Resilience

- **Radicalization** : Individuals exposed to polarizing or extremist narratives may be radicalized, losing their ability to critically evaluate information and interact constructively with those who hold different opinions.
- **Cognitive Isolation** : Those who immerse themselves in online communities based on misinformation may develop cognitive isolation, where their worldview becomes increasingly distant from consensus reality, rendering them unable to participate in constructive dialogue.

5.3 The Social Consequences of Disinformation

Weakening of social cohesion

Disinformation has devastating effects on social cohesion, creating deep divisions between different groups in society. Disinformation narratives that exploit ethnic, religious, or political differences can fuel distrust, hatred, and even violence.

Examples of disinformation causing social divisions

- **Ethnic conflicts** : In several countries, disinformation narratives have been used to inflame tensions between different ethnic groups, leading to intercommunal violence. For example, in India, rumors spread on WhatsApp have been linked to mass lynchings.
- **Political polarization** : In the United States, misinformation surrounding the presidential elections has led to extreme polarization, with entire groups of the population refusing to accept the election results and distrusting government institutions.

Weakening trust in institutions

Disinformation also undermines public trust in key institutions, such as governments, media, and justice systems. When individuals believe that these institutions are corrupt or controlled by malevolent forces, they are less likely to respect their decisions or participate in the democratic process. **Examples of loss of institutional trust**

- **Judicial systems** : Conspiracy theories about judicial corruption or "deep states" can lead to widespread distrust of the justice system, which can make it difficult to resolve disputes and implement the law.
- **Media** : Disinformation that accuses the media of bias or conspiracy can erode public trust in traditional news sources, causing people to turn to alternative, unverified sources, where misinformation is more likely to thrive.

Reinforcement of social inequalities

Disinformation can also exacerbate social inequalities by specifically targeting marginalized or vulnerable groups. For example, disinformation campaigns that spread false information about welfare or public health policies can deter these groups from accessing the services they need.

Examples of inequalities reinforced by misinformation

- **Access to health** : Marginalized communities may be particularly vulnerable to misinformation about health care, which can lead them to avoid vaccines or essential medical treatments, thereby worsening health disparities.
- **Digital exclusion** : Online misinformation can also reinforce digital exclusion, as those who lack the skills to navigate the digital ecosystem may be more easily fooled by false information, putting them at a disadvantage increased social.

5.4 Disinformation and Political Destabilization

Impact on electoral processes

Disinformation has a direct impact on electoral processes, influencing voters' opinions and undermining the legitimacy of electoral results. Disinformation campaigns can target specific candidates, manipulate public perceptions on key issues, or sow doubt about the integrity of the electoral system itself. **Examples of Election Interference via Disinformation**

- **2016 US presidential elections** : Disinformation campaigns by foreign actors have been widely credited with attempting to manipulate voters' opinions and sow social discord in the United States. These efforts have included spreading misinformation about candidates, as well as promoting polarizing narratives on social issues.
- **Brexit Referendum** : In the United Kingdom, the Brexit campaign was marked by the spread of false information, including misleading claims about the United Kingdom's financial contributions to the European Union. These stories played a key role in the referendum result, which deeply divided British society.

Undermining government legitimacy

Disinformation can also undermine the legitimacy of governments by spreading narratives that portray authorities as illegitimate or corrupt. When citizens lose confidence in their leaders, political stability is put at risk, and protest movements can emerge.

Examples of Government Delegitimization

- **Political crisis in Venezuela** : In Venezuela, disinformation spread by state-controlled media, as well as by opponents, has exacerbated the political crisis by undermining trust in the government and further polarizing the population.

- **Arab Spring** : In several countries affected by the Arab Spring revolts, disinformation played a role in organizing protests against existing governments, spreading stories of corruption and abuse of power.

Radicalization and political violence

Continued exposure to misinformation can lead to political radicalization, where individuals take extreme positions and turn to violence to achieve their goals. Disinformation can legitimize this violence by portraying opponents as dangerous or illegitimate enemies.

Examples of political radicalization due to disinformation

- **2021 Capitol Attack** : The January 2021 attack on the U.S. Capitol was largely motivated by misinformation stories about alleged election fraud. The rioters, believing they were defending democracy, were radicalized by online stories that called for direct action against Congress.
- **Election Violence in Kenya** : During Kenya's elections, rumors and misinformation about election results led to inter-ethnic violence, exacerbating existing social and political divisions.

5.5 Resilience and Responses to Misinformation

Resilience Strategies Against Misinformation

To mitigate the psychological and social impacts of misinformation, it is crucial to develop resilience strategies. This includes education, promoting critical thinking, and establishing fact-checking mechanisms. **Examples of effective strategies**

- **Media literacy programs** : Many countries have established media literacy programs to help citizens, especially young people, develop critical thinking skills and recognize misinformation.
- **Fact-checking initiatives** : Organizations like PolitiFact, Snopes, and Le Monde des Décoders provide real-time fact-checks, helping the public discern fact from fiction.

Strengthening online communities

Online communities can also play a role in combating misinformation. By strengthening cohesion and solidarity within these communities, it is possible to promote social norms that value fact-checking and the sharing of reliable information.

Examples of resilient online communities

- **Moderated discussion groups** : Online forums and moderated discussion groups can serve as platforms where users can constructively debate and challenge misinformation. These spaces encourage open dialogue while enforcing strict standards against the spread of misinformation.
- **Awareness campaigns** : Campaigns run by influencers or organizations on social media to promote fact-checking and resilience to misinformation have shown that it is possible to mobilize users online to counter misleading narratives.

Role of governments and institutions

Governments and institutions play a key role in protecting society from the effects of disinformation. This includes regulating online platforms, supporting fact-checking initiatives, and public education. **Examples of government policies**

- **Law against disinformation in France** : France has adopted laws aimed at combating the spread of false information, particularly during election periods. These laws impose fines on online platforms that do not remove identified disinformation content.
- **Government education campaigns** : Many governments have launched campaigns to educate the public about the dangers of misinformation, providing resources to help citizens navigate the information environment.

Conclusion

Misinformation has profound psychological and social consequences that affect both individuals and society as a whole. It can cause stress, anxiety, and depression, while weakening social cohesion, undermining trust in institutions, and destabilizing political processes. However, by developing resilience strategies, strengthening media literacy, and mobilizing online communities, it is possible to counter these effects and build a society that is more informed and more resistant to manipulation.

Chapter 4: Strategies to Combat Disinformation

1. Media and Information Education (MIL)

Introduction

Media and information literacy (MIL) has become a necessity in a world where information travels quickly and often without verification. EMI aims to equip individuals with the skills to navigate a complex and ever-changing media environment. This chapter explores in depth the importance of MIL, its pedagogical approaches, its integration into school curricula, the tools and resources available, and the challenges and opportunities associated with its implementation.

1.1 Importance of Media and Information Literacy

Role of NDE in modern society

EMI plays a central role in creating informed and critical citizens. In a world where misinformation and fake news can have serious consequences, the ability to discern reliable information is essential. EMI enables individuals to understand the mechanisms of media production, distribution and consumption, helping them to make informed decisions.

Objectives and long-term impact of the EMI

The objectives of EMI are not limited to the simple acquisition of technical skills. It is about developing a culture of critical thinking, where individuals are able to evaluate information rigorously and understand the ethical and social issues linked to the media. In the long term, EMI contributes to the creation of a society more resilient to the manipulation of information and more engaged in the democratic process.

Why NDE should start at an early age

The importance of NDE from an early age is crucial to preparing children for a world where they will be constantly exposed to diverse and often contradictory streams of information. Younger generations, especially those growing up with easy access to digital technologies, must be equipped to navigate this complex environment. By starting early, EMI can help form news consumption habits that prioritize fact-checking and critical analysis.

EMI as a prevention tool against radicalization

Another essential aspect of MIL is its role in preventing radicalization. By providing young people with the tools to recognize and resist propaganda and hate speech online, MIL can play a key role in reducing the risks of radicalization. This is particularly important in a context where extremist groups are increasingly using digital platforms to recruit and indoctrinate young people.

1.2 Pedagogical Approaches to Media and Information Education

Approaches based on critical thinking

Critical thinking is at the heart of EMI. This approach encourages students to question what they see, hear and read, rather than passively accepting it. Teaching techniques include class discussions of news articles, analysis of advertisements and media content, and practical exercises where students must verify information and detect bias or manipulation.

Examples of activities based on critical thinking

- **Analysis of media cases** : Students may be asked to analyze real media cases, identifying the different sources of information, the angles of treatment, and possible biases. For example, comparing different newspapers' coverage of the same event can reveal differences in how facts are presented.
- **Debates on journalistic ethics** : Organizing classroom debates on ethical issues related to journalism, such as the role of anonymity of sources or the responsibility of the media in the dissemination of false information, allows students to explore ethical dilemmas faced by journalists.

Learning through media creation

Encouraging students to create their own media content is a powerful method for teaching them the realities of news production. This process helps them understand how editorial choices, source selection, and the way information is presented can influence public perception. **Examples of creative projects in EMI**

- **Making News Videos** : Students can produce video reports on local or school events, focusing on fact-checking and balanced presentation of information. This allows them to confront the challenges of journalism while developing technical skills.
- **Creating Blogs or Podcasts** : Writing blogs or producing podcasts on current topics encourages students to engage critically with the content they create and think about the impact of their words on the public.

1.3 Integration of Media Education into School Curricula

Incorporation of EMI into existing curricula

The integration of EMI into existing school curricula can be done through various subjects. For example, in literature classes, students can analyze how media influence the perception of literary works or historical events. In science classes, they can examine how misinformation can affect understanding of scientific issues, such as climate change or vaccines.

Challenges of integrating EMI into schools

However, integrating MIL into school curricula is not without challenges. Teachers often have to deal with already busy schedules and may lack the time or resources to introduce new subjects. Additionally, the speed with which technology evolves means that educational content must be regularly updated to stay relevant.

Strategies to overcome these challenges

To overcome these challenges, it is essential to provide teachers with ongoing training and appropriate educational resources. Additionally, schools can benefit from partnerships with external experts, such as journalists or media professionals, who can provide practical and current perspectives on media and information issues.

Examples of successful educational partnerships

- **Collaboration with journalists** : Programs such as "Reporters en Herbe" allow students to work directly with professional journalists to produce their own articles or reports, offering them an immersion in the world of journalism.

- **Class projects in partnership with local media** : Schools can collaborate with local media to publish student work, such as articles or radio broadcasts, giving students a platform to express themselves while learning about the realities of the job media.

Digital resources and educational platforms

Digital resources play a crucial role in EMI. Many platforms offer interactive tools that allow students to develop their skills in critical evaluation of information. These resources include online training modules, simulated media scenarios, and fact-checking databases.

Examples of digital platforms and resources

- **MediaSmarts** : A Canadian platform that offers educational resources on digital and media literacy, including lesson plans, interactive activities, and guides for teachers.
- **The News Literacy Project** : A US organization that provides tools and resources to help educators teach news evaluation and critical thinking when dealing with media.

Fact-checking tools

Fact-checking tools are essential for teaching students how to assess the veracity of information they encounter. By using these tools, students learn to verify sources, assess the credibility of authors, and detect manipulations or omissions.

Examples of NDE fact-checking tools

- **Google Fact Check Explorer** : A tool that allows users to search for fact checks from recognized organizations, providing an easy way to verify claims online.
- **First Draft News** : An organization that provides resources and tools to combat misinformation, including guides on fact-checking and training for journalists and educators.

Manuals and teaching guides

The textbooks and teaching guides are valuable resources for teachers looking to integrate MII into their courses. These materials provide detailed lesson plans, case studies, and practical exercises to help students develop their media analysis skills. **Examples of manuals and guides for NDE**

- **"Understanding and Combating Disinformation"** : A manual that provides a comprehensive framework for teaching NDE, with sections on the history of disinformation, mechanisms for manipulating information, and strategies for countering it .
- **"Media Literacy Guide for Schools"** : A practical guide that provides activities and strategies for teaching MIL to students of all ages, with an emphasis on critical evaluation of media and the production of ethical content.

Educational apps and games

Educational apps and games are innovative tools to engage students in EMI learning. These tools provide a fun approach to teaching complex concepts, while strengthening students' critical thinking skills. **Examples of applications and games for NDE**

- **Bad News** : An online game that allows players to simulate the creation of fake news, helping them understand the mechanics of information manipulation.
- **Factitious** : A game that tests players' ability to discern real news from fake news, by offering them realistic scenarios taken from current events.

The challenges of EMI in a changing world

One of the main challenges of EMI is the speed with which the media environment changes. New digital platforms, social media algorithms, and emerging forms of misinformation pose ongoing challenges for educators and institutions. It is essential that EMI programs are flexible and able to adapt quickly to these changes.

The challenge of unequal access to resources

Another major challenge in EMI is unequal access to educational resources. Schools in remote regions or economically disadvantaged areas may not have the means to access the digital tools or training needed to teach MIL effectively. This creates a gap in access to critical media education, exacerbating existing inequalities.

Strategies to overcome these challenges

To overcome these challenges, it is crucial to develop inclusion strategies that ensure that all students, regardless of their socio-economic background, have access to quality EMI education. This may include government initiatives to fund educational resources, partnerships with technology companies to provide digital tools, and training programs for teachers in underserved areas.

Opportunities offered by international collaboration

International collaboration also offers opportunities to strengthen MIL. By sharing resources, ideas, and practices across countries, educators can learn from each other and develop more effective approaches to combating misinformation globally.

Examples of international collaborations in EMI

- **UNESCO and MIL** : UNESCO has played a leading role in promoting MIL globally, developing competency frameworks, educational resources, and training for educators in several countries.
- **Cross-border initiatives** : Programs such as the European "e-Media Education Lab" project bring together teachers and experts from different countries to develop common educational resources and promote the exchange of good practices in EMI.

1.6 The Future of Media and Information Literacy

Towards more inclusive and accessible media education

The future of EMI lies in its ability to become more inclusive and accessible. This means that EMI programs must be tailored to the specific needs of diverse groups of students, including those from disadvantaged backgrounds or with special educational needs. It is also essential to ensure that educational resources are available in multiple languages and formats, to reach as wide an audience as possible.

Inclusion of parents and communities in EMI

MIL does not have to be limited to classrooms. To be fully effective, it must also involve parents, communities, and the media themselves. By educating parents about the importance of critical thinking and encouraging them to actively participate in their children's media education, EMI programs can have a broader and more lasting impact.

Continuous innovation in EMI

Innovation is essential for EMI to remain relevant in the face of emerging challenges. Researchers, educators, and content creators must continue to explore new approaches and develop innovative teaching tools to meet the changing needs of students. This includes the integration of new technologies, such as virtual and augmented reality, into EMI programs, as well as the development of new methods for evaluating the effectiveness of EMI.

The role of public policy in the future of EMI

Public policy will play a crucial role in the future of EMI. Governments must commit to supporting MIL by funding educational programs, promoting partnerships with media and technology companies, and ensuring that MIL is sustainably integrated into education systems. This also includes regulating digital platforms to ensure they play a positive role in promoting trusted information and critical thinking.

Conclusion

Media and information education is an essential component of the fight against disinformation. By equipping individuals with the skills to critically evaluate information, EMI contributes to the creation of a more resilient society, capable of resisting manipulation and attempts at disinformation. For EMI to be fully effective, it must be inclusive, innovative, and supported by strong public policies. The future of EMI depends on our collective ability to adapt educational strategies to the challenges of an ever-changing world.

2. Educational Programs for Schools and High Schools

Introduction

In a global context where disinformation spreads rapidly, it is crucial to integrate educational programs into schools and colleges to prepare young people to identify and combat false information. These programs aim to develop students' critical thinking skills, raise awareness of the dangers of misinformation, and give them the tools to responsibly navigate the modern media ecosystem.

2.1 Objectives of Educational Programs

Strengthening critical thinking

One of the main goals of educational programs is to strengthen critical thinking among students. This means encouraging them not to passively accept the information they receive, but to analyze it, question it, and look for evidence before believing it or sharing it.

Examples of activities to develop critical thinking

- **Comparative Analysis** : Students may be asked to compare news articles from different sources on the same topic to identify potential biases and understand how information may be presented differently depending on the authors' goals.
- **Supported debates** : Organizing debates on controversial topics allows students to develop their ability to argue, listen to divergent opinions, and question the information on which they base their arguments.

Raising awareness about fact-checking

Another key goal is to educate students about the importance of fact-checking. With fake news and conspiracy theories on the rise, it is essential that young people learn how to use fact-checking tools and identify reliable sources of information.

Examples of fact-checking activities

- **Fact-checking workshops** : Students can participate in workshops where they learn how to verify the veracity of information found online, using tools like Google Fact Check Explorer or fact-checking databases.
- **Guided Research Projects** : Have students research current topics and present their findings, making sure they cite their sources and explain how they verified the information.

Promoting digital responsibility

Educational programs should also teach digital responsibility, that is, the importance of acting ethically online. This includes understanding the consequences of sharing unverified information and the importance of protecting one's own and others' privacy.

Examples of digital responsibility activities

- **Online Scenario Simulations** : Create simulations where students must make decisions about posting information online, considering possible impacts on themselves and others.
- **Writing ethical charters** : Invite students to write their own ethical charter for the use of social networks, including commitments to verify information before sharing it and to respect the privacy of others.

2.2 Pedagogical Approaches for Schools and High Schools

Project-based learning

Project-based learning is an effective approach to teaching skills related to countering misinformation. By working on real-world projects, students are actively engaged in their learning and can see the practical application of the skills they develop.

Examples of educational projects

- **Creating a School Newspaper** : Students can create a school newspaper where they are responsible for gathering information, checking facts, and writing articles. This allows them to understand the challenges of journalism and the importance of accuracy in reporting.
- **Developing an awareness campaign** : Students can design and lead an awareness campaign about the dangers of fake news, using posters, videos, and presentations to inform their classmates.

Use of digital technologies

Digital technologies offer many opportunities to make education on countering disinformation more interactive and engaging. Teachers can use online tools, educational apps, and collaborative platforms to create dynamic learning experiences.

Examples of technologies used

- **Collaborative platforms** : Use tools like Google Classroom or Microsoft Teams to organize discussions, interactive quizzes, and group work on the topics of fact-checking and misinformation.
- **Content Creation Apps** : Encourage students to use apps like Canva or Adobe Spark to create visual content and infographics on how to spot and combat misinformation.

Innovative assessment methods

It is important to evaluate the effectiveness of educational programs not only through traditional examinations, but also through innovative methods that reflect the interactive and practical nature of teaching to combat disinformation. **Examples of evaluation methods**

- **Digital Portfolios** : Students can create digital portfolios where they collect their work on fact-checking, campaign projects, and reflections on their learning, allowing for ongoing assessment of their progress.

- **Role plays** : Conduct role plays where students must take on the role of journalists, fact-checkers, or media consumers, to assess their ability to apply the skills they have learned in realistic situations.

2.3 Specific Programs for Primary Schools

Early introduction to information concepts

It is crucial to start teaching information concepts from a young age. Primary schools can use simple, fun activities to introduce students to the concepts of facts, opinions, and sources of information. **Examples of activities for young children**

- **Association games** : Use games where students must associate pictures with sources of information (for example, linking a television picture to the idea of television news), as described in the curriculum activity booklet 【 210†source 】 .
- **Interactive stories** : Read stories to students and invite them to identify real and imaginary information, explaining why it is important to distinguish between the two.

Progressive program for primary schools

A progressive, age-appropriate educational program is essential to ensure a deep understanding of concepts over time. The program can begin with basic concepts in the first year and progress to more complex analyzes as students progress.

Example of a one-year educational program

- **Semester 1** : Introduction to basic concepts, such as what information is and how it is produced. Students learn to recognize sources of information and understand the difference between fact and opinion.
- **Semester 2** : Students explore how to fact-check information, using fun activities to identify fake news and learn the simple steps of fact-checking 【 211†source 】 .

2.4 Programs for Middle and High Schools

Deepening the concepts of disinformation

As students progress through school, educational programs must address more complex concepts related to misinformation, such as media bias, propaganda, and information manipulation strategies. **Examples of topics to cover**

- **Media Bias and Biased Coverage** : Students can learn to identify bias in media reporting, by analyzing how different sources may cover the same event differently.
- **Conspiracy Theories and Their Impact** : An examination of conspiracy theories, including their origin and spread, as well as strategies for refuting them, can help students understand the importance of critical thinking.

Developing fact-checking skills

High school students need to be trained in more advanced fact-checking skills, including using specialized databases, understanding research methods, and analyzing sources. **Examples of advanced activities**

- **Academic Research** : Students may be encouraged to conduct academic research on controversial topics, using primary and secondary sources, and documenting their fact-checking process.
- **Real-time verification workshops** : Organize workshops where students must verify information circulating on social networks or in the media in real time, to develop their verification reflexes.

Preparing for digital citizenship

Educational programs for high school students should also include training in digital citizenship, that is, how to be a responsible and ethical consumer of information in the digital world.

Examples of digital citizenship modules

- **Online Ethics** : Students explore ethical dilemmas related to life online, such as privacy, the spread of misinformation, and the impact of digital behaviors on society.
- **Online Civic Engagement** : High school students learn how to use digital platforms to engage in public debate constructively, promoting trustworthy information and engaging in respectful discussions.

2.5 Parent and Community Involvement

Role of parents in education about misinformation

Parents play a crucial role in educating young people about misinformation. By informing them of the dangers of fake news and involving them in educational programs, schools can strengthen the impact of teaching how to combat disinformation. **Examples of activities to involve parents**

- **Parental Workshops** : Host workshops for parents where they learn the same concepts as their children, allowing them to continue education at home.
- **Guides for Families** : Providing practical guides for families, with advice on how to approach discussions about media and fact-checking with their children.

Community engagement in educational programs

Local communities can also play a role in disinformation education. By collaborating with local organizations, libraries, and media, schools can provide additional resources and enriching experiences for students. **Examples of community collaboration**

- **Library Partnerships** : Local libraries can host events or exhibits on misinformation, providing students and their families with additional resources for learning about the topic.
- **Local Media Engagement** : Inviting local journalists to speak in class or participate in school projects can provide students with practical perspectives on media work and the importance of accuracy in journalism.

2.6 Evaluation and Monitoring of Educational Programs

Importance of continuous assessment

Evaluating educational programs on misinformation is essential to ensure they achieve their goals. Teachers should use continuous assessment methods to monitor student progress and adjust programs accordingly. **Examples of evaluation methods**

- **Regular Quizzes** : Use regular quizzes to test students' understanding of concepts and identify areas where further clarification is needed.
- **Peer Reviews** : Encouraging students to evaluate the work of their peers can help them think critically about their own understanding and learn from the mistakes of others.

Monitoring student progress

It is important to track student progress throughout their education to combat misinformation. This may include regular reports to parents, classroom group discussions to assess collective understanding, and skills tests at the end of programs.

Examples of tracking systems

- **Individual Tracking Sheets** : Each student can have a tracking sheet where teachers note progress made in understanding and applying MIL concepts.

- **Quarterly Meetings** : Hold quarterly meetings with parents and students to discuss progress, identify challenges, and plan targeted interventions for students who need additional support.

Conclusion

Educational programs for schools and colleges play a crucial role in combating misinformation. By integrating educational approaches adapted to each school level, using innovative digital tools, and involving parents and the community, these programs can help train a generation of informed, critical, and responsible citizens. The future of combating disinformation depends on our ability to educate young people about the dangers of manipulating information and giving them the skills to navigate a complex and ever-changing world.

3. The Importance of Critical Thinking and Digital Literacy Skills

Introduction

In a world where the amount of information available continues to grow and misinformation spreads at an alarming rate, critical thinking and digital literacy skills have become indispensable for every citizen. These skills not only allow us to navigate the ocean of information to which we are exposed daily, but also to distinguish the true from the false, the reliable from the doubtful, and the credible from the illusory. This chapter explores in detail the critical importance of these skills, their impact on society, and ways to effectively integrate them into educational programs.

3.1 Understanding Critical Thinking

Definition and Importance of Critical Thinking

Critical thinking is defined as the ability to think clearly, rationally, and independently. It involves questioning claims, examining evidence, evaluating arguments, and drawing conclusions based on careful analysis. Critical thinking is essential not only for personal development, but also for the functioning of a democratic society. It allows individuals to avoid being manipulated by misleading information and to participate actively and in an informed manner in public debate.

History and development of critical thinking

The concept of critical thinking has its roots in ancient Greek philosophy, with figures like Socrates, Plato, and Aristotle laying the foundation for logical reasoning and critical analysis. Over the centuries, this tradition has developed, influencing education and science, and becoming a key component of learning in modern societies. In the 20th century, educators like John Dewey advocated for the teaching of critical thinking in schools, believing that it was essential for preparing citizens to live in a democracy.

The components of critical thinking

Critical thinking is broken down into several essential skills, all of which are interdependent and necessary for complete and rigorous analysis:

- **Analysis** : The ability to break down a situation or information into its constituent elements, in order to better understand how they interact and influence the overall outcome.
- **Evaluation** : The act of examining evidence and arguments critically, considering their validity, relevance, and credibility.
- **Interpretation** : The ability to understand and infer the meaning of information, often by placing it in a broader context or comparing it to other data.
- **Inference** : The ability to draw logical conclusions based on available information, considering possible implications and alternatives.

- **Explanation** : The art of justifying one's conclusions and decisions using clear, coherent, and well-founded arguments.
- **Self-regulation** : The ability to monitor and adjust one's own thought process, recognizing personal biases and correcting errors in judgment.

Practical applications of critical thinking

In everyday life, critical thinking is a valuable skill that helps individuals navigate complex situations, solve problems, and make informed decisions. For example, it is essential when it comes to evaluating financial offers, making medical decisions, or understanding public policies. In an educational context, critical thinking prepares students to be independent learners and engaged citizens.

3.2 Digital Literacy: A Pillar in the Fight Against Disinformation What is digital literacy?

Digital literacy is about more than the ability to use computers or smartphones. It encompasses a set of skills that enable individuals to navigate the digital environment effectively and critically. This includes researching, evaluating, creating, and sharing digital information in a responsible and ethical manner. In an increasingly connected world, digital literacy has become as essential as reading and writing.

The components of digital literacy

Digital literacy includes several key skills that are essential for effective use of digital technologies:

- **Information search and location** : Knowing where and how to find relevant information online, using search engines, databases, and digital libraries.
- **Evaluating Source Credibility** : The ability to distinguish reliable from questionable sources, by examining factors such as the author, purpose, and evidence presented.
- **Understanding algorithms** : Understand how online platform algorithms influence the information presented to us, and how they can be used to manipulate public opinions.
- **Creating and sharing online content** : Know how to create digital content ethically and responsibly, while respecting copyright and protecting the privacy of others.
- **Digital security** : Know and apply best practices to protect personal information online, avoid cyberattacks, and browse safely on the Internet.

The growing importance of digital literacy

With the rise of social media, blogs, and video sharing platforms, digital literacy has become crucial to all aspects of modern life. Whether for professional, educational, or personal reasons, digital literacy skills enable individuals to fully participate in the information society. Without these skills, individuals risk becoming passive consumers of information, vulnerable to manipulation and misinformation.

Case studies on the impact of digital literacy

- **The role of social media in elections** : During the 2016 US presidential elections, social media played a central role in the spread of false information. A study showed that fake news on Facebook was shared more widely than verified news, highlighting the importance of digital literacy to avoid election manipulation.
- **Misinformation about COVID-19** : During the COVID-19 pandemic, misinformation has spread rapidly online, creating confusion and distrust in public health measures. The ability to assess the credibility of information has become essential to understanding and navigating this global crisis.

3.3 The Challenges of Critical Thinking and Digital Literacy in the Fight Against Disinformation Why critical thinking is essential to combat disinformation

Disinformation thrives in environments where people accept information without questioning it. Critical thinking helps break this cycle by encouraging individuals to question the information they receive, seek out evidence, and evaluate sources. By developing these skills, citizens are better equipped to resist manipulation and to contribute to a more informed public debate.

Concrete examples of the application of critical thinking

> **Deconstructing Fake News** : When sensational news appears online, critical thinking pushes individuals to verify sources, seek additional information, and analyze the motivations behind the spread of the news.

- **Analysis of conspiracy theories** : Conspiracy theories are often based on fallacious reasoning and truncated evidence. Critical thinking helps dismantle these theories by exposing logical inconsistencies and demanding solid evidence.

Digital literacy: a bulwark against misinformation

-

Digital literacy is also essential to combating misinformation, as it provides the tools needed to navigate the digital environment critically. By understanding how information is filtered and presented online, individuals can better identify fake news and disinformation campaigns.

Practical cases of digital literacy in action

- **Using fact-checking tools** : Social media users can use tools like Snopes or FactCheck.org to verify the veracity of information before sharing it. This helps reduce the spread of fake news.
- **Algorithm Awareness** : Understanding how YouTube or Facebook recommendation algorithms favor certain content can help users recognize the biases of these platforms and actively seek out alternative sources of information.

Impact on Society of Widespread Adoption of Critical Thinking and Digital Literacy

If critical thinking and digital literacy were widely adopted, society would become more resilient to misinformation. Citizens would be better equipped to participate in fact-based public debates, to make informed decisions, and to resist manipulation attempts by malicious actors. **Examples of large-scale impact**

- **Strengthening democracy** : A well-informed and critical population is essential for a well-functioning democracy. By reducing the spread of misinformation, critical thinking and digital literacy contribute to fairer elections and more informed citizen participation.
- **Reducing social tensions** : Disinformation can exacerbate social tensions by spreading polarizing narratives and false information about minority groups. By adopting critical thinking and digital literacy, society can better manage these tensions and promote stronger social cohesion.

3.4 Integrating Critical Thinking and Digital Literacy into Education

Pedagogical Approaches to Teaching Critical Thinking

Integrating critical thinking into education can be done across various disciplines. For example, in literature classes, students can analyze texts to identify the authors' biases and perspectives. In science classes, they can apply the scientific method to test hypotheses and critically evaluate the results. **Examples of educational activities**

- **Analyzing Historical Debates** : Students can study important historical debates and analyze the arguments of both sides, identifying the strengths and weaknesses of each position.
    Critical Evaluation of Advertising : Students can analyze advertisements to identify the persuasion techniques used and discuss the impact of these techniques on consumers.

Integration of digital literacy into the school curriculum

Digital literacy skills need to be integrated into the curriculum from an early age. This may include lessons on online research, digital safety, and evaluating sources, as well as more advanced projects for older students. **Examples of educational modules in digital literacy**

- **Online Search for Beginners** : A module for younger students that teaches the basics of online search, including how to use search engines, evaluate results, and avoid common pitfalls.
- **Creating Online Content** : Older students can learn how to create and share online content responsibly, taking into account copyright and privacy issues.

Assessment Methods for Critical Thinking and Digital Literacy Skills

-

It is important to regularly assess students' critical thinking and digital literacy skills to ensure they acquire the skills needed to navigate the modern information environment. This may include skills tests, group projects, and peer assessments.

Examples of innovative assessment methods

- **Group Research Projects** : Students work in groups to conduct research on a controversial topic, then present their findings to the class, explaining how they verified the information and evaluated the sources.
- **Digital Portfolios** : Students create digital portfolios that bring together their work on critical thinking and digital literacy, allowing for ongoing assessment of their skills.

3.5 The Impact of Critical Thinking and Digital Literacy on Society

The influence of critical thinking on citizen participation

Critical thinking plays a crucial role in citizen participation. Citizens who are able to think critically are better able to understand political issues, participate in public debate, and make informed decisions in elections. This leads to a more robust democracy and a more engaged society. **Examples of impact on citizen participation**

- **Involvement in electoral processes** : Citizens trained in critical thinking are less likely to be influenced by disinformation campaigns during elections, leading to more informed choices at the voting booth.
- **Participation in public debates** : Citizens who can think critically contribute to more constructive and informed public debates, which can lead to better public policies.

Digital literacy as a driver of social inclusion

Digital literacy plays a key role in social inclusion. It enables individuals from all backgrounds to fully participate in the information society, connect with others, and access educational and economic resources online.

Examples of initiatives for digital inclusion

Digital literacy programs for marginalized communities : Initiatives aimed at providing digital skills to marginalized communities can help reduce inequalities in access to information and opportunities

-

economic.

- **Digital literacy workshops for older adults** : These workshops help older adults become familiar with digital tools, navigate safely online, and avoid the pitfalls of misinformation, thereby contributing to their inclusion in the digital society.

The impact of critical thinking and digital literacy on younger generations

Younger generations, growing up in a digital world, are particularly vulnerable to misinformation. By developing their critical thinking and digital literacy skills, we can prepare them to navigate this complex world with discernment and confidence.

Examples of educational programs for young people

- **Critical Thinking Courses in High School** : Courses dedicated to critical thinking can help high school students develop their skills in evaluating arguments, analyzing sources, and making decisions.
- **Content Creation Workshops for Middle School Students** : Middle school students can participate in workshops where they learn how to create and share content online responsibly, while developing their understanding of issues related to misinformation.

Conclusion

Critical thinking and digital literacy are essential skills for navigating the modern world of information. By fully integrating them into education and promoting them within society, we can create a generation of citizens better prepared to identify, understand and combat misinformation. These skills are not only a shield against fake news, they are also the foundation of a healthy democracy and an informed and resilient society.

4. Technology Initiatives: Fact-Checking, AI and Blockchain

Introduction

The fight against disinformation does not rely solely on education and critical thinking; it also requires the integration of advanced technologies that can help identify, verify and block false information. With the rise of digital technologies, new technology initiatives have emerged, using artificial intelligence (AI), blockchain, and other innovations to combat the spread of misinformation. This chapter explores these technologies, analyzing their functioning, their applications, and their impact on society.

4.1 Fact-Checking: An Essential Tool Against Disinformation

The crucial role of fact-checking

Fact-checking is a journalistic practice that involves verifying the accuracy of information before publication or examining public statements to confirm or deny their veracity. With the explosion of fake news, fact-checking has become an essential tool for media, organizations and citizens seeking to ensure the reliability of the information they consume or share.

Fact-checking organizations: a global overview

Many fact-checking organizations have sprung up around the world to meet the growing demand for transparency and accuracy in information. Among the best known, we find:

- **Snopes** : One of the first fact-checking sites, Snopes has become a go-to for debunking rumors and misinformation circulating online.
- **PolitiFact** : This American organization focuses on verifying political statements, assigning "Pants on Fire" (blatant lies) to the most fallacious claims.

- **Full Fact** : Based in the United Kingdom, Full Fact fact-checks claims made by politicians, media outlets, and public figures, and publishes detailed reports on its findings.
- **AFP Fact Check** : Agence France-Presse (AFP) has set up a team dedicated to fact-checking in multiple languages, to counter disinformation on a global scale.

Fact-checking methodology

Fact-checking typically follows a rigorous methodology, which includes several steps:

1. **Identifying the Claim** : Fact-checkers select a claim that has been widely shared or has a significant impact on the public.
2. **Researching sources** : They look for credible and verifiable sources to examine the accuracy of the claim.
3. **Analysis and Evaluation** : The evidence collected is analyzed, and the claim is evaluated based on the available facts.
4. **Publication of results** : Verification results are published, often with a detailed explanation of the verification process. **Examples of fact-checking initiatives**

- **CrossCheck** : A collaborative project launched by First Draft and several media partners to verify information during the 2017 French elections. The teams verified information in real time to prevent the spread of fake news during the election period.
- **Factmata** : A startup using artificial intelligence to automate fact-checking and identify misleading narratives on social media.

Challenges and Limitations of Fact-Checking

Despite its importance, fact-checking presents several challenges:

- **Speed of Fake News Spread** : Misinformation often spreads faster than corrections, making it difficult for fact-checkers to do their job.
- **Confirmation bias** : Individuals tend to believe information that confirms their pre-existing beliefs, even after it has been verified and disproven.
- **Access to sources** : It is sometimes difficult to obtain reliable information, especially in contexts where press freedom is limited or where data is inaccessible.

4.2 Artificial Intelligence: A Powerful Ally in the Fight Against Disinformation

The introduction of AI in the fight against disinformation

Artificial intelligence (AI) has become a key tool for identifying and combatting disinformation at scale. With its ability to analyze huge amounts of data in real time, AI can detect trends, identify patterns in the spread of fake news, and automate fact-checking.

How AI works in detecting fake news

AI uses several techniques to detect fake news, including:

- **Natural language processing (NLP)** : This technology allows computers to understand, interpret and generate human text. NLP is used to analyze the content of articles, identify keywords associated with fake news, and evaluate the tone and objectivity of texts.
- **Machine Learning** : AI can be trained on large data sets to identify characteristics of fake news, such as sensationalist headlines or questionable sources. Over time, these models improve and become more accurate.
- **Network analysis** : AI can map information distribution networks to identify the original sources of fake news and track its spread across social media and websites.

Concrete applications of AI in the fight against disinformation

Several initiatives use AI to combat misinformation, including:

- **Hoaxy** : A platform developed by Indiana University that uses AI to track the spread of fake news online and visualize its spread on social media.
- **AdVerif.ai** : A startup that uses AI to analyze advertising content and identify fake news before it is distributed on advertising platforms.
- **NewsGuard** : A browser extension that uses AI to assess the credibility of news websites, assigning trust scores based on criteria like transparency and accuracy.

The benefits of using AI

- **Speed and efficiency** : AI can analyze millions of articles, social media posts and videos in real time, quickly detecting fake news and alerting users.
- **Automation** : AI helps automate fact-checking, reducing the workload of journalists and human fact-checkers.
- **Prediction** : Through analyzing trends and patterns, AI can anticipate the spread of misinformation and help prevent it before it goes viral.

The limits and challenges of AI

Despite its many benefits, AI also presents challenges and limitations:

- **Algorithm bias** : AI models can reproduce biases present in training data, which can lead to errors or discrimination.
- **Complexity of human language** : Natural language processing remains a challenge, particularly in understanding nuance, irony, and cultural context, which are often essential for detecting fake news.
- **False positives and false negatives** : AI can sometimes falsely identify true information as fake news (false positives) or fail to detect fake news (false negatives).

Case studies on using AI against disinformation

- **The 2020 US presidential elections** : Several tech companies, including Facebook and Google, used AI to identify and remove fake news circulating on their platforms during the elections.
- **COVID-19 and misinformation** : During the COVID-19 pandemic, AI systems have been deployed to quickly detect and remove misinformation about the virus, vaccines, and treatments.

4.3 Blockchain: Transparency and Traceability of Information

Understanding blockchain

Blockchain is a distributed ledger technology that allows data to be stored securely, transparently and immutably. Each block of data is linked to the previous and next, forming a chain of blocks. This technology is best known for being the basis of cryptocurrencies like Bitcoin, but it also has potential applications in the fight against disinformation.

Blockchain applications for combating disinformation

Blockchain can be used to ensure the authenticity and traceability of information published online. Here are some of the ways it can be applied:

- **Information certification** : Media platforms can use blockchain to certify the origin and veracity of published information. Each article or video could be time-stamped and digitally signed, ensuring that it has not been altered after publication.
- **Traceability of sources** : Thanks to blockchain, it is possible to follow the information distribution chain from its source to its dissemination. This helps identify the origins of fake news and take steps to prevent it from spreading.

- **Decentralization of fact-checking** : Blockchain enables the creation of decentralized platforms where users can check facts collaboratively. These platforms are not controlled by a single entity, which reduces the risk of censorship or manipulation.

Examples of initiatives using blockchain

- **Po.et** : A platform using blockchain to register and manage the copyright of digital content, thus guaranteeing its authenticity and origin.
- **Truepic** : An application that uses blockchain to authenticate photos and videos, ensuring that they have not been modified since they were captured.
- **Civil** : A project that aims to create an ethical and transparent journalism ecosystem using blockchain to guarantee the veracity of information published by its members.

The benefits of blockchain in the fight against disinformation

- **Transparency** : Blockchain provides complete transparency, as all transactions are visible to all participants in the network. This makes it easy to verify the origin and authenticity of the information.
- **Security** : The decentralized nature of blockchain makes it resistant to manipulation and attacks. Once information is recorded on the blockchain, it cannot be modified or deleted without detection.
- **Trust** : By ensuring the authenticity and traceability of information, blockchain can help restore public trust in media and information sources.

The challenges and limitations of blockchain

Like any technology, blockchain also presents challenges and limitations:

- **Complexity and cost** : Implementing blockchain can be complex and expensive, which may limit its adoption, particularly for smaller media organizations.
- **Scalability** : Blockchain networks can have scalability issues, making it difficult to process large amounts of information in real time.
- **Regulation** : The use of blockchain for information management raises regulatory issues, particularly with regard to the protection of personal data and compliance with privacy laws.

Case studies on blockchain and combating disinformation

- **Information traceability during crises** : During crises, such as natural disasters or pandemics, blockchain could be used to ensure the veracity of critical information disseminated to the public, avoiding the spread of false news that could worsen the situation.
- **Decentralized journalism projects** : Initiatives like Civil aim to use blockchain to create a new model of journalism, where journalists are directly rewarded by readers for their work, ensuring transparency and truthfulness of information.

4.4 Impact of Technological Innovation on Society

Transformation of the media ecosystem

The introduction of technologies such as AI and blockchain has already begun to transform the media ecosystem. These technologies enable new forms of journalism, fact-checking, and information distribution. They also offer powerful tools to combat disinformation, but they also raise questions about ethics, privacy, and regulation.

Transformation Examples

- **Automated journalism** : AI enables the creation of automated content, where articles are generated by algorithms based on real-time data. This can speed up the production of information, but raises questions about the quality and ethics of this content.

- **Blockchain-based reputation systems** : Decentralized reputation systems can be developed to assess the credibility of journalists and media outlets, using blockchain to ensure the integrity of the assessments.

Risks and ethical concerns

The use of these technologies raises ethical concerns, particularly regarding surveillance, manipulation of information, and protection of personal data. It is essential that these technologies are developed and used transparently, with safeguards to protect the rights of individuals and ensure the integrity of information.

Examples of Ethical Concerns

- **Algorithmic biases** : AI algorithms can reproduce and amplify biases present in training data, which can lead to discrimination or errors in detecting fake news.
- **Surveillance and Privacy** : Using technologies like AI to monitor online information can raise questions about privacy and mass surveillance.

The future of technology in the fight against disinformation

In the future, it is likely that these technologies will continue to evolve and play an increasingly important role in combating disinformation. It is crucial that developers, regulators, and users work together to ensure these technologies are used ethically and effectively, to build trust in information and protect democracy.

Future outlook

- **Development of ethical AI** : Research into ethical AI will focus on reducing bias and creating more transparent and accountable systems.
- **Expansion of blockchain-based initiatives** : Blockchain could become a standard for information certification, particularly in contexts where data veracity is crucial, such as elections or emergency situations.
- **International collaboration** : Combating disinformation is a global challenge that requires international collaboration. Technologies like AI and blockchain can facilitate this collaboration by providing standardized tools for fact-checking and information traceability.

Conclusion

Technologies such as AI and blockchain offer powerful tools to combat misinformation, enabling faster fact-checking, better traceability of information, and greater transparency in the media ecosystem. However, these technologies are not without challenges and must be developed and used ethically and responsibly. By integrating these technologies into the fight against disinformation, we can create a safer, more reliable, and more democratic information environment. **5. International Collaboration for Regulation and Surveillance**

Introduction

The fight against disinformation is a global challenge that can only be effectively addressed through close international collaboration. As information flows without borders through digital platforms, it has become essential that governments, international organizations, technology companies and civil society work together to regulate and monitor the spread of fake news. This chapter explores the various international initiatives, existing regulations, the challenges these efforts face, and the critical importance of cooperation to protect the integrity of information on a global scale.

5.1 The Importance of International Regulation

Why international regulation is necessary

With the rise of digital technologies, information, whether true or false, can now be disseminated instantly across the world. This reality has made national approaches to information regulation largely ineffective, as content can easily bypass borders through the Internet. For this reason, coordinated international regulation is necessary to ensure that standards and rules for combating disinformation are applied uniformly, regardless of national borders.

The risks of a lack of international regulation

Without international regulation, efforts to combat disinformation are fragmented, which can lead to disparities in the application of laws and regulations, creating safe havens for malicious actors. Additionally, the lack of consistent regulation can lead to a "race to the bottom" where less regulated countries become hubs for the spread of false information, thereby undermining the effectiveness of measures taken by other nations. .

Examples of existing international regulations

- **The General Data Protection Regulation (GDPR)** : Although focused on the protection of personal data, the European Union's GDPR has implications for the regulation of digital platforms and the responsibility of companies in the management of information .
- **The Budapest Convention on Cybercrime** : This convention, adopted by the Council of Europe, aims to harmonize national legislation on cybercrime, including offenses related to the dissemination of false information online.

5.2 International Initiatives to Combat Disinformation

International organizations and their role

Several international organizations play a key role in coordinating efforts to combat disinformation. These organizations work not only to create standards and guidelines, but also to facilitate cooperation between member states for effective regulation.

- **UNESCO** : The United Nations Educational, Scientific and Cultural Organization (UNESCO) leads initiatives to promote media and information literacy across the world, providing educational resources and organizing awareness campaigns.
- **The European Union** : The EU has several initiatives in place to combat disinformation, including the Code of Practice Against Disinformation, which sets standards for online platforms and advertisers.
- **The Organization for Security and Co-operation in Europe (OSCE)** : The OSCE monitors elections in its member states to prevent and counter electoral interference, including the spread of fake news.

International cooperation programs

Cooperation between nations is essential to develop common strategies and share resources and information on best practices in combating disinformation. Here are some examples of international cooperation programs:

- **The G7 Disinformation Working Group** : This working group, made up of foreign ministers from G7 countries, works to develop strategies to counter disinformation, particularly that originating from foreign interference.
- **The Global Fact-Checking Partnership** : Launched by several major fact-checking organizations, this partnership aims to standardize fact-checking methods globally and strengthen cooperation between fact-checkers in different countries.

The challenges of international cooperation

Although international cooperation is crucial, it is not without challenges. Among the main obstacles are cultural differences, divergent political priorities, and questions of national sovereignty. Additionally, economic disparities between countries may limit the ability of some nations to fully participate in these initiatives. **Examples of challenges encountered**

- **Regulatory differences** : Media and information regulations vary widely between countries, which can complicate efforts to implement common international standards.
- **Political interference** : In some cases, efforts to combat disinformation can be hampered by internal political considerations, where governments use disinformation as a propaganda tool.

5.3 Digital Platforms and their Responsibility in the Fight against Disinformation

The role of digital giants

Large digital platforms such as Facebook, Twitter, Google and YouTube play a central role in the dissemination of information across the world. Given their global reach, these companies have a particular responsibility in combating disinformation. However, regulating these platforms on an international scale remains a major challenge. **Digital platform initiatives to combat disinformation**

- **Facebook** : Facebook has launched several initiatives to combat misinformation, including using AI systems to identify fake news, partnering with fact-checking organizations, and introducing warning labels on content doubtful.
- **Google** : Google has developed algorithms to demote low-quality content in its search results and created the Google News Initiative program to support quality journalism.
- **Twitter** : Twitter has policies in place to limit the spread of misleading content, including labeling tweets containing disputed information and suspending accounts that consistently spread false news.

Limitations of current initiatives

While these initiatives are a step in the right direction, they also have limitations. For example, the AI systems used by these platforms are not infallible and can miss harmful content or, on the contrary, censor legitimate content. Additionally, content moderation is often perceived as opaque, with little transparency on the criteria used to decide what content is removed or labeled.

The need for stricter regulation of platforms

There is growing recognition that stricter regulations are needed to hold digital platforms accountable for the spread of disinformation. Legislative initiatives like the European Union's Digital Services Act aim to establish clearer rules for online content moderation and increase the transparency of algorithms.

Examples of current regulations

- **The Digital Services Act (DSA)** : This EU regulation imposes increased transparency and accountability obligations on large digital platforms, including reporting on content moderation and algorithms used to classify information. .
- **Australia's Digital Platforms Act** : This law requires digital platforms to pay media companies for the news content they share, strengthening funding for quality journalism and reducing reliance on user-generated content , often of lower quality.

5.4 The Challenges of International Collaboration

Cultural and political obstacles

International collaboration in combating disinformation is often hampered by cultural and political differences between countries. These differences can affect how information is perceived and processed, as well as the priorities of different governments.

Examples of cultural barriers

- **Perception of freedom of expression** : In some countries, efforts to regulate online information are seen as an attack on freedom of expression, which can complicate the implementation of common regulations.
- **Language differences** : Language differences can also pose a challenge, as misinformation can take very different forms across languages, requiring specific verification approaches.

The issues of national sovereignty

The question of national sovereignty is another major obstacle to international cooperation. Governments may be reluctant to cede some of their control over information to international bodies, fearing that this will weaken their authority or expose their country to foreign influence.

Examples of tensions linked to sovereignty

- **Foreign interference** : Allegations of foreign interference in the electoral processes of different countries have exacerbated international tensions, making collaboration more difficult.
- **Divergent regulations** : Countries have very different media and internet regulations, making it difficult to create common standards. For example, what is considered censorship in one country may be seen as necessary regulation in another.

Economic disparities

Economic disparities between countries pose another major challenge for international collaboration. Developing countries, in particular, may lack the resources necessary to implement measures to combat disinformation or to fully participate in international initiatives. **Examples of economic disparities**

- **Access to technology** : In many developing countries, limited access to information technology and digital infrastructure complicates efforts to monitor and combat disinformation.
- **Funding for initiatives** : International initiatives often require substantial funding, which can be an obstacle for countries with limited resources.

5.5 The Role of Civil Society and NGOs

The contribution of non-governmental organizations

Non-governmental organizations (NGOs) play a crucial role in combating disinformation, particularly in contexts where governments are constrained by resources or political considerations. NGOs can act as independent gatekeepers of information, providing fact-checking, raising public awareness, and advocating for stricter regulations. **Examples of NGO initiatives**

- **Reporters Without Borders (RSF)** : RSF campaigns for press freedom and the fight against disinformation around the world, offering support to journalists and denouncing violations of freedom of expression.
- **First Draft** : An NGO focused on fact-checking and media literacy, providing resources to help journalists, educators, and the public identify and combat misinformation.

Challenges faced by NGOs

NGOs face several challenges in their fight against disinformation, including lack of funding, political pressure, and security risks for journalists and activists working in hostile environments. **Examples of specific challenges**

- **Threats against journalists** : In many countries, journalists who work on fact-checking or reporting disinformation face threats, intimidation, and even violence.
- **Access to Resources** : NGOs, particularly those operating in developing countries, may have limited access to the technological and financial resources needed to carry out their missions.

The role of civil society

Civil society, including citizen groups, educators, and activists, also plays a key role in combating disinformation. Active citizen participation in fact-checking, reporting fake news, and educating others is essential to creating a culture of vigilance and accountability. **Examples of civil society initiatives**

- **Crowdsourced fact-checking projects** : Initiatives like "TruthBuzz" encourage citizens to participate in fact-checking and share the results with their communities.
- **Media literacy campaigns** : Citizen groups organize workshops and awareness campaigns to educate the public about the dangers of misinformation and how to recognize it.

5.6 The Future of International Collaboration

Towards closer collaboration

In the future, it is likely that international collaboration in combating disinformation will become even more essential. As technologies continue to evolve, new forms of disinformation will emerge, requiring globally coordinated responses. **Examples of potential future initiatives**

- **Creation of a dedicated international agency** : One proposal could be the creation of an international agency dedicated to the fight against disinformation, which would coordinate the efforts of governments, digital platforms, and civil society.
- **Developing global standards** : Developing global standards for online information regulation, including guidelines for algorithm transparency and data protection, could help harmonize international efforts.

The challenges ahead

Despite the progress made, several challenges will need to be overcome for international collaboration to be effective:

- **Evolution of disinformation techniques** : Disinformation techniques are becoming more and more sophisticated, particularly with the use of deepfakes and artificial intelligence, which will complicate the task of regulators.
- **Maintaining the balance between regulation and freedom of expression** : A major challenge will be to ensure that efforts to regulate online information do not undermine freedom of expression, a fundamental principle in many democracies.

The role of research and innovation

Research and innovation will play a crucial role in developing new technologies and strategies to combat disinformation. Universities, research laboratories, and technology companies will need to work closely together to find innovative solutions to this global problem.

Examples of promising research areas

- **AI for deepfake detection** : Developing AI tools that can detect deepfakes in real time will be crucial to preventing the spread of this misleading content.

- **Blockchain for information transparency** : Exploring the use of blockchain to ensure the authenticity and traceability of information could offer a lasting solution against misinformation.

Conclusion

International collaboration is the key to effectively combating disinformation on a global scale. By joining forces, governments, international organizations, digital platforms, and civil society can implement robust regulations, develop innovative technologies, and raise public awareness of the importance of verified information. Going forward, overcoming challenges of sovereignty, economic disparities, and cultural differences will be essential to create a united front against the growing threat of disinformation.

1. Analysis of Conspiracy Themes Around the Covid-19 Pandemic

Introduction

The Covid-19 pandemic, which began at the end of 2019, has caused not only a global health crisis, but also an "infodemic" marked by an unprecedented proliferation of misinformation and conspiracy theories. These theories, often based on distortions of reality or erroneous interpretations, have resonated strongly with various online communities, exacerbating the crisis by sowing distrust, confusion, and sometimes even hatred. The speed with which these theories have spread shows how vulnerable contemporary society is to fake news, especially in times of crisis. In this section, we will explore in depth the main conspiracy theories that have emerged during the Covid-19 pandemic, their spread, their public acceptance, and their social and health impact.

5.1 The Origin of Conspiracy Theories Linked to Covid-19

The First Rumors and Their Emergence

The first conspiracy theories around Covid-19 began to emerge as soon as news of the outbreak was first reported in late 2019 and early 2020. One of the first theories to gain popularity was the idea that the SARS-CoV-2 virus was intentionally created in a laboratory in Wuhan, China, and was deliberately released as a biological weapon. This theory has been fueled by a combination of distrust of the Chinese government, legitimate concerns about the safety of virology labs, and speculation about the unusual origins of the virus. Although scientists quickly dismissed this theory, explaining that the virus has characteristics typical of a zoonosis (transmission of a pathogen from an animal to humans), it has continued to spread, particularly among communities online suspicious of the authorities.

Theories of Creation in the Laboratory

The idea that SARS-CoV-2 was manufactured in a laboratory is not unprecedented in the history of pandemics. Similar theories emerged during the HIV/AIDS crisis in the 1980s, where some claimed the virus was created as a biological weapon. These theories often exploit fear of the unknown and distrust of scientific and governmental institutions. In the case of Covid-19, the geographic proximity of the epicenter of the epidemic to the Wuhan Institute of Virology provided an easy pretext for those seeking to promote this theory. Supporters of the idea have often cited the fact that the institute was conducting research on coronaviruses, but without presenting solid evidence to support the hypothesis of a deliberate or accidental leak.

In fact, the majority of scientific experts, including those at the World Health Organization (WHO), agree that the virus most likely has a natural origin. Genetic studies have shown that the virus is closely related to coronaviruses found in bats, suggesting a natural jump from an animal host to humans, possibly via an intermediate host such as the pangolin. However, despite this evidence, the lab theory continued to be fueled by public figures and alternative media, which contributed to its widespread dissemination.

Theories of Population Control and Vaccines

Another major conspiracy theory that has emerged during the pandemic concerns vaccines. These theories have often been linked to existing fears regarding government control, mass surveillance, and public health. One of the most popular theories was that Covid-19 vaccines were used as a tool for population control. Some claimed, without evidence, that vaccines contained microchips intended to track individuals, a theory often associated with Bill Gates because of his philanthropic commitment to global health.

These theories have been fueled by a growing distrust of pharmaceutical companies and governments, exacerbated by the rapid and unprecedented nature of the development of Covid-19 vaccines. While vaccines were seen by most as the key to ending the pandemic, these theories cast doubt on their safety and effectiveness, contributing to vaccine hesitancy in many communities.

Theories on 5G and the Spread of the Virus

Among the most absurd yet popular conspiracy theories is the idea that 5G technology was responsible for the spread of SARS-CoV-2. This theory, which has no scientific basis, gained popularity online, where videos and articles claimed that 5G towers weakened people's immune systems or even that 5G airwaves could carry the virus. This theory has led to acts of vandalism against telecommunications infrastructure in several countries, showing the concrete impact that such ideas can have on society.

This theory combines irrational fears about new technologies with a distrust of large telecommunications companies. The 5G phenomenon has already sparked concerns about the possible health effects of radiation, and the pandemic has provided fertile ground for those fears to morph into broader conspiracy theories.

The Spread of Conspiracy Theories on Social Media

Social media has played a central role in the propagation of these theories. Facebook, Twitter, YouTube, and other platforms became channels for these ideas, which spread quickly thanks to algorithms designed to maximize user engagement. Conspiracy theories, often sensationalistic, have proven particularly engaging, prompting users to share them widely. Platforms have implemented measures to limit the spread of this false information, such as adding warning labels or removing certain content, but these efforts have often been deemed insufficient or applied inconsistently.

5.2 Factors Facilitating the Spread of Conspiracy Theories

The Role of Fear and Uncertainty

Fear and uncertainty are powerful drivers for the spread of conspiracy theories. In times of crisis, such as a global pandemic, these emotions are heightened, pushing individuals to seek answers that offer them a sense of control or explanation in the face of the unknown. Conspiracy theories often provide simple, understandable narratives, scapegoating and offering simplistic explanations for complex problems. This reduction in complexity allows those overwhelmed by fear and uncertainty to find some comfort, even if it leads them to adopt erroneous beliefs.

Confirmation Bias

Confirmation bias is a well-documented psychological phenomenon where individuals tend to favor information that confirms their existing beliefs, while ignoring or rejecting information that contradicts them. During the Covid-19 pandemic, this bias has played a crucial role in the spread of conspiracy theories. People already distrustful of governments, mainstream media, or official science were more likely to believe and share conspiracy theories that seemed to confirm their suspicions. This phenomenon has been amplified by social media, where algorithms create "filter bubbles" that expose users to content that reinforces their existing opinions.

The Echo Chamber Effect

The echo chamber effect is another important factor that has contributed to the spread of conspiracy theories during the pandemic. In echo chambers, beliefs and ideas are amplified and repeated, often without being questioned. Social media and online forums, where users are often surrounded by like-minded people, create environments ripe for the reaffirmation of conspiracy theories. In these spaces, users can find support for their beliefs, strengthen their convictions, and become more resolute in rejecting conflicting information.

The Influence of Public Figures and Alternative Media

Public figures, including politicians, celebrities, and online influencers, have played a significant role in spreading Covid-19 conspiracy theories. In some cases, politicians have adopted elements of these theories to mobilize their electoral base or to oppose their opponents. These public figures have a significant platform and audience, which allows them to legitimize misconceptions and disseminate them widely. Furthermore, alternative media, often less regulated than traditional media, have served as conduits for these theories, publishing articles, videos, and podcasts that resonated with audiences wary of established media.

5.3 The Consequences of Conspiracy Theories on Society

Impact on Public Health

Conspiracy theories have had serious consequences for public health during the Covid-19 pandemic. One of the most visible consequences has been vaccine hesitancy, fueled by false theories about the safety and intentions behind vaccines. In some countries, disinformation campaigns have led to a significant drop in vaccination rates, undermining efforts to achieve herd immunity and allowing the virus to continue to circulate. Additionally, the spread of misinformation about treatments, such as the idea that unproven remedies could cure or prevent Covid-19, has led some to avoid appropriate medical care, worsening the health situation.

Legitimacy Effect of Erroneous Beliefs

One of the indirect consequences of conspiracy theories is that they can legitimize erroneous beliefs and dangerous behavior. For example, the theory that the virus is an invention or exaggeration has led some people to ignore public health measures, such as wearing masks or social distancing, thereby increasing their risk of infection and that of others. Additionally, the spread of these theories undermined health authorities' efforts to communicate accurate information and health advice, creating confusion that complicated management of the pandemic.

Polarization and Social Conflict

Conspiracy theories have exacerbated social and political polarization during the Covid-19 pandemic. In many countries, the pandemic has become an ideological battleground, where political divisions have been amplified by differences of opinion over the severity of the virus, containment measures, and vaccines. These divisions have sometimes led to open conflict, including protests against health restrictions that degenerated into violence. Polarization has also affected personal relationships, with families and communities divided over issues related to the pandemic

Distrust of Institutions and the Media

Conspiracy theories have helped erode trust in public institutions, health authorities, and traditional media. In some cases, this distrust has been exploited by malicious actors, including foreign governments, to weaken social cohesion and sow disorder. Furthermore, widespread distrust has made it more difficult to communicate public health messages and implement pandemic control measures. This erosion of trust risks having long-term consequences, making societies more vulnerable to future misinformation.

Economic Consequences

Conspiracy theories have also had economic repercussions, particularly for the healthcare, tourism, and entertainment industries. Misinformation about Covid-19 has fueled economic uncertainty, discouraging investment and slowing economic recovery. Additionally, theories that encouraged the use of unproven treatments resulted in unnecessary expenses for consumers and diverted resources away from proven treatments.

5.4 Responses and Countermeasures to Disinformation

Fact-checking initiatives

Faced with the rapid spread of misinformation during the pandemic, numerous fact-checking initiatives have been put in place to verify information and correct fake news. These initiatives have played a crucial role in providing the public with reliable information and exposing the inaccuracies of conspiracy theories. However, the work of fact-checkers has been complicated by the enormous volume of misinformation online and the speed with which it spreads. Additionally, some proponents of conspiracy theories have dismissed fact-checks, perceiving them as part of a larger conspiracy.

Regulation of Online Platforms

Governments and digital platforms have also taken steps to regulate the spread of disinformation. Facebook, Twitter, YouTube, and other platforms have introduced new policies to remove or label misleading content related to Covid-19.

However, these efforts have been controversial, with some perceiving them as an attack on free speech. Additionally, the implementation of these policies has been uneven, with some conspiracy theories continuing to flourish despite efforts to limit them.

Educational Initiatives to Promote Critical Thinking

Education is one of the most promising strategies for combating disinformation in the long term. By teaching individuals from a young age to critically evaluate sources of information and recognize bias, it is possible to reduce their vulnerability to conspiracy theories. Many media literacy programs have been launched in response to the pandemic, aiming to strengthen critical thinking skills and raise public awareness of the dangers of misinformation. These programs include online courses, workshops, and educational resources for schools and universities.

International Collaborations to Combat Disinformation

The fight against misinformation during the Covid-19 pandemic has also led to increased collaboration between governments, international organizations, and technology companies. Initiatives such as the Global Fact-Checking Partnership have helped coordinate verification efforts globally. Additionally, organizations like the WHO have worked with digital platforms to promote accurate information about Covid-19 and counter misinformation. These collaborations have shown the importance of a comprehensive approach to combating disinformation, which transcends national borders.

Conclusion

The Covid-19 pandemic has revealed how quickly conspiracy theories can spread and cause widespread harm. They have not only harmed public health, but they have also exacerbated social divisions, undermined trust in institutions, and disrupted the economy. Although considerable efforts have been made to counter these theories, much remains to be done to strengthen the resilience of societies to disinformation. This will require a multifaceted approach, combining education, regulation, international collaboration, and the development of new technologies to monitor and counter fake news. Ultimately, combating disinformation is a crucial issue for public health, democracy, and social stability in an increasingly interconnected world. **2. The Impacts of Disinformation on Modern International Conflicts**

Introduction

In an increasingly interconnected world, where information circulates at unprecedented speed, disinformation has become a powerful weapon in international conflicts. Disinformation campaigns, often orchestrated by states or non-state actors, aim to manipulate public opinion, sow confusion, destabilize adversaries, and influence the outcomes of geopolitical conflicts. This section explores in depth the various aspects of disinformation in the context of modern international conflicts, examining its origins, its diffusion mechanisms, its actors, and its long-term consequences for global stability.

5.1 The Origin and Evolution of Disinformation in International Conflicts

The First Uses of Disinformation in Conflicts

The use of disinformation as a tool of war is not a new phenomenon. Since ancient times, leaders have understood the importance of controlling information to manipulate the enemy and influence perceptions. However, with the advent of the press, radio, television, and more recently the Internet, the reach and effectiveness of disinformation campaigns have increased significantly.

For example, during World War II, propaganda played a crucial role, with powers such as Nazi Germany, the Soviet Union, and the Allies using carefully crafted messages to galvanize support among their populations while demoralizing the enemy. Leaflets, radio broadcasts, and propaganda films were common ways to spread misleading or biased information to influence the course of the war.

The Cold War Era: A Laboratory for Disinformation

The Cold War marked a period of intense competition between the United States and the Soviet Union, where disinformation became a key weapon of psychological warfare. Both superpowers have conducted sophisticated disinformation campaigns to destabilize the other side, manipulate global public opinion, and gain strategic advantages. One of the most famous examples is Operation Infektion, a disinformation campaign led by the KGB in the 1980s that aimed to make people believe that the AIDS virus was created by the United States as a weapon. biological. Although this allegation has been denied, it has caused confusion and mistrust globally.

The Cold War also saw the emergence of "fake news" before the Internet era, with fabricated or biased newspaper articles, books, and documentaries circulating around the world. These efforts aimed not only to discredit the adversary, but also to create divisions within alliances and influence social and political movements in various countries.

The Digital Revolution and the Amplification of Disinformation

The rise of the Internet and social media has transformed the way disinformation is created and disseminated in international conflicts. New technologies have made it possible to reach global audiences on an unprecedented scale, making disinformation more difficult to detect and counter. Modern disinformation campaigns often leverage bots, trolls, and recommendation algorithms to amplify misleading messages, creating an information ecosystem where the truth becomes difficult to discern.

Conflicts like the war in Syria have illustrated how disinformation can be used to manipulate international perceptions. Doctored videos, photoshopped photos, and false testimonies have been widely distributed to influence global public opinion and the political decisions of foreign powers. These campaigns not only affected perceptions of the conflict, but they also had an impact on immigration policies, military interventions, and humanitarian aid.

The Use of Traditional and Digital Media

Disinformation campaigns in international conflicts use a combination of traditional and digital media to maximize their reach and impact. Traditional media, such as newspapers, television channels, and radio stations, continue to play a crucial role, especially in regions where Internet access is limited. In some cases, governments or insurgent groups directly control these media, disseminating biased or fabricated information to support their strategic goals.

With the rise of digital media, misinformation has found fertile new ground. Social networks like Facebook, Twitter, and YouTube have become key platforms for the rapid spread of false information. These platforms allow disinformation campaigns to bypass traditional editorial filters and directly target specific segments of the population. For example, during the 2016 US presidential elections, Russian actors used targeted ads on Facebook to spread false or misleading information, aimed at influencing voters and sowing division.

The Role of Bots and Trolls

Bots and trolls play a central role in modern disinformation campaigns. Bots are automated programs that can distribute content widely, while trolls are individuals or groups who deliberately spread misleading or provocative information to sow discord. These tools make it possible to artificially manipulate online discussions, create false impressions of popular support, and polarize debates.

In the context of international conflicts, bots and trolls are often used to amplify narratives aligned with the interests of a particular state or group. For example, during the conflict in Ukraine, Russian bots were used to spread pro-Russian messages and to discredit the Ukrainian government. These efforts were aimed at weakening international support for Ukraine and justifying Russia's annexation of Crimea.

Handling Recommendation Algorithms

Recommendation algorithms, which determine what content is shown to users on digital platforms, play a key role in the spread of misinformation. These algorithms are designed to maximize engagement by showing users content they might be interested in, often based on their past behaviors. However, this can create echo chambers where users are exposed to increasingly extreme or biased content, reinforcing their existing beliefs.

Disinformation actors exploit these algorithms by creating content that is designed to go viral, often using sensationalist headlines, shocking images, or memes. Once this content starts to gain traction, the algorithms amplify it, reaching a much wider audience. This can have devastating consequences in the context of international conflicts, where public perception and political decision-making can be influenced by false or misleading information.

Fake News and Hybrid Conflicts

Hybrid conflicts, which combine conventional military tactics with information warfare operations, have become a hallmark of modern conflicts. Disinformation plays a central role in these conflicts, where it is used to blur the lines between fact and fiction, creating confusion and paralyzing opposing responses. In conflicts like those in Ukraine or Syria, fake news has been used to create competing narratives, where each side accuses the other of war crimes, human rights violations, or military provocations.

These competing narratives make it difficult for the international community to discern the truth and make informed decisions. Additionally, disinformation in hybrid conflicts can be used to justify military actions or to discredit peace efforts, thereby prolonging conflicts and exacerbating humanitarian suffering.

States as Main Actors of Disinformation

States are often the main instigators of disinformation campaigns in international conflicts. They use disinformation as a strategic tool to weaken their adversaries, influence international public opinion, and achieve their geopolitical goals. States have vast resources at their disposal to carry out these campaigns, including intelligence agencies, state-controlled media networks, and alliances with non-state actors.

Russia, for example, is well known for its use of disinformation in international conflicts. Since the Cold War, Russia has developed sophisticated information warfare strategies, which it has used to influence elections, sow division in the West, and justify its military actions. The 2014 annexation of Crimea and intervention in Syria are examples where Russia has used disinformation campaigns to shape international perception and achieve its strategic goals.

Insurgent and Terrorist Groups

Insurgent and terrorist groups also use disinformation as a tool to promote their causes, recruit members, and destabilize their adversaries. These groups often use social media to spread their messages, attracting a global audience and bypassing traditional media. Disinformation allows them to create narratives that justify their violent actions, discredit their enemies, and build support among their supporters.

For example, the Islamic State (Daesh) has used disinformation prolifically in its propaganda efforts. The videos and messages posted by Daesh on social media were designed to inspire terror, attract recruits, and present an image of strength and victory, even when the group suffered military defeats. These propaganda efforts have had a significant impact, not only on the ground, but also on the overall perception of the war on terrorism.

Businesses and Non-State Actors

In addition to states and insurgent groups, corporations and other non-state actors also play a role in the spread of disinformation in international conflicts. Some companies, particularly in the media and technology sectors, have been accused of enabling or even facilitating the spread of false information for profit. Other non-state actors, such as criminal organizations, use disinformation to protect their illicit activities or to manipulate financial markets.

Individual Actors: Influencers and Journalists

Individuals, including influencers and journalists, can also play a role in spreading misinformation, whether intentionally or not. Influencers with large audiences can amplify misleading narratives, either out of ignorance or for personal or political gain. Journalists, particularly in media environments where pressure to publish quickly is high, may accidentally relay unverified information, contributing to the spread of misinformation.

Destabilization of Regions in Conflict

One of the most direct consequences of disinformation in international conflicts is the destabilization of regions in conflict. The spread of false information can exacerbate ethnic, religious, or political tensions, transforming local disputes into large-scale violent conflicts. For example, in Myanmar, disinformation spread on social media helped fuel hatred against the Rohingya minority, leading to mass violence and a humanitarian crisis.

Impact on Political and Military Decisions

Disinformation can also influence political and military decisions, misleading decision-makers or shaping public opinion in ways that support or oppose military intervention. In some cases, misleading information led to military interventions based on erroneous premises, which had disastrous consequences for local populations. The 2003 invasion of Iraq, justified in part by incorrect information about weapons of mass destruction, is a tragic example.

Erosion of Trust in International Institutions

Disinformation in international conflicts can also erode trust in international institutions, such as the UN or the International Criminal Court, by discrediting them or sowing doubt about their impartiality. This can weaken mediation and conflict resolution efforts, prolong wars, and complicate post-conflict reconstruction efforts.

Economic Consequences

The economic impacts of disinformation in international conflicts are also significant. Financial markets can be destabilized by false information, leading to significant economic losses. Additionally, economic sanctions based on incorrect information can worsen humanitarian situations and prolong conflicts. **Humanitarian Consequences**

Finally, disinformation in international conflicts has serious humanitarian consequences. By sowing confusion about the intentions of belligerents, military objectives, or the security of humanitarian corridors, disinformation can hamper relief efforts and worsen the suffering of civilian populations. Aid workers themselves can be targeted or manipulated by disinformation campaigns, complicating their work and putting lives at risk.

5.5 Responses and Countermeasures to Disinformation in International Conflicts

International Initiatives to Counter Disinformation

The international community has become aware of the destructive role of disinformation in conflicts and has put in place several initiatives to confront it. Organizations such as the UN, NATO, and the European Union have developed strategies to detect and counter disinformation, including by forming specialized teams and cooperating with digital platforms to limit the spread of false information.

Regulation of Digital Platforms

The regulation of digital platforms is a key element in the fight against disinformation in international conflicts. Legislation like the Digital Services Act in Europe aims to impose stricter responsibilities on platforms to act quickly against misleading content. However, the application of these regulations remains a challenge, particularly in contexts where geopolitical interests are at stake.

Strengthening Societal Resilience

Strengthening the resilience of societies to disinformation is essential to limit its impact. This includes media literacy, promoting critical thinking, and supporting quality, independent journalism. By strengthening citizens' abilities to discern reliable information from false information, it is possible to reduce the vulnerability of societies to disinformation campaigns.

International Collaboration

International collaboration is crucial to combating disinformation in conflicts. Countries must share information, coordinate efforts, and work together to counter transnational disinformation campaigns. Initiatives like the G7 Disinformation Working Group or the Global Fact-Checking Partnership show the importance of international cooperation in this area.

Using Technology to Detect and Counter Disinformation

Cutting-edge technologies, including artificial intelligence and data analytics, are playing an increasingly important role in detecting and neutralizing disinformation. These technologies can be used to analyze patterns of misinformation dissemination, identify responsible actors, and provide fact-based counter-narratives. However, these tools must be used ethically and transparently to avoid abuse and human rights violations.

Conclusion

Disinformation in modern international conflicts poses a serious threat to global peace and security. It destabilizes regions in conflict, influences political and military decisions, and exacerbates humanitarian suffering. Although significant efforts have been made to counter this threat, much remains to be done to strengthen the resilience of societies and promote truthful and reliable information. As technology evolves, combatting disinformation will require innovative approaches, strengthened international collaboration, and a strong commitment to the truth.

3. Study on the Impact of Deepfakes in Modern Media

Introduction

Deepfakes represent one of the most worrying technological developments in recent years. Using advanced artificial intelligence techniques, they create videos, images, or audio recordings that appear realistic, but are in fact entirely fabricated. This technology, which first emerged as a curiosity in tech circles, has quickly transformed into a potential weapon of massive disinformation, with profound implications for politics, national security, and society at large.

The impact of deepfakes in modern media is vast and multidimensional. They have the potential to undermine trust in institutions, manipulate public opinions, and provoke conflict. As this technology becomes more accessible, its malicious use increases, posing complex challenges to governments, media, and technology platforms. This section examines in detail the different facets of the impact of deepfakes, focusing on their role in disinformation and the risks they pose for democracy.

5.1 Origin and Evolution of Deepfakes

Early Technological Developments

Deepfakes get their name from the combination of the terms "deep learning" and "fake". Deep learning, a branch of artificial intelligence, allows machines to learn from large amounts of data. This technology was first used in areas such as image recognition, natural language processing, and recommendation systems, before being misused to create falsified audiovisual content.

The first deepfakes appeared in 2017, when an anonymous user posted manipulated videos on an online forum. These videos showed celebrities in compromising situations, using technology to superimpose the faces of these celebrities onto the bodies of actors in adult films. Although these videos quickly gained attention due to their sensational nature, they also highlighted the destructive potential of this technology when used for malicious purposes.

Expansion and Growing Sophistication

Since those early days, deepfake technology has evolved rapidly. The tools needed to create deepfakes have become more accessible, and the videos themselves have become increasingly difficult to detect, even by experts. Free software and online tutorials now make it possible for virtually anyone, even without advanced technical skills, to create convincing deepfakes.

One reason for this growing sophistication is the continued improvement of deep learning algorithms. These algorithms can now analyze and reproduce the smallest details of facial expressions, body movements, and even human voices. Additionally, the neural networks used to create deepfakes improve with each iteration, learning from past mistakes to produce even more realistic results.

The First Malicious Uses

Early uses of deepfakes focused on online harassment, particularly against women, whose faces were superimposed on pornographic videos without their consent. However, it soon became clear that the technology could be used for much broader and potentially dangerous purposes. In 2018, a doctored video of President Barack Obama appeared online, in which he appeared to say things he never said. Although this video was quickly identified as a fake, it served as a warning about the potential dangers of deepfakes in politics.

This Obama video showed that deepfakes could be used to manipulate public opinion, discredit political figures, or sow confusion during critical events, like elections. The technology has since been used to create videos of political leaders around the world, in which they appear to make inflammatory statements or make controversial decisions. These deepfakes have the potential to provoke diplomatic crises, incite violence, or destabilize governments.

5.2 Deepfakes Propagation Mechanisms

Social Media Platforms as Catalysts

Social media plays a crucial role in the spread of deepfakes. Platforms like Facebook, Twitter, and YouTube allow these manipulated videos to reach a global audience in record time. The viral nature of social media amplifies the impact of deepfakes, as they can be shared thousands of times in a matter of minutes, reaching millions of people before their authenticity is even questioned.

A striking example is Ukrainian President Volodymyr Zelensky's deepfake video released in 2022, in which he appeared to call on his troops to lay down their arms. Although the video was quickly denied, it sowed doubt and confusion among the public, exacerbating tensions in an already volatile context. This incident shows how deepfakes can be used to influence the course of a conflict by manipulating public opinion.

Using Recommendation Algorithms

Social media platforms' recommendation algorithms also play a key role in the spread of deepfakes. These algorithms are designed to maximize engagement by showing users content they might be interested in. However, this means that sensationalist content, like deepfakes, is often favored because it elicits strong emotional reactions and encourages users to interact more with the platform.

This dynamic creates a vicious cycle where deepfakes become more and more visible and reach a wider and wider audience, thus strengthening their impact. Users, often unaware that they are viewing a fake, share these videos, unwittingly contributing to the spread of misinformation.

Online Communities and Broadcast Forums

Online communities, such as Reddit or 4chan, play a crucial role in the creation and distribution of deepfakes. These platforms allow users to share techniques, tools, and tutorials for creating deepfakes, while providing a space to distribute this content anonymously. These communities can be places of radicalization, where users are exposed to extremist or hateful content, and where deepfakes are used to spread toxic ideologies.

In 2019, a deepfake video of President Donald Trump was shared on Reddit, in which he appeared to declare war on North Korea. Although the video was quickly identified as fake, it was viewed by thousands of people before being removed, illustrating how effective these online communities can be at spreading deepfakes.

Anonymity and Difficulty of Tracing

The anonymity offered by the Internet complicates the fight against the spread of deepfakes. Deepfake creators may operate under pseudonyms or use obfuscation technologies to conceal their identities. This makes it difficult for authorities to trace the origin of these videos and hold those responsible accountable. Additionally, even when deepfakes are identified and removed, they may reappear on other platforms or in other forms, making combating this threat even more complex.

5.3 Actors Involved in the Creation and Dissemination of Deepfakes

Governments and State Actors

Governments, particularly those of authoritarian regimes, see deepfakes as a powerful tool to manipulate public opinion, both domestically and internationally. They can use this technology to discredit political opponents, influence elections in other countries, or justify controversial actions. For example, reports have suggested that Russia used deepfakes as part of its disinformation operations aimed at influencing the United States presidential elections in 2016 and 2020.

Deepfakes offer governments a way to conduct false flag operations, where they can create content that appears to come from other actors, such as terrorist groups or rival countries. This can sow confusion, create diplomatic tensions, or provoke international crises. The opacity of the origin of deepfakes complicates the task of investigators and analysts, making it difficult to respond quickly and appropriately to these threats.

Criminal Groups and Hackers

Criminal groups and hackers also exploit deepfakes for their own purposes. They can use this technology to extort money, discredit individuals, or disrupt businesses. For example, deepfakes have been used to simulate the voices of corporate executives, tricking their subordinates into transferring large sums of money to fraudulent bank accounts. These attacks, known as "CEO fraud," have cost victim companies millions of dollars.

Hackers can also use deepfakes to manipulate public opinion or provoke online crises. For example, they may create videos of public figures making controversial statements or engaging in illegal activities, with the aim of tarnishing their reputation or provoking mass reactions. These deepfakes can be distributed on social networks, online forums, or even traditional media, thus amplifying their impact.

Individuals and Amateurs

Finally, individuals and amateurs also play a role in the creation and dissemination of deepfakes. Thanks to the increasing availability of deepfake creation tools and software, it is now possible for anyone, even without advanced technical skills, to create fake videos. These users may be motivated by a variety of reasons, ranging from simple amusement to personal revenge, political or ideological motivations.

One infamous example is that of an anonymous user who created and distributed pornographic deepfakes of celebrities. These videos, which superimposed the faces of female celebrities onto the bodies of adult film actresses, caused widespread outrage and raised questions about the ethical and legal implications of deepfakes. These cases show how individuals can use this technology to cause real harm, even outside of any political or criminal context.

The Erosion of Trust in the Media

One of the most worrying consequences of deepfakes is the erosion of trust in the media. As deepfakes become more sophisticated and harder to detect, the public is likely to become increasingly skeptical of all forms of media content, including legitimate news. This skepticism can lead to "reality erosion," where individuals no longer know what information to trust and end up retreating into bubbles of misinformation or conspiracy theories.

This loss of trust can have serious consequences for democracy and society in general. When citizens can no longer trust the information they receive, it becomes difficult to maintain informed public debate, make fact-based policy decisions, or respond effectively to crises. Deepfakes therefore threaten not only specific individuals or institutions, but also the very fabric of democratic society.

Psychological Impacts on Victims

Deepfakes can also have devastating psychological consequences for the individuals who fall victim to them. Deepfake videos, especially those of a sexual or defamatory nature, can cause irreparable harm to a person's reputation, affect their career, personal relationships, and mental health. Victims of deepfakes may suffer from anxiety, depression, and other psychological disorders, in addition to public humiliation and social stigma.

A particularly tragic case is that of a young woman whose face was superimposed on the body of an actress in a deepfake pornographic video. The video was widely shared online, leading to ridicule and harassment against him. Although the victim attempted to have the video removed, it continued to circulate on various sites, exacerbating her trauma. This case highlights the legal and technical challenges of protecting victims of deepfakes and achieving justice.

Polarization and Radicalization

Deepfakes can also exacerbate political and social polarization, providing ammunition for extremists and fueling divisions within society. Deepfake videos can be used to stoke anger, fear, or hatred by showing political leaders, ethnic groups, or religious communities in an unfavorable light. This content can radicalize individuals by reinforcing their prejudices and encouraging them to adopt more extreme positions.

The dissemination of deepfakes during politically charged events, such as elections, protests, or international crises, can have particularly serious consequences. For example, a deepfake showing a political candidate making racist or sexist statements could mobilize opponents, provoke violent protests, or even spark riots. Similarly, a deepfake showing law enforcement using excessive force against protesters could exacerbate tensions and lead to violent clashes.

Gaps in the Current Legal Framework

The current legal framework is often ill-equipped to deal with the challenges posed by deepfakes. In many countries, laws on defamation, publicity rights, and privacy protections do not adequately cover deepfakes, leaving victims with little legal recourse. Additionally, the transnational nature of the Internet complicates enforcement of existing laws, as deepfake creators may operate from jurisdictions where regulations are lax or non-existent.

Some jurisdictions have begun to take steps to address these gaps. For example, in 2019, the state of California passed a law prohibiting the distribution of political or pornographic deepfakes without the consent of the individuals involved. However, these laws remain rare and often limited in their scope. It is therefore crucial to develop international legal frameworks capable of responding to the challenges posed by deepfakes.

The Ethical Issues of Deepfake Technology

Deepfakes also pose complex ethical questions. Although they can be used in harmless or even creative ways, such as in arts or entertainment, their potential for harm is considerable. Deepfakes raise questions about the responsibility of creators and disseminators of this content, as well as the limits of free expression in a world where fake news can cause real harm.

It is also important to consider the ethical implications of the use of deepfakes by governments and businesses. For example, the use of deepfakes by intelligence services to conduct psychological warfare operations or by companies to manipulate public opinion raises questions about the boundaries between ethics and legality. These issues require in-depth reflection and appropriate regulation to protect the rights of individuals and preserve the integrity of democratic institutions.

The Responsibility of Technological Platforms

Technology platforms, such as social media and video-sharing sites, play a crucial role in the spread of deepfakes. They therefore have an ethical and legal responsibility to minimize the damage caused by this content. However, implementing effective policies to detect and remove deepfakes is a considerable challenge, due to the technical complexity of these videos and the speed with which they spread.

Some platforms have started to take steps to combat deepfakes. For example, Facebook has implemented a policy to remove identified deepfakes, while YouTube has developed detection tools based on artificial intelligence. However, these efforts are often reactive rather than proactive, and deepfakes continue to proliferate online. It is therefore necessary to strengthen cooperation between technology companies, governments, and civil society organizations to develop more effective solutions.

5.6 Strategies to Combat Deepfakes

The Role of Media Literacy

One of the most promising strategies to combat deepfakes is media literacy. By teaching citizens to recognize the signs of falsified video, verify sources, and understand how deepfakes work, it is possible to reduce the impact of this content. Media literacy programs should be integrated into schools, universities, and professional training, to equip individuals with the skills needed to navigate an increasingly complex media environment.

Educational initiatives, such as those led by non-governmental organizations, academic institutions, and online platforms, have already begun to raise public awareness of the dangers of deepfakes. For example, massive open online courses (MOOCs) on disinformation and deepfakes have been developed to teach users how to analyze and verify digital content. These programs should be expanded and supported by governments and technology companies.

Technological Innovations for Deepfake Detection

Alongside education, technological innovations play a crucial role in detecting deepfakes. Artificial intelligence-based tools, such as those developed by companies like Microsoft and Adobe, can analyze videos and detect anomalies characteristic of deepfakes. These tools use computer vision techniques to identify inconsistencies in movements, facial expressions, or image quality, which may indicate that a video has been tampered with.

However, the race between deepfake creators and detection technology developers is constantly evolving. As deepfakes become more sophisticated, detection tools must also improve to remain effective. This requires continued investment in research and development, as well as collaboration between private sector actors, universities, and governments.

Regulatory Policies and International Cooperation

Finally, regulation and international cooperation are essential to combat the threat of deepfakes. Governments must enact clear and enforceable laws to criminalize the creation and dissemination of malicious deepfakes, while ensuring the rights to freedom of expression and privacy are protected. In addition, international cooperation is necessary to harmonize regulations, share information, and coordinate responses to deepfake incidents.

International organizations, such as the UN or the European Union, can play a key role in promoting comprehensive regulatory frameworks to combat deepfakes. They can also provide a platform for cooperation between states, technology companies, and civil society organizations. Initiatives such as creating shared databases of known deepfakes, or developing common protocols for incident response, could help mitigate the risks associated with this technology.

Conclusion

Deepfakes represent a growing threat to modern society, with profound implications for democracy, security, and social cohesion. Their potential to manipulate public opinion, destabilize institutions, and cause psychological and social harm is immense. To respond to this threat, it is essential to combine education, technological innovation, and regulation, while strengthening international cooperation.

It is also crucial to develop a culture of vigilance and accountability, where individuals, businesses, and governments recognize the dangers of deepfakes and take action to counter them. In the digital age, where information travels at unprecedented speed, it is more important than ever to protect the integrity of media content and preserve public trust in information sources.

Ultimately, the fight against deepfakes is a fight for truth and transparency. By overcoming this threat, we can not only protect our societies against manipulation, but also strengthen the foundations of our democracies and promote a future where information is a tool of progress and justice, rather than a weapon of division and deception.

4. Disinformation and Elections: Cases of the United States, Brazil and the European Union

Introduction to Election Disinformation

Electoral disinformation has become a worrying phenomenon in modern democracies, where the integrity of electoral processes is put to the test by the dissemination of false information, unfounded rumors, and media manipulation. Elections, key moments in the political life of any country, are particularly vulnerable to attempts to manipulate public opinion. The objective of electoral disinformation is often twofold: on the one hand, to influence the results of elections in favor of a candidate or a party, and on the other hand, to weaken citizens' confidence in the democratic process itself. even.

Over the past decades, the rapid evolution of information and communication technologies has transformed the disinformation landscape. Social media platforms, messaging apps, and video sharing sites have become prime vectors for the spread of fake news, reaching millions of people in record time. This new reality has led to a proliferation of sophisticated disinformation campaigns, often orchestrated by internal and external actors, seeking to disrupt elections for geopolitical, economic, or ideological purposes.

In this section, we will examine three emblematic cases of electoral disinformation: the presidential elections in the United States in 2016 and 2020, the presidential election in Brazil in 2018, and the elections within the European Union. Each case offers valuable lessons on the disinformation strategies used, the mechanisms by which false information spreads, and the responses provided by governments and digital platforms.

2. The United States: The Case of the 2016 and 2020 Presidential Elections

Context and Conduct of Elections

The presidential elections in the United States, particularly those of 2016 and 2020, marked a turning point in the history of electoral disinformation. These elections were the scene of large-scale disinformation campaigns, aimed at influencing voters, sowing division, and calling into question the legitimacy of the results. The polarized political context, combined with the rise of social media, has created fertile ground for the spread of false information.

In 2016, the election between Hillary Clinton and Donald Trump was marked by unprecedented foreign interference, mainly attributed to Russia. U.S. intelligence reports revealed that Russian actors carried out a complex disinformation campaign, using platforms like Facebook, Twitter, and YouTube to spread content aimed at weakening Clinton's candidacy and favoring Trump's. This content included fabricated articles, targeted advertisements, and memes intended to polarize the electorate.

The 2020 election, pitting Donald Trump against Joe Biden, saw a new wave of misinformation, this time centered around mail-in voting. Due to the Covid-19 pandemic, postal voting was widely used, but it quickly became a subject of misinformation, with unfounded claims that this method of voting was susceptible to massive fraud. These claims, amplified by social media and statements by Trump himself, led to widespread distrust of the electoral process, culminating in the events of January 6, 2021, with the storming of the Capitol.

Disinformation Mechanisms Used by Internal and External Actors

Disinformation campaigns during the US presidential elections used a variety of techniques, from fake news and deepfakes to ad microtargeting and automated bots. These techniques made it possible to manipulate public opinion in a subtle but effective way, by playing on fears, prejudices, and existing divisions within American society.

Russian interference in 2016 was particularly sophisticated. Groups like the Internet Research Agency (IRA) have created fictitious social media accounts to spread polarizing content, even organizing opposing protests to exacerbate social tensions. Additionally, Russian hackers stole emails from the Democratic National Committee (DNC) and posted them on WikiLeaks, damaging Clinton's campaign by portraying it in an unfavorable light.

In 2020, misinformation focused on mail-in voting, with false reports claiming millions of ballots were thrown out or tampered with. These assertions, although denied by electoral authorities, were widely relayed on social networks and by certain conservative media, helping to create a climate of suspicion and distrust with regard to the electoral results.

Impact on Election Results and Public Perception

The impact of disinformation on the results of the US presidential elections is difficult to quantify precisely, but it is clear that it played a significant role in polarizing the electorate and calling into question the legitimacy of the results. In 2016, Russia's disinformation campaign helped confuse voters, amplify internal divisions, and weaken Clinton's candidacy.

In 2020, misinformation about mail-in voting not only undermined trust in the electoral process, but it also led to violent actions, such as the storming of the Capitol, where Trump supporters attempted to overturn the results of the election. This event highlighted the dangers of electoral disinformation, not only for American democracy, but also for social stability.

The Role of Tech Companies and Media in the Fight Against Disinformation

Faced with the scale of misinformation during the presidential elections, technology companies have been criticized for their role in spreading false information. Facebook, Twitter, and YouTube, in particular, have been accused of not doing enough to prevent the spread of misleading content and false political ads.

In response to these criticisms, these platforms have implemented measures to combat misinformation, such as adding warning labels on misleading content, removing automated accounts, and suspending accounts that violate the rules . However, these measures were often found insufficient or applied inconsistently, and misinformation continued to proliferate.

Additionally, mainstream media has played a crucial role in fact-checking and correcting misinformation. Organizations like PolitiFact, FactCheck.org, and Snopes have worked tirelessly to debunk rumors and fake news, but they have faced a daunting challenge with the speed and scale of misinformation online.

3. Brazil: The 2018 Presidential Election

Political and Social Context of Brazil before the 2018 Election

The 2018 Brazilian presidential election took place in a context of political, economic and social crisis. After years of corruption scandals, economic instability, and increasing urban violence, the country was deeply divided. This climate of distrust and disillusionment has created fertile ground for disinformation, which has become a key tool in the electoral campaign.

Jair Bolsonaro, a far-right candidate, emerged as a central figure in the election, presenting himself as a political outsider capable of restoring order and fighting corruption. His campaign benefited greatly from the use of social networks, particularly WhatsApp, to disseminate political messages, mobilize his supporters, and attack his opponents.

The Rise of Social Networks, notably WhatsApp, in the Dissemination of Disinformation

WhatsApp, a popular messaging app in Brazil, became a major channel for the spread of disinformation during the 2018 presidential election. Unlike Facebook or Twitter, where content is public and can be monitored, WhatsApp allows private communications and encrypted, making it difficult to detect and verify false information.

Millions of Brazilians have received messages containing fake news, conspiracy theories, and doctored videos via WhatsApp. These posts were often presented as truthful information, shared by friends or family members, which gave them additional credibility. Among the most widespread misinformation were claims that electronic ballot boxes had been rigged, or that Bolsonaro's opponents were involved in criminal activity.

Types of Disinformation Spread: Fake News, Personal Attacks, and Manipulation of Public Opinion

Disinformation spread during the 2018 Brazilian presidential election took various forms, from fake news to personal attacks. Bolsonaro's supporters have used smear campaigns to discredit his rivals, particularly Fernando Haddad, the Workers' Party (PT) candidate. Messages circulating on WhatsApp claimed, for example, that Haddad planned to teach "gender theory" in schools and distribute "gay kits" to children, an allegation that was widely denied but had a significant impact on public opinion.

Additionally, doctored videos showing violent protests or falsified speeches have been widely shared, reinforcing social and political divisions. These videos, often edited to appear authentic, have been used to manipulate public opinion, playing on voters' fears and prejudices.

Impact of Misinformation on Election Results

The impact of disinformation on the 2018 Brazilian presidential election was considerable. Jair Bolsonaro won the election with a large majority, but the disinformation campaign left deep scars on the Brazilian political landscape. The spread of false information has not only polarized the electorate, but it has also weakened trust in democratic institutions, particularly the electoral system.

After the election, surveys were conducted to determine the extent of the use of disinformation, but the results were mixed. Although some fines have been issued and accounts suspended, efforts to regulate misinformation on WhatsApp and other platforms have encountered significant obstacles, particularly due to the private nature of communications on these apps.

Post-Election Measures to Limit the Spread of False Information in Subsequent Elections

In response to the scale of misinformation during the 2018 election, Brazilian authorities took steps to limit the spread of false information in subsequent elections. Electoral justice has worked with digital platforms to monitor and remove misleading content, and awareness campaigns have been launched to educate the public about the dangers of misinformation.

WhatsApp, in particular, has taken steps to limit the spread of viral messages, reducing the number of times a message can be forwarded, and putting systems in place to detect and block suspicious accounts. However, despite these efforts, disinformation remains a major challenge for Brazilian democracy, and it is essential to continue efforts to strengthen the resilience of the electoral system.

4. The European Union: Challenges and Responses to Disinformation

Context of European and National Elections in Member States

The European Union, as a complex and multicultural political entity, faces unique challenges when it comes to electoral disinformation. European elections, which determine the composition of the European Parliament, as well as national elections in member states, are prime targets for disinformation campaigns, both internal and external.

The 2019 European elections were marked by a series of disinformation campaigns, aimed at influencing voters in different member countries. These campaigns have often exploited national and cultural divides, seeking to weaken EU cohesion and promote populist or Eurosceptic agendas. National elections, such as those in France, Germany, and Italy, have also been targets of disinformation, particularly from foreign actors seeking to influence European politics.

Examples of Disinformation Campaigns at the European Union Level

A prominent example of disinformation during the 2019 European elections was the campaign led by Eurosceptic groups, who spread false information on sensitive topics such as immigration, security, and national sovereignty. These campaigns have often used social networks like Facebook and Twitter to target specific voters with personalized messages, amplifying existing divisions and fears.

For example, in Italy, false information about an alleged "secret pact" between the EU and some African countries to transfer millions of migrants to Europe was widely shared, contributing to a rise in anti-immigration sentiment. In France, rumors about an alleged "dilution" of French culture by European policies have been used to mobilize the far-right electorate.

The Role of Foreign Interference, Particularly Russia, in the Spread of Disinformation

Foreign interference, notably from Russia, was a key factor in the spread of disinformation during European and national elections within the EU. European intelligence services have reported several attempts by Russia to influence elections by supporting populist and Eurosceptic parties, spreading misinformation on sensitive issues, and hacking election systems.

In Germany, for example, disinformation campaigns aimed at weakening Chancellor Angela Merkel have been attributed to Russian actors. These campaigns have used social media to spread misinformation on issues such as the migration crisis and economic policies, with the aim of polarizing public opinion and strengthening political forces opposed to the EU.

EU Initiatives to Counter Disinformation: Code of Good Conduct on Disinformation, Cooperation with Online Platforms, and Strengthening Media Literacy

In response to these challenges, the European Union has put in place several initiatives to counter electoral disinformation. In 2018, the European Commission adopted a "Code of conduct on disinformation", to which several major digital platforms, including Facebook, Google, and Twitter, have signed up. This code provides measures to improve the transparency of political advertisements, reduce the dissemination of false information, and promote reliable sources of information.

Additionally, the EU has strengthened its cooperation with online platforms to monitor and remove misleading content during election periods. EU-funded fact-checking teams have also been set up to identify and debunk fake news circulating online. At the same time, awareness campaigns have been launched to educate European citizens about the dangers of disinformation and encourage them to verify information before sharing it.

Strengthening media literacy has also been a priority for the EU. Educational programs aimed at developing critical thinking and the ability to discern reliable information have been integrated into the education systems of Member States. These initiatives aim to create a population that is better informed and more resilient to attempts at manipulation.

Impact of Disinformation on EU Cohesion and Election Results

Disinformation has had a significant impact on the cohesion of the European Union, exacerbating internal divisions and strengthening populist and Eurosceptic movements. Disinformation campaigns have often exploited cultural, economic, and political differences between member states, creating tensions that have weakened the unity of the EU.

When it comes to election outcomes, it is difficult to precisely quantify the impact of misinformation, but it is clear that it influenced voters' perceptions and, in some cases, their voting decisions. The 2019 European elections saw a rise in the power of populist and Eurosceptic parties, who used disinformation as a tool to mobilize their electoral base and weaken their opponents.

5. Comparison of Strategies to Combat Electoral Disinformation

Comparison of Approaches Adopted by the United States, Brazil, and the European Union

The United States, Brazil, and the European Union have all taken different approaches to combating electoral disinformation, depending on their respective political and cultural contexts. In the United States, emphasis has been placed on regulating digital platforms and fact-checking, although these efforts have been hampered by internal political divisions. In Brazil, the fight against disinformation has focused on regulating messaging apps like WhatsApp, while the EU has opted for a more comprehensive approach, combining regulation, international cooperation, and citizen education.

Each approach has its strengths and weaknesses. In the United States, political polarization has made it difficult to adopt consistent and effective measures, while in Brazil, the private nature of communications on WhatsApp has complicated the monitoring and regulation of disinformation. In contrast, the EU has managed to put in place a more comprehensive regulatory framework, although challenges related to the linguistic and cultural diversity of member states persist.

Lessons Learned from Each Case and Their Applicability to Other Electoral Contexts

The experiences of the United States, Brazil, and the European Union offer several important lessons for other countries facing electoral disinformation. First, regulation of digital platforms is essential to limit the spread of disinformation, but it must be accompanied by efforts to strengthen media literacy and citizen resilience.

Second, international cooperation is crucial to countering foreign interference and transnational disinformation campaigns. Countries must share information, coordinate efforts, and work together to develop effective responses to disinformation threats.

Finally, it is important to recognize that electoral disinformation cannot be eradicated by technical or legislative means alone. A continued commitment to transparency, truth, and integrity of electoral processes is necessary to preserve democracy and protect voters' rights.

6. Conclusion: Towards Strengthened Election Protection

Election disinformation is a growing threat to democracies around the world, exacerbated by digital technologies and geopolitical tensions. The cases of the United States, Brazil, and the European Union show the extent to which disinformation can influence voters' perceptions, polarize societies, and weaken democratic institutions.

To counter this threat, it is essential to strengthen regulatory frameworks, promote media literacy, and foster international cooperation. At the same time, citizens, technology companies, and governments must actively engage in protecting the integrity of elections and combating disinformation in all its forms.

Only a collective approach, based on transparency, education, and accountability, will protect elections and preserve democracy in a world increasingly interconnected and vulnerable to media manipulation.

5. Case Studies on Disinformation and Ecological Crises

Introduction: The Ecological Crisis and the Role of Disinformation

Ecological crises, notably climate change, deforestation, loss of biodiversity, and ocean pollution, have become major challenges of the 21st century. These crises are not only environmental challenges, but also social, economic and political. In this context, disinformation plays a disruptive role, exacerbating misunderstandings, sowing confusion and slowing down the actions needed to mitigate these crises. The following case studies examine how misinformation enters into debates about ecological crises, the impacts it creates, and strategies to combat it.

1. Climate Change: Fertile Ground for Disinformation

Climate change is one of the topics most affected by misinformation. For decades, various actors, including some governments, businesses and advocacy groups, have sought to downplay, deny or distort the scientific facts about global warming. These efforts have far-reaching repercussions, influencing public opinion, delaying the adoption of crucial environmental policies, and undermining the credibility of scientists and international institutions.

The Genesis of Climate Denial: The First Movements

Climate disinformation campaigns date back to the 1970s, when the first studies of global warming began to attract attention. At that time, some industries, notably fossil fuel producers, funded research and campaigns aimed at sowing doubt about scientific findings. These industries had a clear economic interest in preserving the status quo in terms of energy consumption.

Internal documents, made public decades later, revealed that some oil giants were aware of the potential effects of global warming as early as the 1970s. Despite this, these companies chose to finance disinformation campaigns, highlighting researchers and think tanks who minimized the impact of climate change or contested its existence. These efforts contributed to delaying global awareness of global warming and weakening early attempts to regulate greenhouse gas emissions.

Disinformation Strategies: Climate Skepticism and Creating Controversies

Climate disinformation campaigns have adopted several strategies to sow confusion. One of the most effective tactics has been to present climate change as a controversial topic, exaggerating scientific uncertainties and pitting skeptical "experts" against climate scientists. This strategy, known as "false balance," was widely used in the media, where skeptical voices received disproportionate visibility compared to their actual representation in the scientific community.

Another aspect of climate misinformation involves simplifying or distorting scientific data to make it more ambiguous or controversial than it actually is. For example, graphs showing an apparent pause in warming in the early 2000s were widely circulated to suggest that global warming had stopped, when this period was simply part of normal temperature fluctuations in a context of global warming in the long term.

Impact of Climate Disinformation: Political and Societal Delays

Misinformation about climate change has had profound consequences. By delaying awareness and action, these campaigns have contributed to the worsening of the climate crisis. Governments, under pressure from public opinion influenced by disinformation, have often hesitated to adopt restrictive measures to reduce greenhouse gas emissions. This political inertia has not only prolonged dependence on fossil fuels, but also made the transition to renewable energy more costly and complex.

On a societal level, disinformation has divided public opinion. In many countries, a significant part of the population remains skeptical about the reality of climate change, or doubts the anthropogenic causes of warming. This division makes it difficult to implement ambitious climate policies, as governments face public opposition fueled by misinformation.

Case Study: Climategate

An emblematic example of climate misinformation is the "Climategate" scandal of 2009. Stolen emails between climate scientists were published online, and their contents were presented out of context to suggest that the scientists were manipulating the data to exaggerate global warming. . Climate skeptics and some media outlets have exploited this situation to attack the credibility of the scientific community and question the validity of the evidence for climate change.

Although subsequent investigations exonerated the scientists involved and confirmed that the emails had been taken out of context, the impact on public opinion was significant. Climategate has strengthened the positions of climate skeptics and helped delay international climate negotiations, including crucial discussions at the 2009 Copenhagen Conference.

Combating Climate Misinformation: Initiatives and Challenges

To combat misinformation about climate change, several initiatives have emerged. Scientific and environmental organizations have stepped up efforts to communicate the evidence of climate change in a clear and accessible way. Fact-checking platforms proliferated, and media outlets were encouraged to abandon the "false balance" in favor of a more accurate representation of the scientific consensus.

Governments and international institutions, such as the United Nations, have also recognized the importance of climate literacy and have launched educational campaigns to raise public awareness. However, these efforts face significant challenges, including the persistence of disinformation networks, the role of social media in the dissemination of misleading content, and the inherent complexity of climate science.

2. Deforestation and Disinformation: Case of the Amazon

Deforestation, particularly in the Amazon, is another area where misinformation plays a major role. Tropical forests, often referred to as the "lungs of the planet," are crucial for regulating the global climate and conserving biodiversity. However, deforestation continues to threaten these vital ecosystems, exacerbated by permissive policies and misinformation that downplays the dangers or denies the reality of the ongoing destruction.

Actors of Disinformation on Deforestation

Multiple actors are involved in disinformation about deforestation, including governments, extractive industries, and local interest groups. In the case of the Amazon, some governments have tried to downplay data on deforestation to avoid international criticism and to promote policies favorable to the exploitation of natural resources.

Industries, such as agriculture, logging, and mining, also have an interest in spreading misleading information that suggests their activities have minimal impact on the environment. For example, public relations campaigns were used to promote the idea that deforestation practices were "sustainable" or that deforested areas were quickly reforested, which is often far from reality.

Disinformation Strategies: Reducing Impact and Glorifying Development

Disinformation campaigns about deforestation use several strategies to manipulate public opinion and influence policy makers. One common tactic is to downplay the extent of deforestation by using cherry-picked data or challenging the methodology of studies that document forest loss. For example, some governments have accused NGOs and scientists of exaggerating deforestation rates to obtain international funding.

Another strategy is to glorify economic development projects, such as agriculture and mining, as essential drivers of economic growth and social well-being. This rhetoric emphasizes short-term economic benefits while ignoring long-term environmental costs, including loss of biodiversity, soil erosion, and alteration of hydrological cycles.

Impact of Disinformation on Amazon Deforestation

Misinformation has devastating consequences for forest ecosystems, particularly in the Amazon. By minimizing the effects of deforestation or promoting destructive practices as sustainable, these campaigns slow conservation and reforestation efforts. Additionally, they weaken international pressure to protect these forests, allowing destructive activities to continue.

Misinformation also contributes to the marginalization of indigenous populations who depend on these forests for their survival. By presenting forest lands as areas available for development, disinformation campaigns ignore the rights of indigenous communities and undermine their efforts to protect their traditional territories.

Case Study: The Amazon Fires of 2019

In 2019, the Amazon was ravaged by large-scale fires, drawing global attention to the deforestation crisis. However, the responses of local governments, notably that of Brazil, have been marked by strong misinformation. The Brazilian president accused NGOs of starting the fires to attract international attention, while his supporters downplayed the significance of the fires, saying they were "normal" for the dry season.

These statements were widely reported by pro-government media, sowing confusion and weakening international calls for immediate action. Although satellite images showed the unprecedented scale of the fires, misinformation delayed the policy response, worsening the ecological damage.

Combating Misinformation on Deforestation

Combating misinformation about deforestation requires a multi-faceted approach. Conservation organizations play a crucial role in collecting and disseminating accurate data on the condition of forests and exposing destructive practices. Technology, including satellites and drones, makes it possible to independently monitor forests and provide indisputable evidence of environmental changes.

Governments and international institutions must also strengthen laws and regulations to protect forests, while ensuring that information released to the public is accurate and based on scientific evidence. Finally, public awareness is essential to counter misinformation. By educating citizens about the realities of deforestation and providing them with the tools to verify information, it is possible to reduce the impact of misinformation on public opinion.

3. Misinformation about Ocean Pollution

The oceans, which cover more than 70% of the Earth's surface, are essential for climate regulation, oxygen production, and biodiversity. However, they are seriously threatened by pollution, including plastics, chemicals, and oil spills. Misinformation around ocean pollution makes these threats worse by downplaying the dangers, delaying action, and distorting possible solutions.

Sources of Misinformation about Ocean Pollution

Several sources contribute to misinformation about ocean pollution. Polluting industries, such as plastics manufacturers, oil companies, and chemical industries, have a vested interest in minimizing the impact of their activities on the oceans. They fund biased studies and public relations campaigns to present their activities in a favorable light and to challenge environmental regulations.

Governments, particularly in countries where the plastics or fossil fuel industry is a key economic sector, can also be complicit in misinformation by weakening environmental standards and downplaying the risks of marine pollution. Additionally, some NGOs, while generally well-intentioned, may unintentionally contribute to disinformation by exaggerating certain threats or promoting solutions that are not evidence-based.

Disinformation Tactics: Risk Minimization and Illusory Solutions

A common misinformation tactic is to downplay the risks associated with ocean pollution. For example, some companies have funded studies claiming that marine plastics break down faster than they actually do, or that toxic chemicals are diluted and become harmless when dumped into the oceans. These messages are often amplified by the media, which may be influenced by advertisements or partnerships with these industries.

Another strategy is to promote simplistic or ineffective solutions to the problem of ocean pollution. For example, some campaigns promote recycling as a universal solution to the problem of plastic waste, while failing to mention that most plastics are not recyclable or that recycling infrastructure is often inadequate. This approach distracts from more systemic solutions, such as reducing plastic production or strictly regulating industrial discharges.

Impact of Disinformation on Ocean Protection

Misinformation about ocean pollution slows progress toward effective protection of these vital ecosystems. By sowing doubt about the scale of the problems or promoting inadequate solutions, these campaigns divert resources and attention from efforts that could have a real impact. Additionally, they create a false sense of security, which can lead to complacency among the public and decision-makers.

The consequences are serious: ocean pollution continues to worsen, with devastating impacts on marine life, coastal economies, and communities that depend on ocean resources. Plastic, in particular, has become ubiquitous in the oceans, affecting thousands of marine species and entering the human food chain.

Case Study: The Myth of "Plastic Islands"

An example of common misinformation is the myth of "plastic islands," often described as gigantic masses of floating trash in the Pacific Ocean. Although these waste concentration zones do exist, they are often misunderstood or exaggerated in the media. The reality is that these "islands" are largely composed of microplastics, invisible to the naked eye, which disperse throughout the water column and are much more difficult to clean than media portrayals suggest.

This misinformation has perverse effects: by focusing on the idea of "cleaning up" these islands, efforts are diverted from more effective solutions, such as reducing plastic production at source or improving management systems. land waste. Furthermore, it reinforces the false idea that the problem of marine plastics can be solved through simple and visible actions, whereas it requires a profound transformation of industrial practices and consumer behavior.

Combating Misinformation on Ocean Pollution

Combating misinformation about ocean pollution requires concerted action at multiple levels. Scientists and NGOs play a key role in providing accurate data and raising public awareness of the real challenges and solutions. Journalists have a responsibility to fact-check and provide balanced coverage that reflects the complexity of marine issues.

Governments and international bodies must strengthen regulations on plastics, chemicals and industrial spills, while ensuring policies are based on sound scientific evidence. Furthermore, it is essential to promote global solutions, such as the circular economy, which reduce waste production at source.

Conclusion: Towards Sustainable Management of Ecological Crises

Ecological crises represent one of the greatest challenges of the 21st century, and misinformation represents a major obstacle to solving them. Whether by downplaying the impact of climate change, justifying deforestation, or presenting simplistic solutions to ocean pollution, misinformation delays the actions needed to protect our planet.

To overcome these challenges, it is essential to strengthen environmental literacy, promote transparency and accountability in public communications, and support international efforts to combat misinformation. Only a coordinated approach, based on science and global cooperation, will protect our planet's vital ecosystems and ensure a sustainable future for future generations.

1. Integration of Media Education into School Curricula

Introduction: The Importance of Media Literacy in Today's Context

Media education is no longer content to be a simple addition to the school curriculum; it has become a central component in the training of citizens of the 21st century. In a world where information flows are omnipresent and young people are increasingly exposed to varied content, often without adult mediation, media education is a necessity. This education aims not only to teach students to decode media messages, but also to arm them against the manipulations and disinformation that abound in the current media ecosystem.

Today, children and adolescents consume media in diverse and omnipresent ways: social networks, online videos, blogs, forums, and even video games, all convey messages that they must learn to analyze critically. This challenge is all the greater since younger generations are often more comfortable with digital technologies than their elders, but this ease does not necessarily translate into an ability to discern truth from falsehood, or to understand the mechanisms. complexities that underlie the creation and distribution of media content.

Faced with this reality, educational systems must evolve to integrate media education in a systematic and structured manner from an early age. This is not limited to simple technical education on the use of digital tools, but encompasses comprehensive training in digital citizenship, critical thinking, and understanding information dynamics in a democratic society. This chapter explores ways to effectively integrate media education into school curricula, taking into account the specificities of each level of education, educational objectives, teaching methods, available resources, and modes of delivery. assessment.

1.1 Pedagogical Objectives for Media Education

The educational objectives of media education are multiple and varied, but all share a common goal: to prepare students to become critical and informed actors in a society where information circulates at high speed and where the boundaries between reality and fiction are often blurry. Objectives should be adapted based on students' ages and levels of understanding, but certain guiding principles remain constant.

For Primary School:

- **Introduction to Basic Concepts** : At this level, students begin to be exposed to media in more direct ways, including through television, the Internet, and the social media that their parents or siblings use. The goal is to teach them to distinguish between facts and opinions, to recognize different sources of information, and to understand that not all information is reliable or verified. It is essential to instill in them the idea that information must be verified before it is accepted as true.

  Practical examples: Through simple activities such as role-playing where students play the role of journalists, television presenters or media consumers, they can learn to differentiate a factual report from an advertisement or fiction. Board games or interactive quizzes can also be used to teach these concepts in a fun way.

- **Awareness of the Reliability of Sources** : Young students must be introduced to the notion of reliable sources of information. This may include discussions about types of sources (books, newspapers, teachers, parents) and how to distinguish a reliable source from a questionable source, such as an anonymous Internet post or an advertisement disguised as information. Teachers should emphasize the importance of seeking advice from several trusted people or verifying information in reputable books or websites.

  Teaching approaches: For example, an activity could involve comparing a short story told by a student to a story told by an adult or found in a book, to show how information can vary depending on the source and reliability of the story. -this.

- **Development of Critical Thinking** : From a young age, it is crucial to encourage students to ask questions about what they see, hear, or read. They must learn not to take all information at face value and to develop a skeptical but constructive attitude. This critical thinking will not only help them navigate the world of media, but also develop analytical thinking skills that will serve them well throughout their lives.

  Practical activities: Teachers can organize class discussions on current topics appropriate to the age of students, encouraging them to ask questions and express their doubts. For example, a simple topic like "Why are TV commercials trying to sell us toys?" can open a discussion about the intentions behind media messages.

For the College:

- **Development of Critical Thinking in the Face of Social Media** : In middle school, students are increasingly exposed to social media, often without adult supervision. It is crucial that they learn to analyze the information they find there, to understand the mechanisms of dissemination of fake news, and to identify credible sources of information. Teachers need to help them understand that not everything they see or read on social media is necessarily true or trustworthy.

  Teaching Strategies: Workshops where students analyze social media posts, identify original sources, and discuss the credibility of those sources can be particularly effective. They could, for example, compare a rumor spread on social networks to verified information found in a reputable newspaper.

- **Introduction to Fact-Checking Techniques** : Middle school students should be introduced to methods of verifying information. This includes learning to research alternative sources, analyzing the intentions behind posts, and verifying images and videos. These skills are essential for navigating the world of digital information, where misinformation can be pervasive.

  Concrete examples: Teachers can organize sessions where students must verify the veracity of certain information using fact-checking tools available online. For example, they might be asked to verify a viral claim by searching for credible news articles or using fact-checking sites like Snopes or Les Décoders.

- **Encouragement of Active Participation** : It is essential that students are encouraged to actively participate in discussions on the media and express their opinions in a reasoned manner. Supervised classroom debates are a great way to develop this skill, teaching students to respect different points of view and construct arguments based on facts.

  Suggested activities: Teachers can organize debates on current issues where students must defend a position, drawing on evidence and reliable sources. For example, a debate on "Does social media do more harm than good?" would allow students to think critically about the pros and cons of these platforms.

For high school:

- **In-Depth Analysis of Disinformation Techniques** : High school students must gain a thorough understanding of the techniques used to manipulate information. This includes analyzing deepfakes, manipulating statistics, and selectively disseminating facts. They must be able to break down these techniques, understand their implications, and discuss how they can influence public opinion.

  Case studies: Teachers can use real-life case studies where students must analyze examples of misinformation in the media, discuss techniques used to manipulate information, and suggest strategies to counter these techniques. For example, an analysis of how disinformation campaigns have influenced elections or political decisions may be a relevant topic.

- **Preparation for Digital Citizenship** : High school students must be prepared to exercise their role as citizens in a digital environment. This involves understanding the responsibilities associated with disseminating information, knowing how to contribute positively to the information society, and respecting ethical principles in the use of digital media.

  Digital Citizenship Projects: Students may be asked to create awareness campaigns on topics related to misinformation, using social media responsibly to inform their peers about important topics. For example, they could design a campaign about the importance of checking facts before sharing information online.

- **Research and Verification Skill Development** : High school students should be trained to use advanced research tools, assess the credibility of online sources, and produce responsible media content. These skills are essential for their higher education and future professional life.

  Research Projects: Students may be tasked with conducting in-depth research on topics related to media and disinformation, using academic databases, newspaper archives, and fact-checking sites. The result could be a research report, presentation or documentary, showing their ability to analyze and synthesize complex information.

1.2 Methodologies for Teaching Media Literacy

Teaching media literacy must rely on varied and interactive methodologies to capture students' attention and actively involve them in their learning. Teaching methods must be adapted to the age of the students and the context in which they are used, while being flexible enough to meet the specific needs of each class.

Fun and Interactive Approach for Primary School:

- **Educational Games** : Educational games are at the heart of learning for young students. They help make learning fun while teaching essential skills. For example, card games where students must match statements to reliable or unreliable sources can be used to strengthen their fact-checking skills.

  Example game: A role play called "Budding Journalist" where students must collect information and verify its authenticity before publishing it in a class "newspaper" can be very educational. Each student can play a different role (journalist, editor, news source), which helps understand the complex process of creating news.

- **Explanatory Cartoons** : Cartoons can be used to explain complex concepts, such as fake news or the distinction between facts and opinions, in a simple and engaging way. Students can then discuss the messages in the cartoons and identify times when the characters need to verify information.

  Example Resource: A cartoon about a character who shares rumors without verifying the facts, causing problems in their community, can be a good starting point for a class discussion on the importance of verifying information.

- **Creative Workshops** : Creative workshops allow students to express what they have learned in a tangible way. For example, students can create their own "journals" by pasting pictures and writing captions that distinguish facts from opinions.

  Suggested activity: A workshop where students create a poster entitled "The golden rules of good information readers," on which they illustrate the steps to follow to verify information before believing it or sharing it.

Case Studies and Framed Debates for College:

- **Case Studies** : Middle school students can be exposed to real-life case studies where they analyze examples of disinformation, discuss the impacts on society, and propose solutions to combat these phenomena. These case studies can include analyzes of disinformation campaigns on current topics, such as health, politics, or the environment.

  Case Example: A case study on the spread of misinformation during a flu epidemic, where students must analyze the different types of information shared online, identify reliable sources, and discuss the consequences of misinformation on public health.

- **Use of Digital Tools** : Digital tools, such as fact-checking software and information tracking apps, can be introduced to teach students how to verify the authenticity of information online. Students can learn to use these tools to analyze articles, videos, and images.

  Educational tool: A workshop where students use tools like Google Fact Check Explorer to verify claims circulating on social media can be very informative. They can learn to analyze articles, verify images with tools like TinEye, and look for additional information to confirm or deny a rumor.

- **Supervised Debates** : Class debates, supervised by the teacher, allow students to express their opinions on current issues related to the media, while learning to respect different points of view and construct arguments based on facts.

Example of a debate: A debate on the subject "Influencers on social networks: reliable sources of information or vectors of disinformation?" where students are divided into teams to defend opposing points of view, drawing on research and real-life examples.

Documentary Research and Critical Analysis for High School:

- **Documentary Research** : High school students should be encouraged to conduct in-depth documentary research on topics related to media and disinformation. This includes researching reliable sources, critically analyzing content, and writing evidence-based reports.

  Research project: Students could be asked to complete a research project on a famous case of disinformation, such as the Iraq "weapons of mass destruction" affair. They will have to analyze the different sources of information, identify biases and errors, and write a report on the lessons to be learned from this episode.

- **Analysis of Biased Videos and Articles** : Students can be trained to identify biases in videos and articles, understand how these biases influence public opinion, and discuss strategies to counter these influences.

  Practical exercise: Students could analyze extracts from television news, political debates or online press articles to identify potential biases, omissions of information, and manipulation techniques used. They could then discuss in class the impact of these biases on public perception.

- **End of Year Projects** : End of year projects, such as creating documentaries or writing investigative articles, allow students to practice their media literacy skills while contributing to a dialogue broader on societal issues.

  Suggested project: Students could create a mini-documentary on a current topic related to misinformation, using research, fact-checking, and video editing techniques. This project would help them develop skills in communication, critical analysis, and use of digital technologies.

1.3 Educational Resources for Media Education

Educational resources play a key role in implementing a media literacy program. Resources should be appropriate for student level and designed to encourage interactive learning and engagement. Here are some examples of suggested resources for each grade level, based on the materials provided.

For Primary School:

- **Activity Booklets** : Activity booklets include interactive exercises where students must separate fact from opinion, identify sources of information, and think critically about the media content they consume. These booklets can be used in class or at home, in addition to the lessons taught by the teacher.

  Suggested content: An activity booklet could include short stories followed by reflection questions, matching exercises where students match statements to reliable or unreliable sources, and guessing games where students must decide whether information is true or false.

- **Posters and Educational Games** : Interactive posters and educational games are valuable tools for reinforcing learning in a fun and visual way. For example, a poster entitled "How to know if information is true?" could be posted in the classroom to remind students of the steps to follow to verify the information.

  Educational game: A board game where students must collect "evidence" to verify a rumor before publishing it in their class "newspaper" can be very engaging. Students must navigate the game board, collecting clues and evidence, while avoiding the pitfalls of false information.

- **Drawings and Creative Workshops** : Creative workshops where students draw situations related to information and reflect on the veracity of the information received are essential for integrating concepts in a practical way.

    Suggested Workshop: A workshop where students create a comic strip about a character who learns to verify the information they receive could be a great way to consolidate learning. Each student could create a page from the comic strip, illustrating a different step in the fact-checking process.

For the College:

- **Workbooks** : Workbooks can include case studies, source credibility quizzes, and online fact-checking activities. These workbooks allow students to practice the skills they learned in class and think critically about the information.

    Workbook Content: Exercises could include questions on comparing different news sources, case studies on famous disinformation campaigns, and brainstorming activities where students discuss the social and political impacts of fake news.

- **Instructional Videos** : Educational videos on topics such as fake news, media bias, and information manipulation techniques are important resources for capturing student attention and illustrating the concepts being taught.

    Example video: A series of short videos explaining how fake news is created, spread and why it is dangerous could be very useful. Each video could end with reflection questions or challenges for students, encouraging them to apply what they have learned.

- **Digital Tools** : Digital tools, such as fact-checking software or information tracking platforms, should be integrated into the curriculum to teach students how to navigate the digital world critically.

    Example tool: A mobile application where students can check information in real time using databases of verified articles could be introduced. Students could be encouraged to use this app to check news they see on their own social media accounts.

For high school:

- **Methodological Guides** : Methodological guides, which explain the steps of documentary research, critical analysis of sources, and writing articles, are essential for high school students who must develop advanced skills in media education.

    Guide Content: A guide detailing advanced research techniques, methods for assessing the credibility of academic and journalistic sources, and the steps of writing an investigative article could be very useful for students working on science projects. research.

- **Online Resources** : Online resources, including academic article databases, fact-checking sites, and educational platforms, are indispensable tools for independent research and learning.

    Suggested Resource: A database of verified resources on controversial topics (like climate change, vaccination, etc.) could be made available to students, allowing them to conduct in-depth research while ensuring their sources are reliable.

- **Presentation Materials** : Presentation materials, such as slides, charts, and videos, are used to help students effectively communicate their ideas and argue about complex media topics.

    Example material: A digital presentation kit including slide templates, interactive graphics, and explanatory videos could be provided to students to help them prepare their presentations on misinformation topics. This kit could include tutorials on using presentation software like PowerPoint or Prezi.

1.4 Evaluation and Monitoring of Media Education Programs

Continuous evaluation is crucial for measuring the effectiveness of media education programs and for adapting teaching methods according to students' needs. The documents provided suggest several approaches for evaluation and monitoring.

For Primary School:

- **Playful Assessments** : Educational games and quizzes are used to assess students' skills in fact-checking and understanding media concepts. These gamified assessments allow teachers to measure student progress informally, while making learning fun and engaging.

  Example assessment: An interactive quiz where students answer questions about the truth of information they have studied in class could be used regularly to assess their understanding. Results could be displayed in class chart format, encouraging healthy and motivating competition.

- **Progress Monitoring** : Student progress is documented through monitoring sheets, which are shared with teachers and parents. Quarterly meetings allow us to discuss progress and areas for improvement. These sheets may include observations on class participation, results of activities and quizzes, as well as feedback on the development of students' critical thinking skills.

  Tracking method: Teachers can use a digital logbook where they record daily or weekly observations of student participation and progress. This journal can be shared with parents during parent-teacher meetings, facilitating communication and support for parents in the learning process.

For the College:

- **Group Projects** : Group projects where students work together to analyze cases of misinformation and present their findings are important assessment tools. These projects assess not only individual skills, but also the ability to collaborate and communicate effectively.

  Example project: A group project where students must create a presentation on an example of misinformation they found online, explaining how they checked the facts, what sources they used, and what solutions they propose to counter it. this type of misinformation.

- **Presentations and Debates** : Oral presentations and class debates are used to assess students' ability to defend their opinions, analyze complex information, and respond critically to the arguments of others.

  Debate Example: Students could be assessed on their ability to structure their arguments, use credible evidence, and respond thoughtfully to counterarguments in a debate on a current media issue.

For high school:

- **Research Projects** : Research projects, where students are required to carry out in-depth investigations into media-related topics, are a key assessment method. These projects require students to apply all the skills they have learned, from literature research and critical analysis to writing and presenting.

  Example research project: Students could be asked to write a report on the impact of disinformation in a recent election campaign, analyzing the different disinformation strategies used, the effects on public opinion, and the measures taken to counter this misinformation.

* **Real-Life Scenario-Based Assessments** : Real-world scenario-based assessments, where students must analyze cases of misinformation in real-time and propose solutions, help assess their ability to apply their knowledge in practical contexts.

  Example scenario: Students could be presented with a scenario where they must respond to viral misinformation circulating on social media. They should identify the original sources, verify the facts, and propose a communications strategy to correct the information and limit the damage.

Conclusion: Towards a Systematic Integration of Media Education

Integrating media education into school curricula is essential to preparing students to become critical and informed citizens in a society where information is omnipresent. Interactive methodologies, adapted educational resources and continuous assessments are key elements for successful integration.

It is crucial that teachers, educators, and policymakers work together to develop media literacy programs that meet the needs of students at all grade levels. By investing in media literacy, we can help create a generation capable of navigating the complex world of digital information, recognizing misinformation, and actively participating in democracy.

2. Guide for Teachers: Tools and Resources for Teaching Media and Information Literacy (MIL)

Introduction: The Crucial Role of Teachers in Media Literacy

The rise of digital technologies has transformed the educational landscape, making media and information literacy (MIL) more essential than ever. In this context, teachers play a central role in helping students navigate the flow of information, discern right from wrong, and become informed and critical citizens. However, for teachers to successfully meet this challenge, they must be equipped with the appropriate tools and resources, as well as teaching methodologies suited to each level of education.

This guide aims to provide teachers with the tools and resources necessary to integrate EMI into their classes, whether they teach in primary school, middle school or high school. It is based on the educational objectives defined in educational files, as well as best practices in terms of methodology, evaluation, and monitoring of student progress. This guide also aims to strengthen teachers' ability to adapt to the specific needs of their students and create an interactive and engaging learning environment.

1. Pedagogical Tools for Teaching Media and Information Literacy

Teaching tools are essential instruments for teaching MIL effectively. They must be selected and adapted according to the age of the students, their digital skills, and the educational objectives specific to each school level. Tools can range from simple visual supports, such as posters and activity booklets, to more advanced digital tools, such as fact-checking software and interactive platforms.

1.1 Primary School Tools

In primary school, the aim is to introduce students to the basic concepts of MIL in a fun and accessible way. Educational tools must be simple, visual, and designed to capture the attention of young students while facilitating their understanding.

- **Activity Booklets** : Activity booklets are valuable educational tools for young students. They can include interactive exercises where students must distinguish facts from opinions, identify sources of information, and think critically about the media content they consume. Booklets should be colorful, attractive, and include illustrations to keep students interested.

    Example content: An activity booklet could include short stories followed by reflection questions, matching exercises where students match statements to reliable or unreliable sources, and guessing games where students must decide whether a information is true or false. For example, an activity could ask students to match a picture of an information source (such as a television or a book) to the correct category, thereby strengthening their understanding of different information sources.

- **Educational Posters and Posters** : Posters and posters are visual tools that can be used to reinforce concepts taught in class. A poster entitled "How to know if information is true?" could be posted in the classroom to remind students of the steps to follow to verify the information.

    Example poster: An interactive poster where students can add stickers or notes to complete the fact-checking steps, making learning more interactive. Teachers can also use these posters for class discussions, asking students to give examples of information they have checked recently.

- **Educational Games** : Educational games are particularly effective for teaching NDE to young children because they transform learning into a fun and engaging activity. Card games where students must match statements to reliable or unreliable sources can be used to strengthen their fact-checking skills.

    Example of a game: A role-playing game entitled "Budding Journalist" where students must collect information and verify its authenticity before publishing it in a class "newspaper". Each student can play a different role (journalist, editor, news source), which helps understand the complex process of creating news.

- **Cartoons and Explanatory Videos** : Cartoons and explanatory videos are powerful tools for explaining complex concepts in a simple and engaging way. They can be used to introduce topics like fake news or the distinction between facts and opinions.

    Example video: A cartoon where a character shares rumors without verifying the facts, causing problems in their community, can be a good starting point for a class discussion on the importance of verifying information. Teachers can then ask students to discuss the lessons they learned from the video and suggest ways to avoid spreading rumors.

1.2 College Tools

In middle school, students begin to have a more nuanced understanding of media and are often exposed to information from a variety of sources, including social media. Educational tools must therefore be designed to help students develop critical thinking when faced with this information and learn to use digital tools to check the facts.

- **Workbooks** : Workbooks for middle school students should include case studies, source credibility quizzes, and online fact-checking activities. These workbooks allow students to practice the skills they learned in class and think critically about the information.

    Example content: A workbook could include questions on comparing different sources of information, case studies on famous disinformation campaigns, and brainstorming activities where students discuss the social and political impacts of fake news.

- **Instructional Videos** : Educational videos on topics such as fake news, media bias, and information manipulation techniques are important resources for capturing student attention and illustrating the concepts being taught.

  Example video: A series of short videos explaining how fake news is created, spread and why it is dangerous could be very useful. Each video could end with reflection questions or challenges for students, encouraging them to apply what they have learned.

- **Applications and Digital Tools** : Digital tools are essential for teaching middle school students how to verify the authenticity of information online. Students should be trained to use fact-checking software, academic article databases, and interactive platforms to analyze and validate the information they encounter.

  Example application: A mobile application where students can check information in real time using databases of verified articles could be introduced. Students could be encouraged to use this app to check news they see on their own social media accounts.

- **Collaborative Projects** : Collaborative projects are effective teaching tools for encouraging students to work together to analyze information, verify facts, and present their findings. These projects also assess students' communication and teamwork skills.

  Example project: A group project where students must create a presentation on an example of misinformation they found online, explaining how they checked the facts, what sources they used, and what solutions they propose to counter it. this type of misinformation.

1.3 Tools for High School

In high school, students are expected to develop advanced MIL skills, including documentary research, critical analysis of sources, and production of media content. Educational tools for this level must be more sophisticated and adapted to more complex projects.

- **Methodological Guides** : Methodological guides are essential tools for high school students. They explain the stages of documentary research, critical analysis of sources, and writing articles. These guides should be comprehensive, including real-world examples and practical exercises to help students master these skills.

  Sample guide: A methodological guide detailing advanced research techniques, methods for assessing the credibility of academic and journalistic sources, and the steps for writing an investigative article. This guide could include real-life case studies, fact-checking exercises, and tips on presenting research.

- **Online Resources** : Online resources, including academic article databases, fact-checking sites, and educational platforms, are indispensable tools for independent research and learning. High school students must learn to navigate these resources, select relevant information, and use it to support their arguments.

  Example resource: A database of verified resources on controversial topics (like climate change, vaccination, etc.) could be made available to students, allowing them to conduct in-depth research while ensuring that their sources are reliable.

- **Content Production Tools** : High school students must also be trained to use content production tools, such as video editing software, blog creation platforms, and interactive presentation tools. These skills are essential for preparing students to produce responsible and engaging media content.

  Example of tool: A workshop where students learn how to use video editing software to create a short documentary on a current topic could be very educational. Students would learn not only the technical aspects of video production, but also how to structure a narrative, check facts, and present information in a clear and compelling manner.

- **End of Year Projects** : End of year projects allow students to practice their MIL skills while contributing to a broader dialogue on societal issues. These projects may include creating documentaries, writing investigative articles, or designing awareness campaigns on topics related to disinformation.

  Example project: Students could create a mini-documentary on a current topic related to misinformation, using research, fact-checking, and video editing techniques. This project would help them develop skills in communication, critical analysis, and use of digital technologies.

2. Methodologies for Teaching Media and Information Literacy

The methodologies used to teach MIL must be varied and adapted to different levels of education. They must be designed to engage students, encourage their active participation, and develop their critical thinking.

2.1 Fun and Interactive Approaches for Primary School

In primary school, learning must be fun and interactive to capture the attention of young students. Teaching methods should include games, hands-on activities, and classroom discussions to make MIL concepts accessible and engaging.

- **Educational Games** : Educational games are particularly effective for teaching NDE to young children. They help make learning fun while teaching essential skills, like checking facts and recognizing reliable sources.

  Example game: A board game where students must collect "evidence" to verify a rumor before publishing it in their class "newspaper." Students must navigate the game board, collecting clues and evidence, while avoiding the pitfalls of false information.

- **Creative Workshops** : Creative workshops allow students to express what they have learned in a tangible way. For example, students can create their own "journals" by pasting pictures and writing captions that distinguish facts from opinions. *Example workshop:* A workshop where students create a poster titled "The Golden Rules of

  good reader of information," on which they illustrate the steps to follow to verify information before believing it or sharing it.

- **Class Discussions** : Class discussions are essential for encouraging students to ask questions, share their own experiences with the media, and think critically about the information they encounter.

  Discussion example: Teachers can organize age-appropriate discussions on current topics, encouraging them to ask questions and express their doubts. For example, a simple topic like "Why are TV commercials trying to sell us toys?" can open a discussion about the intentions behind media messages.

2.2 Case Studies and Framed Debates for College

By middle school, students are ready to tackle more complex topics and develop a more nuanced understanding of media. Methodologies should include case studies, guided discussions, and collaborative projects to help students analyze information and develop critical thinking skills.

- **Case Studies** : Case studies allow students to analyze real examples of disinformation, discuss the impacts on society, and propose solutions to combat these phenomena.

  Case Example: A case study on the spread of misinformation during a flu epidemic, where students must analyze the different types of information shared online, identify reliable sources, and discuss the consequences of misinformation on public health.

- **Supervised Debates** : Class debates, supervised by the teacher, allow students to express their opinions on current issues related to the media, while learning to respect different points of view and construct arguments based on facts.

  Example of a debate: A debate on the subject "Influencers on social networks: reliable sources of information or vectors of disinformation?" where students are divided into teams to defend opposing points of view, drawing on research and real-life examples.

- **Collaborative Projects** : Collaborative projects are effective teaching tools for encouraging students to work together to analyze information, verify facts, and present their findings.

  Example project: A group project where students must create a presentation on an example of misinformation they found online, explaining how they checked the facts, what sources they used, and what solutions they propose to counter it. this type of misinformation.

2.3 Documentary Research and Critical Analysis for High School

In high school, students are expected to develop advanced MIL skills, including documentary research, critical analysis of sources, and production of media content. Methodologies must include research projects, critical analysis, and content production to prepare students to become critical and informed citizens.

- **Documentary Research** : High school students should be encouraged to conduct in-depth documentary research on topics related to media and disinformation. This includes researching reliable sources, critically analyzing content, and writing evidence-based reports.

  Example of a research project: Students could be invited to carry out a research project

  research on a famous case of disinformation, such as the "weapons of mass destruction" affair in Iraq. They will have to analyze the different sources of information, identify biases and errors, and write a report on the lessons to be learned from this episode.

- **Analysis of Biased Videos and Articles** : Students can be trained to identify biases in videos and articles, understand how these biases influence public opinion, and discuss strategies to counter these influences.

  Practical exercise: Students could analyze extracts from television news, political debates or online press articles to identify potential biases, omissions of information, and manipulation techniques used. They could then discuss in class the impact of these biases on public perception.

- **End of Year Projects** : End of year projects, such as creating documentaries or writing investigative articles, allow students to practice their NDE skills while contributing to a broader dialogue on societal issues.

  Suggested project: Students could create a mini-documentary on a current topic related to misinformation, using research, fact-checking, and video editing techniques. This project would help them develop skills in communication, critical analysis, and use of digital technologies.

3. Evaluation and Monitoring of Media and Information Education Programs

Continuous evaluation is crucial for measuring the effectiveness of media education programs and for adapting teaching methods according to students' needs. Teachers must be equipped with the tools necessary to assess students' skills in fact-checking, critical analysis, and media content production.

3.1 Assessment in Primary School

In primary school, assessment should be fun and continuous, allowing teachers to measure student progress while making learning fun and engaging.

- **Educational Games** : Educational games can be used to assess students' fact-checking skills. For example, a game where students must guess whether information is true or false using tools learned in class can serve as a fun assessment.

    Example assessment: An interactive quiz where students answer questions about the truth of information they have studied in class could be used regularly to assess their understanding. Results could be displayed in class chart format, encouraging healthy and motivating competition.

- **Monitoring Sheets** : Student progress must be documented through monitoring sheets, which are shared with teachers and parents. Quarterly meetings allow us to discuss progress and areas for improvement.

    Tracking method: Teachers can use a digital logbook where they record daily or weekly observations of student participation and progress. This journal can be shared with parents during parent-teacher meetings, facilitating communication and support for parents in the learning process.

3.2 College assessment

In middle school, assessment should include group projects, presentations, and debates to measure students' critical analysis and communication skills.

- **Group Projects** : Group projects where students work together to analyze cases of misinformation and present their findings are important assessment tools. These projects assess not only individual skills, but also the ability to collaborate and communicate effectively.

    Example project: A group project where students must create a presentation on an example of misinformation they found online, explaining how they checked the facts, what sources they used, and what solutions they propose to counter it. this type of misinformation.

- **Presentations and Debates** : Oral presentations and class debates are used to assess students' ability to defend their opinions, analyze complex information, and respond critically to the arguments of others.

    Debate Example: Students could be assessed on their ability to structure their arguments, use credible evidence, and respond thoughtfully to counterarguments in a debate on a current media issue.

3.3 High school assessment

In high school, assessment should include research projects, critical analyses, and media content productions to measure students' advanced MIL skills.

- **Research Projects** : Research projects, where students are required to carry out in-depth investigations into media-related topics, are a key assessment method. These projects require students to apply all the skills they have learned, from literature research and critical analysis to writing and presenting.

    Example research project: Students could be asked to write a report on the impact of disinformation in a recent election campaign, analyzing the different disinformation strategies used, the effects on public opinion, and the measures taken to counter this misinformation.

- **Real-Life Scenario-Based Assessments** : Real-world scenario-based assessments, where students must analyze cases of misinformation in real-time and propose solutions, help assess their ability to apply their knowledge in practical contexts.

    Example scenario: Students could be presented with a scenario where they must respond to viral misinformation circulating on social media. They should identify the original sources, verify the facts, and propose a communications strategy to correct the information and limit the damage.

Conclusion: Strengthening the Role of Teachers in Media Education

Media and information education is an essential element in the training of citizens of the 21st century. Teachers play a crucial role in helping students develop the skills needed to navigate a complex and ever-changing media world. By providing teachers with the appropriate tools, resources, and methodologies, we can strengthen their ability to teach MIL effectively and meaningfully.

This guide, with a focus on best teaching practices and available resources, aims to support teachers in this important mission. By working together, teachers, educators and policy makers can help create a generation of critical, informed and responsible citizens capable of contributing positively to the information society.

3. Practical Activities and Exercises for Students

Introduction: The Importance of Practical Activities in Media Literacy

Media and information literacy (MIL) is a key skill for 21st century citizens, where access to information is both a blessing and a challenge. Younger generations, immersed in a constant flow of digital data, must learn to discern fact from fiction, identify reliable sources, and understand media manipulation techniques. Practical activities play a crucial role in the acquisition of these skills, as they allow students to put theoretical knowledge into practice, develop critical thinking, and prepare to navigate a complex and ever-changing media environment.

1. Activities for Primary School

In primary school, the aim is to introduce the fundamental concepts of MIL in a fun and accessible way. Activities should be designed to capture the attention of young students while allowing them to understand the basics of checking facts, distinguishing between sources of information, and critically analyzing media messages. These activities should also encourage the active participation of students and foster their natural curiosity about the media.

1.1 Activity: "True or False?"

- **Objective:** The main objective of this activity is to help students develop the ability to distinguish facts from opinions and false information. This helps them understand that it is important not to believe everything they see or hear, but rather to think critically about the information presented to them.

- **Duration:** 30 minutes

- **Materials:** Personalized activity booklet, pencils, whiteboard, projector to present examples in class.

- **Procedure:**

- **Introduction:** The teacher begins by explaining to students the difference between a fact, an opinion, and false information. A fact is something that can be proven or verified, an opinion is what someone thinks or feels, and misinformation is something that is presented as fact but is incorrect or misleading.

- **Individual Activity:** Each student receives an activity booklet containing a series of simple affirmations. For example, "The sun rises in the east" (fact), "Chocolate is the best treat" (opinion), and "If you eat carrots, you will be able to see in the dark" (false information). Students should check the "True" or "False" box based on what they think for each statement.
- **Class Discussion:** Once all students have completed the booklet, the teacher leads a class discussion to review each statement. For example, for the statement "The sun rises in the east," the teacher can show a video or animation to explain why this is a fact. For the statement "Chocolate is the best treat," the teacher can encourage students to share their opinions and understand that it is subjective. For the statement "If you eat carrots, you will be able to see in the dark", the teacher can explain how this idea came about (perhaps from an exaggeration of a quality of carrots) and why it is incorrect.
- **Follow-up Activity:** Students are then encouraged to ask questions about other information they have encountered outside of school, whether on television, on the Internet, or in family discussions. The teacher can create a "wall of truth" in the classroom where students can paste information they find and classify it as fact, opinion, or misinformation.
- **Assessment:** The teacher assesses students' understanding by asking them to give personal examples of facts, opinions, and misinformation they have heard recently, and to explain them to the class.

1.2 Activity: "Where does information come from?"

- **Objective:** This activity aims to help students identify different sources of information and understand their reliability. This includes distinguishing between primary and secondary sources, as well as recognizing traditional media versus new forms of digital media.

- **Duration:** 20 minutes

- **Materials:** Activity booklet, images representing different sources of information (television, books, Internet, teacher), cards to use in an association game.

- **Procedure:**

- **Introduction:** The teacher explains to students that information can come from many different sources, and that it is important to know where that information comes from to determine if it is reliable. It presents examples of common sources of information, such as books, newspapers, television, and the Internet.
- **Association Game:** Students participate in an association game where they must link each source of information to the corresponding image in their activity booklet. For example, an image of a professor may be associated with the category "reliable source", while an image of an Internet advertisement may be discussed in terms of questionable reliability.
- **Discussion:** After the game is completed, a class discussion is conducted to explain why certain sources are considered more reliable than others. The teacher can introduce examples of reliable sources (such as encyclopedias or scientific articles) and less reliable sources (such as online forums or disguised advertisements).
- **Creative Activity:** Students are invited to create their own "source tree" where they draw or paste images representing different sources of information, ranking them in order of reliability. This project can be displayed in the classroom as a constant visual reminder of the importance of verifying the provenance of information.
- **Assessment:** Students are assessed on their ability to explain why certain sources are more reliable than others, giving specific examples and justifying their choice.

1.3 Activity: "Game of truth and lies"

- **Objective:** Develop critical thinking skills in students by teaching them to identify misleading information and understand the consequences of misinformation.

- **Duration:** 30 minutes

- **Materials:** Specially designed deck of cards with true, false, and ambiguous statements, scoreboard.

- **Procedure:**

- **Introduction:** The teacher explains the concept of truth and lies in the media, emphasizing the importance of checking the facts before believing or sharing information. It discusses why some people or organizations might spread false information intentionally.
- **Group Play:** Students are divided into small groups and given a deck of cards with various statements. Each group must decide whether each statement is true or false using the tools and knowledge learned in class. For example, a card might say "Elephants can fly" (wrong), and students should explain why this is incorrect using scientific facts.
- **Discussion and Debriefing:** Each group then presents their findings to the class, explaining how they verified the information and why they judged certain statements to be false or true. The teacher leads a discussion about the importance of fact-checking and explains errors to clarify concepts.
- **Follow-up:** Students are encouraged to continue this activity at home by talking with their parents or guardians about information they find online or on television, and trying to verify this information together.
- **Assessment:** Students are assessed on their ability to identify false information, justify their choices, and explain the importance of fact-checking in daily life.

2. Activities for the College

In middle school, students begin to interact more with digital media, requiring more complex activities that engage their critical thinking and ability to analyze information from different sources. These activities should also encourage collaboration among students and allow them to explore the social and political impacts of media.

2.1 Activity: "Case Analysis: Fake News on Social Networks"

- **Objective:** Learn to analyze and verify information found on social media, using fact-checking tools and developing a critical understanding of digital media.

- **Duration:** 45 minutes

- **Materials:** Access to social media posts (print or digital), worksheets for analysis, internet access for fact checking, projector for classroom presentation.

- **Procedure:**

- **Introduction:** The teacher presents a brief history of social networks and discusses their role in the dissemination of information, emphasizing the advantages and disadvantages. It also introduces the concept of fake news and explains why it can be dangerous.
- **Group Analysis:** Students are divided into groups and given examples of social media posts potentially containing fake news. Each group must analyze the post, identify red flags of misinformation, and use online tools to fact-check. For example, they can research the source of information, verify the authenticity of images, and compare with credible news articles.

- **Presentation of Results:** Each group presents their results to the class, explaining why they think the post is fake news or not, and detailing the verification process used. The teacher can ask questions to deepen the analysis and encourage critical thinking.
- **Discussion:** A group discussion is conducted to explore why fake news spreads easily on social media, and how users can protect themselves against misinformation. Students are encouraged to share their own experiences with fake news and discuss how this information impacts their opinions.
- **Follow-up:** Students are invited to create a poster or digital presentation explaining how to fact-check information on social media, which can be shared with the school community to educate their peers about the importance of fact-checking.
- **Evaluation:** The evaluation is based on the quality of the analysis, the rigor of the verification process, and the clarity of the presentation. Students are also assessed on their ability to collaborate and communicate effectively within their group.

2.2 Activity: "Debate: Social Media and Disinformation"

- **Objective:** Encourage critical thinking and the ability to argue about the impacts of social media on the spread of disinformation, by developing communication and analysis skills.

- **Duration:** 60 minutes

- **Material:** Documentation on the impacts of social media, preparation sheets for the debate, access to academic articles or study reports, projector for presentation.

- **Procedure:**

- **Preparation:** The class is divided into two groups: one defending the idea that social media is mainly beneficial for society, and the other that they are an important vector of disinformation. Each group spends preparation time to collect arguments, based on facts, studies, and real examples. They use academic resources, news articles, and study reports to strengthen their arguments.
- **Class Debate:** The debate is then conducted in class, with a moderator (the teacher) who asks questions, gives speaking time, and ensures that each student can express themselves. Students must not only present their arguments, but also respond to the other group's counterarguments. The debate covers aspects such as the impact of fake news on elections, the role of social media algorithms, and the responsibilities of digital platforms.
- **Post-Debate Discussion:** At the end of the debate, a discussion is conducted to learn lessons and clarify the points raised. The teacher encourages students to reflect on what they have learned and how it influences their own use of social media.
- **Writing a Report:** Each student is invited to write a personal report on the debate, explaining their position, the arguments they found most convincing, and how their opinions may have evolved during the activity.
- **Assessment:** Students are assessed on the quality of their arguments, their ability to use credible evidence, their participation in debate, and the clarity of their written report.

2.3 Activity: "Research Project: Analysis of a Disinformation Campaign"

- **Objective:** Develop skills in research, critical media analysis, and presentation, through the in-depth study of a disinformation campaign.

- **Duration:** 1 week (work in class and at home)

- **Materials:** Access to the school library, online resources for research, methodological guides, presentation software.

- **Procedure:**

- **Choice of Topic:** Students choose a historical disinformation campaign
  or contemporary to study, in consultation with the teacher. The choice could be topics like war propaganda, election disinformation, or health misinformation (e.g., vaccine misinformation).
- **Research:** Students conduct in-depth research on their chosen campaign, using books, academic articles, digital archives, and media reports. They must identify the disinformation techniques used, analyze the motivations behind the campaign, and study the impacts on public opinion and the events that followed.
- **Writing and Presentation:** The research results are presented in the form of a written report or multimedia presentation to the class. The report should include an introduction to the context of the campaign, an analysis of disinformation techniques, a discussion of the consequences, and conclusions on lessons for the future.
- **Class Discussion:** After the presentations, a class discussion is conducted to compare the different campaigns studied, identify common trends, and brainstorm ways to combat such practices in the future.
- **Evaluation:** Projects are evaluated based on depth of analysis, rigor of research, quality of presentation, and students' ability to defend their findings during class discussion.

3. Activities for high school

In high school, students are able to conduct in-depth research and participate in complex projects that prepare them for their future roles as informed and critical citizens. These activities should include advanced research projects, specialized workshops, and media content productions that encourage students to apply their knowledge practically and develop skills that will benefit them in their professional and personal lives.

3.1 Activity: "Documentary Project: Investigating Fake News"

- **Objective:** Produce a short documentary that analyzes a case of fake news, focusing on fact-checking techniques, storytelling, and video production.

- **Duration:** 3 weeks (group work)

- **Equipment:** Cameras, video editing software, access to digital archives and the Internet for research, studio or room equipped for filming.

- **Procedure:**

- **Initial Training:** Students begin with a training session on fact-checking techniques, video production, and documentary storytelling. A professional in the field (journalist or documentary filmmaker) may be invited to lead this workshop.
- **Choice of Subject:** Each group chooses a subject for their documentary, based on a real case of fake news. Topics may include misinformation about political events, health crises, or social phenomena. The choice must be validated by the teacher to ensure the relevance and feasibility of the project.
- **Research and Script:** Students carry out in-depth research to understand the origins of fake news, the reasons for its dissemination, and its consequences. They then write a detailed script for their documentary, ensuring that each assertion is supported by verified evidence.
- **Filming and Editing:** Groups film the necessary scenes, which may include expert interviews, testimonials, and re-enactments.
  Editing must be done carefully, using professional software, to produce a quality documentary.

- **Screening and Debate:** Once the documentary is finalized, it is screened in front of the class, followed by a question-and-answer session where students must defend their work and respond to constructive criticism from their peers and the teacher.
- **Rating:** The documentary is rated based on the quality of the research, the rigor of the fact-checking, the originality of the storytelling, and the technical quality of the filming and editing. Students are also assessed on their ability to collaborate effectively in groups and manage different aspects of production.

3.2 Activity: "Fact-Checking Workshop"

- **Objective:** Train students in professional fact-checking techniques used by journalists and fact-checking experts.

- **Duration:** 2 days (intensive workshop)

- **Materials:** Access to online fact-checking tools, press articles, fact database, laptops for each student, methodological guides.

- **Procedure:**

- **Introduction:** The workshop begins with an introduction to fact-checking, explaining its importance in modern journalism and how it contributes to the quality of information in a democracy. Concrete examples of fact-checking carried out by the media are presented to illustrate the process.
- **Practical Training:** Students learn the different stages of fact-checking, from verifying sources to analyzing evidence, including searching for original documents and consulting experts. Practical cases are used to allow students to apply the techniques learned, with close supervision from the teacher or guest expert.
- **Fact-Checking Exercise:** Each student must verify the accuracy of a press article or public statement, using the tools and methods presented during the workshop. They must write a detailed report explaining their verification process, the sources consulted, and the conclusions drawn.
- **Presentation of Results:** Students present their fact-checking reports to the class, explaining how they approached the process, challenges encountered, and lessons learned. A discussion is held on the importance of transparency and integrity in fact-checking.
- **Evaluation:** The evaluation is based on the precision of the fact-checking, the methodological rigor, the clarity of the explanations, and the students' ability to defend their conclusions during the presentation.

3.3 Activity: "Critical Analysis of the Media"

- **Objective:** Develop an in-depth understanding of media bias and information manipulation techniques, encouraging students to adopt a critical attitude towards media content.

- **Duration:** 1 month (class project)

- **Material:** Press articles, television reports, access to academic databases, critical analysis tools, presentation software.

- **Procedure:**

- **Introduction to Media Bias:** The teacher begins with a series of

> course on media bias, explaining how and why it occurs, and how it can influence public perception. Historical and contemporary examples are used to illustrate different types of bias, such as confirmation bias, framing bias, and ideological bias.

- **Media Content Analysis:** Students are invited to choose several articles or reports on the same subject from different media (national and international). They analyze differences in coverage, identify possible biases, and assess the impact of these biases on public perception. Students are encouraged to use critical analysis tools to structure their work, such as bias assessment grids or narrative analysis models.
- **Report Production:** Each student writes a detailed report on their analyses, discussing the biases identified, how they influence news storytelling, and possible solutions for more balanced media coverage. The reports must be argued with concrete examples and academic references.
- **Class Discussion:** Once the reports are completed, a series of class discussions are held to compare the analyses, discuss the findings, and brainstorm ways to improve critical media consumption among young people. Students may also be asked to suggest guidelines for media consumers to minimize the influence of media bias.
- **Evaluation:** Reports are evaluated based on depth of analysis, originality of ideas, use of credible evidence and references, and clarity of presentation. Class discussions are also assessed to measure students' ability to argue and think critically.

Conclusion

The practical activities and exercises proposed in this chapter aim to provide students with the tools necessary to navigate a complex and constantly changing media environment. By developing skills in fact-checking, critical analysis, and media content production, these activities prepare students to become informed and engaged citizens. Integrating these activities into the school curriculum is essential to strengthening students' critical thinking and cognitive resilience in the face of misinformation.

4. Using the "Toolkit for Teachers_Disinformation_FR"

Introduction: The Importance of Toolkit in Media and Information Education

In a world increasingly dominated by digital news and social media, media and information literacy (MIL) has become essential in preparing students to navigate a complex media landscape in a critical and informed manner. Teachers play a crucial role in this process, and to support them, specific resources, such as the "Toolkit for Teachers_Disinformation_FR", have been developed. This toolkit is designed to provide educators with the tools needed to teach the critical skills required to identify, analyze, and counter misinformation.

This chapter explores the use of this toolkit in depth, detailing each section and offering practical strategies for integrating the proposed activities and resources into school curricula. The goal is to maximize the educational impact of EMI and prepare students to become informed citizens, capable of actively participating in a democratic society.

1. Structure and Content of the Toolkit

The "Toolkit for Teachers_Disinformation_FR" is structured into several key sections, each aimed at providing teachers with practical tools, ready-to-use activities, and educational resources for teaching MIL. This toolkit is designed to be flexible, allowing teachers to tailor it to the specific needs of their students, while covering a wide range of topics related to misinformation.

1.1 Introduction to the Toolkit

- **Objective:** The first section of the toolkit provides a general introduction to disinformation, explaining why it is crucial to teach it in MIL. This section contextualizes the phenomenon of disinformation, presenting concrete examples and exposing the challenges it poses in the current media environment.

- **Strategy for Use:** Teachers can use this section as a starting point for a class discussion about misinformation. By introducing the topic in an engaging way, they can capture students' interest and make them aware of the importance of NDE. A suggested activity would be to ask students to share examples of misinformation they have encountered, whether online or in traditional media, and discuss their impacts.

1.2 Educational Activities

- **Objective:** This section is the heart of the toolkit, offering a series of educational activities designed to help students develop skills in fact-checking, critical analysis of sources, and understanding the mechanisms by which disinformation spreads. The activities are suitable for different grade levels and can be used as is or modified according to the specific needs of the class.

- **Usage Strategy:** Teachers are encouraged to select activities based on students' age and level of understanding. Each activity comes with detailed instructions, necessary materials, and suggestions for class discussions. An effective strategy would be to start with simple activities, such as role-playing or simulations, to introduce basic concepts, then progress to more complex exercises, such as analyzing disinformation campaigns or creating content verified.

1.3 Additional Resources

- **Purpose:** The toolkit includes a variety of complementary resources, such as academic articles, case studies, how-to videos, and links to online fact-checking tools. These resources are designed to enrich lessons and provide teachers and students with additional information to deepen their understanding of misinformation.

- **Use Strategy:** Teachers can integrate these resources into their lessons to reinforce the concepts covered in the educational activities. For example, after completing an activity on fact-checking, students might be invited to read an academic article on the effects of disinformation on democracy, or watch a video on the manipulation techniques used by spreaders of fake news. news. These resources can also be used for research projects or in-depth class discussions.

1.4 Evaluations and Monitoring

- **Objective:** The section on evaluations and monitoring provides tools to measure the impact of MIL activities on students. It offers assessment criteria, questionnaires, and observation grids to help teachers monitor student progress in critical skills and understanding misinformation.

- **Strategy for Use:** Teachers can use these tools to assess student knowledge before and after activities, to measure the effectiveness of lessons and identify areas needing attention. Assessments can be formal, such as tests or graded projects, or informal, such as group discussions or reflective journals. Regular monitoring ensures that students integrate the skills taught and are able to apply them independently.

2. Integration of the Toolkit into School Programs

One of the main advantages of the "Toolkit for Teachers_Disinformation_FR" is its flexibility. It can be integrated into various school programs, whether in social sciences, language, or technology courses. This section explores how teachers can incorporate the toolkit into their daily teaching to maximize its impact.

2.1 Use in Social Sciences Classes

- **Approach:** Social sciences courses are an ideal context for introducing the concepts of disinformation, as they allow for exploring the sociopolitical impacts of the dissemination of false information. Teachers can use the toolkit activities to illustrate how misinformation has influenced historical events or how it continues to shape public opinions today.

- **Practical Example:** A lesson could focus on studying a historical disinformation campaign, such as propaganda during World War II or fake news during the Cold War. Students could use the toolkit to analyze the disinformation techniques used, understand the motivations behind these campaigns, and discuss their impacts on the course of history.

2.2 Use in Language Classes

- **Approach:** In language classes, the toolkit can be used to teach skills in critical analysis of texts and discourses. Teachers can encourage students to deconstruct news articles, political speeches, and digital content to identify bias, manipulation, and false information.

- **Practical Example:** An activity could consist of analyzing a political speech or an editorial using the tools in the toolkit. Students would be asked to identify fallacious arguments, deliberate omissions, and persuasion techniques used to manipulate public opinion. This activity could be followed by a discussion on the importance of journalistic rigor and integrity in public communications.

2.3 Use in Technology Classes

- **Approach:** Technology courses provide a platform for teaching technical aspects of disinformation, such as image manipulation, creating deepfakes, and using algorithms to spread fake news. The toolkit can be integrated to educate students about the dangers of these technologies and train them to use fact-checking tools.

- **Practical Example:** A project could involve analyzing how social media algorithms amplify misinformation. Students could use case studies provided in the toolkit to understand how fake news spreads on digital platforms and propose solutions to counter these effects, such as developing ethical algorithms or improving fact-checking tools .

2.4 Interdisciplinary Projects

- **Approach:** The toolkit can also be used for interdisciplinary projects, where students apply skills learned in different fields to solve complex problems related to misinformation. These projects enhance collaborative learning and show students how EMI skills are relevant in various academic and professional contexts.

- **Practical Example:** An interdisciplinary project could involve creating a misinformation awareness campaign for the school or local community. Students would work in teams to research examples of misinformation, create educational content (articles, videos, infographics), and use digital platforms to spread their message. The toolkit would serve as a guide throughout the project, offering resources and examples for each step.

3. Practical Examples of Using the Toolkit

To illustrate how the "Toolkit for Teachers_Disinformation_FR" can be used effectively in a school context, this section provides case studies and detailed usage scenarios. Each example is designed to show how the activities and resources in the toolkit can be adapted to different teaching levels and educational objectives.

3.1 Case Study: Use in College

- **Context:** A middle school teacher wants to introduce his students to the dangers of misinformation online, particularly on social media.

- **Strategy:** The teacher decides to use a combination of activities from the toolkit to create a series of lessons on misinformation. It begins with a basic activity where students analyze examples of fake news they have found online. Then, they use the toolkit resources to fact-check and understand how fake news spreads. Finally, students are encouraged to create their own awareness campaigns to share what they have learned with their peers.

- **Outcome:** By the end of the project, students not only gained a better understanding of the dangers of misinformation, but they also developed practical skills in fact-checking and producing responsible content. Their awareness campaigns are presented at a school open day, where they receive praise from parents and teachers.

3.2 Case Study: Use in High School

- **Context:** A high school teacher wants to deepen students' understanding of the sociopolitical mechanisms behind misinformation, focusing on historical and contemporary examples.

- **Strategy:** The teacher uses the toolkit to organize a research project where students choose an example of historical disinformation (e.g., Nazi propaganda) and a contemporary example (e.g., fake news during the 2016 U.S. election). They use the toolkit resources to analyze the techniques used, the motivations of disinformation spreaders, and the impacts on society.

- **Outcome:** Students produce comprehensive research reports, which they present to the class in mock lecture format. This project not only allows them to deepen their understanding of disinformation, but also to develop skills in academic research, critical analysis, and oral presentation.

3.3 Scenario: Specific Activities for Primary Schools

- **Context:** A primary school teacher seeks to introduce MIL at a basic level, focusing on simple and accessible concepts.

- **Strategy:** The teacher uses educational games and group activities from the toolkit to teach students to distinguish facts from opinions and identify reliable sources of information. For example, one activity could be to create a class "newspaper" where students must verify information before posting it. The teacher also uses explanatory videos to illustrate the dangers of misinformation in a fun way.

- **Outcome:** Students begin to develop critical thinking skills at a young age, learning to ask questions about the information they receive and discussing the importance of fact-checking with their parents at home.

4. Challenges and Solutions in Using the Toolkit

Integrating the "Toolkit for Teachers_Disinformation_FR" into school curricula may present some challenges. This section explores these potential challenges and offers practical solutions to overcome them, drawing on examples from educational practice.

4.1 Challenge: Lack of Time for Integration

- **Problem:** Teachers may feel overwhelmed by the busy school schedule and struggle to find time to incorporate additional activities on misinformation.

- **Solution:** To overcome this challenge, teachers can start by integrating elements of the toolkit into existing lessons, rather than creating entirely new units. For example, a fact-checking exercise might be added to a critical reading lesson or a media analysis project might be integrated into a social studies course. By using the toolkit in a modular way, teachers can gradually introduce EMI concepts without overwhelming the curriculum.

4.2 Challenge: Level Differences Among Students

- **Problem:** Students in the same class may have varying skill levels in media literacy and technology, making it difficult to consistently apply the toolkit activities.

- **Solution:** To address this problem, teachers can differentiate activities based on student skills. The toolkit offers resources that can be adapted to different levels, allowing advanced students to work on more complex projects while those who need more support can focus on basic activities. Teachers can also organize heterogeneous groups where more experienced students help their peers, thus promoting collaborative learning.

4.3 Challenge: Resistance to Change

- **Problem:** Some teachers or students may be reluctant to adopt new teaching methods, particularly if they involve technologies or concepts with which they are unfamiliar.

- **Solution:** To encourage adoption of the toolkit, it is important to start with simple and accessible activities, demonstrating their relevance and effectiveness. Trainings for teachers can also be organized to familiarize them with digital tools and EMI concepts. Success stories from other teachers using the toolkit can be shared to inspire confidence and motivation.

Conclusion: Maximizing the Impact of the Toolkit

The "Toolkit for Teachers_Disinformation_FR" is a valuable resource for teachers wishing to integrate EMI into their lessons. By using it strategically and tailoring its resources to the specific needs of their students, teachers can strengthen their students' critical skills and prepare them to navigate a complex media world informedly.

Successful toolkit integration requires a flexible approach and a willingness to experiment. By overcoming potential challenges and taking advantage of the many resources available, teachers can transform their classroom into a dynamic learning space where students develop the skills needed to become critical and responsible consumers of information.

5. EMI Skills Assessment

Introduction: The Crucial Importance of Assessment in Media and Information Literacy

Media and information literacy (MIL) plays an increasingly vital role in shaping 21st century citizens. In a world where misinformation spreads rapidly, students must be equipped with the skills to discern fact from falsehood, analyze information critically, and make informed decisions. However, teaching these skills is not enough: it is equally crucial to assess them rigorously and systematically to ensure that students truly integrate the concepts and practices taught.

Evaluation within the framework of the EMI is not limited to the simple verification of the knowledge acquired; it should include an assessment of analytical skills, cognitive resilience in the face of misinformation, and the ability to apply these skills in real-world contexts. This section explores the different methods and tools for assessing MIL skills, drawing on the resources available in the "Toolkit for Teachers_Disinformation_FR" as well as proven educational practices.

1. Fundamental Objectives of MIL Assessment

EMI skills assessment must pursue several key objectives to be effective:

- **Measuring Conceptual Understanding:** It is essential to check that students understand the fundamental concepts of information, such as the distinction between facts and opinions, the reliability of sources, and different techniques for manipulating information. This conceptual understanding forms the foundation on which analytical and critical skills can be built.

- *Practical example:* A written test could include multiple choice questions where students must identify whether a statement is a fact, an opinion, or false information. Additionally, MCQ-type exercises could be used to assess students' ability to recognize manipulation techniques used in various media.

- **Assess Critical Skills:** Students' critical skills, such as analyzing information, identifying bias, and the ability to independently check facts, should be assessed regularly. These skills are essential for students to navigate the digital world effectively.

- *Practical example:* An assessment exercise could involve analyzing a news article or social media post. Students should identify potential biases, verify facts using reliable sources, and write a short essay explaining their findings.

- **Develop Cognitive Resilience:** Assessment must also ensure that students develop cognitive resilience in the face of misinformation. This means that they must not only be able to recognize false information, but also resist attempts at emotional and cognitive manipulation.

- *Practical example:* A classroom simulation where students are exposed to a disinformation campaign could be used to assess their ability to remain critical and not be influenced by misleading information.

- **Promote Active Engagement:** The assessment should encourage students to actively engage in the fight against misinformation. This includes producing verified informative content, participating in critical discussions, and engaging in outreach projects.

- *Practical example:* A final year project could involve creating a misinformation awareness campaign, where students must design posters, videos, and presentations to inform their peers and the community. **2. EMI Skills Assessment Methods**

Assessing EMI skills can be carried out through a variety of methods, each tailored to a specific aspect of learning. These methods should be designed to assess not only factual knowledge, but also students' analytical, critical, and practical skills.

2.1 Formative Assessment: An Continuous Process

Formative assessment is an ongoing process that occurs throughout the school year. It aims to provide regular feedback to students to help them improve their skills in real time.

- **Quizzes and Written Tests:** Quizzes and tests are common tools for assessing understanding of basic NDE concepts. They allow you to quickly check whether students have properly integrated the fundamental concepts.

- *Practical example:* After a lesson on distinguishing facts from opinions, a quiz might ask students to classify a series of statements as facts or opinions. Another test could assess their understanding of different sources of information and their relative reliability.

- **Practical Exercises:** Practical exercises, such as critical analysis of a press article or checking the veracity of information on social networks, make it possible to assess students' analytical skills. These exercises can be integrated into regular lessons and corrected in class to provide immediate feedback.

- *Practical example:* An exercise might involve checking a viral news story on social media. Students should research reliable sources, compare the information, and write a short report explaining their verification method.

- **Educational Games:** Educational games, like those described in the "Educational File - Primary School", can be used to assess fact-checking skills in a fun way. For example, the "Truth and Lies Game" helps students apply what they have learned in an interactive way.

- *Practical example:* A role play where students take on the role of journalists who must verify information before publishing it could be used to assess their ability to identify reliable sources and avoid the spread of false information.

2.2 Summative Assessment: A Review of Acquired Learning

The summative evaluation takes place at the end of a teaching unit or a project. It aims to evaluate the skills acquired by students and to determine their level of mastery of the concepts taught.

- **Group Projects:** Group projects provide an opportunity to assess students' collaborative skills and ability to apply what they have learned in a real-world context. These projects assess not only understanding of concepts, but also student engagement and ability to communicate complex ideas.

- *Practical example:* A group project could involve creating a misinformation awareness campaign, where each student is responsible for fact-checking part of the project. Students would be assessed on their ability to work in a team, seek reliable information, and produce quality content.
- **Research Reports:** Research reports are an excellent way to assess students' ability to explore a topic related to NDE. For example, students might be asked to write a report on the impact of fake news on elections, using reliable sources to support their arguments.

- *Practical example:* A research report could focus on the analysis of a historical or contemporary disinformation campaign. Students should identify the disinformation techniques used, analyze the motivations of the spreaders, and discuss the social and political impacts of the campaign.
- **Oral Presentations:** Oral presentations make it possible to assess students' ability to explain and defend their points of view. During these presentations, students may be asked to analyze a disinformation campaign and propose solutions to remedy it. Communication and argumentation skills are thus put to the test.

- *Practical example:* A presentation could consist of an analysis of widely distributed fake news. Students would be asked to explain how they identified the misinformation, what verification methods they used, and what strategies they recommend to prevent the spread of such information in the future.

3. Assessment Tools and Resources

The "Toolkit for Teachers_Disinformation_EN" offers a range of tools and resources to help teachers assess EMI skills. These tools are designed to be flexible and suitable for various educational contexts.

- **Evaluation Grids:** Standardized evaluation grids for projects and practical exercises make it possible to evaluate criteria such as accuracy, relevance of sources, and methodological rigor. These grids can be adapted to the specific needs of each class.

- *Practical example:* An evaluation grid for a research project could include criteria such as clarity of presentation, quality of sources used, critical analysis, and ability to draw conclusions based on evidence.
- **Self-Assessment Quizzes:** Self-assessment quizzes allow students to reflect on their own learning and identify areas where they need to improve. These questionnaires also promote awareness of NDE skills.

- *Practical example:* A self-assessment quiz might ask students to rate their own ability to check facts, analyze information critically, and identify bias in the media they consume.
- **Online Tests:** Online platforms offer automated skills tests

  in fact-checking and critical media analysis. These tests can be used for quick and effective assessment of student knowledge, while providing immediate feedback.

- *Practical example:* An online test could include scenarios where students must identify false information, verify sources, and answer questions about manipulation techniques used in digital media.

4. Strategies for Integrating Assessment into the Curriculum

Integrating MIL skills assessment into the school curriculum requires strategic planning. Here are some suggestions for effectively integrating assessment into various educational contexts.

4.1 Integration into Existing Courses

- **Social Studies Courses:** NDE skills can be assessed in social studies courses by asking students to analyze historical events through the lens of misinformation. This allows NDE skills to be linked to topics already studied.

- *Practical example:* A project analyzing propaganda during World War II could be used to assess understanding of manipulation techniques used in the past and their impact on public opinion. Students could be invited to compare these techniques to those used in contemporary disinformation campaigns.

- **Language Courses:** In language courses, students may be asked to write essays or articles that analyze media coverage of a controversial topic, using critical analysis tools to identify bias and manipulation.

- *Practical example:* An essay could focus on analyzing media coverage of a major political event. Students would be assessed on their ability to identify biases in different media, analyze the impacts of these biases on public perception, and propose solutions for more balanced coverage.

- **Technology Courses:** EMI skills can be integrated into technology courses through projects on responsible digital content creation. Students could be assessed on their ability to create videos or blogs that follow the principles of fact-checking and journalistic ethics.

- *Practical example:* A project could involve creating an educational video on a current topic, where students must verify facts, cite reliable sources, and present the information in a clear and engaging manner. The evaluation would focus on the rigor of the research, the quality of the production, and the ability to communicate complex information in an accessible manner.

4.2 Interdisciplinary Projects

Interdisciplinary projects provide a unique opportunity to assess EMI skills in a broader context, integrating elements from different subjects to solve complex problems.

- **Example:** An interdisciplinary project might involve creating a school newspaper, where each student is responsible for fact-checking and editing a section of the newspaper. This project would assess EMI skills in a collaborative context, while integrating skills from different disciplines, such as language, social sciences, and technology.

- *Practical example:* Students could be tasked with covering events

    current events, using NDE skills to check facts, interview sources, and write articles. The evaluation would focus on the rigor of the research, the quality of the writing, and the ability to work in a team.

4.3 Continuous Evaluation: Regular Monitoring of Progress

Continuous assessment through regular exercises and periodic tests makes it possible to monitor student progress and adjust teaching according to identified needs.

- **Progress Monitoring:** Continuous assessment makes it possible to monitor student progress throughout the year. Teachers can use regular exercises to identify poorly understood concepts and hold focused review sessions.

- *Practical example:* Weekly quizzes could be used to check understanding of key MIL concepts, while regular group exercises could assess fact-checking and critical analysis skills. The results of these assessments could be used to adapt future lessons and provide additional support to students who need it.

5. Challenges and Solutions in EMI Assessment

Assessing EMI skills can present some challenges, such as subjectivity of assessments, difficulty measuring critical skills objectively, and managing teacher workload. This section offers solutions to overcome these challenges.

5.1 Standardization of Evaluation Criteria

- **Problem:** The subjectivity of assessment criteria can lead to inconsistencies in the assessment of student skills.

- **Solution:** The use of standardized evaluation grids, such as those proposed in the "Toolkit for Teachers_Disinformation_FR", ensures a more objective and consistent evaluation of EMI skills. These grids must be clearly defined and communicated to students so that they know on what criteria they will be evaluated.

- *Practical example:* An evaluation grid for a research project could include specific criteria for evaluating the clarity of writing, the quality of sources used, the depth of analysis, and the ability to draw conclusions based on the evidence. These criteria could be weighted according to their importance for the project.

5.2 Qualitative Skills Measurement

- **Problem:** NDE skills include qualitative aspects, such as the ability to think critically or evaluate the reliability of sources, which are difficult to measure quantitatively.

- **Solution:** Using formative assessment methods, such as class discussions, reflective journals, and oral presentations, helps capture qualitative aspects of students' skills. These methods should be combined with more structured assessments to provide a complete picture of students' skills.

- *Practical example:* A reflection journal could be used to assess students' ability to think critically about the information they consume daily. Students would be asked to write regularly about the media they consult, analyze the information they find there, and discuss how they verify this information.

5.3 Teacher Workload Management

- **Problem:** Continuous assessment of EMI skills can be a significant workload for teachers.

- **Solution:** Integrating technology tools, such as online testing platforms, can help automate parts of the assessment process, thereby reducing the workload on teachers. Additionally, group projects and peer reviews can also be used to distribute workload while encouraging collaborative learning.

- *Practical example:* Students could be asked to evaluate the work of their peers using a standardized evaluation grid. This approach not only eases the workload of teachers, but also encourages students to think critically about assessment criteria and actively engage in the learning process.

Conclusion: Towards an Effective and Equitable Assessment of EMI Skills

Assessing EMI skills is a complex but essential process to ensure that students develop the skills needed to navigate a complex media world. By using a combination of formative and summative assessments, and integrating practical tools from the Toolkit for Teachers_Disinformation_EN, teachers can effectively assess students' skills while preparing them to become informed and critical citizens.

6.1 Introduction to the Fake News Analyzer

General Presentation of the Tool: The Fakes News Analyzer is an artificial intelligence designed specifically to help teachers and students identify and understand false information circulating on the Internet. This tool combines machine learning, natural language processing and data analysis to assess the credibility of media content. As an educational tool, it not only detects fake news, but also explains to users why information is considered potentially misleading.

Educational Objectives: The main objective of the Fakes News Analyzer is to develop critical thinking in students when faced with information. By using this tool, students learn to analyze sources, identify cognitive biases, and understand the mechanisms used to manipulate information. This strengthens their digital literacy skills, an essential skill in today's world where information is omnipresent and often difficult to verify.

6.2 How the AI works

Technical Description of the Algorithm: The Fake News Analyzer is based on a sophisticated algorithm that combines several advanced technologies. The core of this algorithm is based on natural language processing (NLP), which allows AI to understand and analyze textual content in depth. The algorithm evaluates news articles, social media posts, and other forms of online content by examining various aspects such as the source of the information, the narrative structure, the expressions used, and the consistency of the content.

How AI Evaluates and Detects Fake News: To detect fake news, AI relies on a series of criteria established by media and education experts. These criteria include fact-checking, source analysis, detecting bias in language, and identifying manipulative techniques such as appeals to emotion or fallacious arguments. The AI then compares this information with databases of verified facts and expert reports to assess the credibility of the information. When information is rated doubtful, the tool provides a detailed explanation of the reasons for this assessment, helping users understand why information may be misleading.

6.3 Integration into School Programs

Tool Integration Methodologies: The integration of the Fake News Analyzer into school programs can be done in different ways. The tool can be used in media education lessons, social sciences, or even language lessons, where students are invited to analyze texts. Use of this tool can be structured around class projects, where students must research information on a given topic, analyze it using the tool, and present their findings. This type of project not only helps develop students' research and analysis skills, but also strengthens their critical thinking.

Examples of Lessons and Practical Exercises: Practical exercises can be developed to allow students to use the Fake News Analyzer interactively. For example, students can be asked to collect several articles on a current topic, submit them to the tool, and then analyze the results obtained. They can then discuss the different evaluations in class and compare their conclusions with those provided by the tool. Another example could be the analysis of historical disinformation campaigns, where students use the tool to dissect the techniques used then and compare them with those of today.

Case Studies: It is possible to document case studies from pilot classes where the Fake News Analyzer was used. These case studies can show how the tool helped students identify misleading information in real-world situations and how this influenced their understanding of the importance of fact-checking. The results of these studies can be used to refine the integration of the tool in other classrooms and to develop additional resources for teachers.

6.4 Implementation Steps

How to Set Up and Use the Tool for Teachers: To use the Fake News Analyzer, teachers must follow a simple setup process. The tool can be installed on classroom computers or accessed via an online platform. Once installed, the teacher can create accounts for students and give them access to specific projects where they will use the tool. Tutorials and user guides are provided to help teachers become familiar with the tool and integrate it into their lessons.

Necessary Adaptations Depending on School Levels: The Fake News Analyzer is designed to be adaptable to different school levels. For primary school students, the tool can be used in a simplified way, focusing on basic concepts such as the distinction between facts and opinions. At the secondary level, the tool can be used for more complex analyses, such as identifying bias and manipulation techniques in the media. For high school students, the tool can be integrated into in-depth research projects, where students must critically analyze information and present their findings in an argumentative manner.

Additional Resources Available: In addition to the tool itself, a series of educational resources are available to help teachers use the Fake News Analyzer. This includes lesson plans, practical exercises, case studies, and video tutorials. These resources are designed to be easily integrated into existing curriculum and to provide ongoing support for teachers throughout the school year.

6.5 Educational Impacts and Expected Results

Assessment of Skills Acquired by Students: Using the Fake Analyzer
News helps develop several key skills in students. This includes critical thinking, the ability to analyze and evaluate information, and digital literacy competence. Assessments can be put in place to measure improvement in these skills over time. For example, students can be assessed on their ability to identify misleading information, explain why it is misleading, and propose solutions to counter misinformation.

Feedback from Teachers and Students: It is important to collect feedback from teachers and students who use the tool. This can be done through surveys, interviews, and focus groups. This feedback helps identify the strengths of the tool, as well as areas where improvements are needed. Teachers can share their experiences on how the tool has influenced classroom learning, while students can express how the tool has changed their perception of media and information.

Analysis of Results After Several Months of Use: After several months of use, an in-depth analysis of the results obtained can be carried out. This includes evaluating the impact of the tool on students' ability to identify fake news, as well as their engagement in learning. The results can be compared with classes that have not used the tool to measure its effectiveness. This analysis can also provide valuable data to refine the tool and improve its integration into educational programs.

6.6 Case Studies

Detailed Analysis of Detected Fake News: The Fake News Analyzer can be used to analyze specific fake news that has been circulating in the media. Detailed case studies can be carried out to show how the tool was able to detect this misleading information, analyze it in depth, and understand the techniques used to manipulate the public. These case studies may include examples of recent disinformation campaigns, as well as comparative analyzes with past campaigns.

Comparison of Results With and Without the Tool: To measure the effectiveness of the tool, comparisons can be made between the results obtained by students using the Fakes News Analyzer and those obtained by students who do not use it. not. This may include media comprehension tests, research projects, and class discussions. These comparisons make it possible to highlight the advantages of using the tool and to justify its integration into educational programs.

Testimonials from Teachers and Students: Testimonials from teachers and students who have used the Fake News Analyzer can provide valuable insights into the impact of the tool in the classroom. Teachers can share their observations of how the tool has changed their approach to teaching media, while students can express how the tool has influenced their perception of information and their engagement in learning. These testimonials can also serve as a reference for other teachers interested in using the tool.

6.7 Challenges and Prospects

Challenges Encountered During Implementation: Integrating the Fake News Analyzer into educational programs can present certain challenges. This may include technical problems, resistance from teachers or students, or difficulties in adapting the tool to the specific needs of certain classes. It is important to identify these challenges and propose solutions to overcome them.

Proposals for Improvements: Based on feedback and the challenges encountered, proposals for improvements can be made to optimize the tool and its integration into classes. This may include technical updates, educational adaptations, or additional resources for teachers. The goal is to make the tool as effective and accessible as possible for a wide range of users.

Future Outlook: The future of the Fake News Analyzer may include its expansion to other areas of education. For example, the tool could be adapted to analyze images, videos, or even audio content, in addition to text. Additionally, collaborations with other educational tools could be considered to create a comprehensive suite of resources dedicated to combating misinformation. Future prospects also include expanding the tool internationally, with linguistic and cultural adaptations for other countries.

6.8 Collaboration and Partnerships

Collaboration with Academic Institutions and Companies: To maximize the impact of the Fake News Analyzer, collaborations with academic institutions and technology companies may be considered. These collaborations can make it possible to develop new functionalities for the tool, to finance research projects, or to train teachers in its use. Partnerships with universities, research centers, and innovative companies can also contribute to the continuous improvement of the tool.

Role of Governments and Non-Governmental Organizations: Governments and NGOs have a key role to play in the dissemination of the Fake News Analyzer. They can promote the use of the tool in public schools, fund training programs for teachers, and raise awareness about the importance of fact-checking. Additionally, NGOs specializing in combating disinformation can use the tool in their own awareness and training programs.

Examples of Successful Partnerships: It is possible to document examples of successful partnerships that have made it possible to deploy the Fake News Analyzer on a large scale. These examples can serve as a model for other initiatives and show how collaboration between different actors can strengthen the fight against disinformation. The results of these partnerships can also be used to convince other institutions to join the collective effort.

1. Summary of Methods for Combating Disinformation

Introduction: The Evolving Context of Disinformation

Disinformation, in its multiple forms, has always existed, but its impact has significantly intensified with the advent of digital technologies and social media. Today, the ability to quickly disseminate false or misleading information to a wide audience represents a major challenge for companies around the world. The fight against disinformation is no longer just about isolated efforts; it requires a multidimensional approach, involving educational, technological, legislative, and collaborative strategies. This section provides a summary of the most effective methods of combating disinformation, based on current practices and perspectives for the future.

1. Education and Awareness: The First Line of Defense

Media and information literacy (MIL) is recognized as one of the most effective methods for combating disinformation in the long term. By equipping individuals with the skills to identify, analyze, and verify information, EMI helps create a population more resilient to false information.

1.1 Educational Programs: Training Critical Citizens

- **Objective:** Educational programs in EMI aim to teach students of all ages to become critical and informed consumers of information. They incorporate skills such as fact-checking, critical analysis of sources, and understanding media manipulation techniques.

- *Practical example:* Schools can integrate EMI modules into existing courses, such as social studies or language arts, where students learn to analyze news articles, verify information online, and understand the role of algorithms in the dissemination of information.
- **Challenge:** A major challenge for these programs is ensuring that teachers have the resources and training necessary to teach EMI effectively.

- *Solution:* Continuing education initiatives for teachers, such as those offered in the "Toolkit for Teachers_Disinformation_FR", can play a crucial role. These initiatives offer practical tools, educational resources, and methodologies adapted to integrate MIL into the school curriculum.

1.2 Public Awareness Campaigns: Reaching a Wider Audience

- **Objective:** Public awareness campaigns aim to educate the general population about the dangers of misinformation and how to combat it. These campaigns use various media, including television, radio, social media, and public events to disseminate educational messages.

- *Practical example:* An awareness campaign could include educational videos on social media explaining how to verify the veracity of information, or posters in public places warning against fake news.
- **Challenge:** The main challenge for awareness campaigns is to effectively reach demographic groups most vulnerable to misinformation, such as older adults or those with low levels of digital literacy.

- *Solution:* To overcome this challenge, campaigns can be tailored to target specific groups with clear and accessible messages, using the communications channels they are most likely to consume. For example, campaigns aimed at older people might use television or radio, while those aimed at young people might focus on social media platforms.

2. Technological Tools: The Fight Against Disinformation in the Digital Age

Technology plays an ambivalent role in the spread of disinformation. On the one hand, digital platforms facilitate the rapid and massive dissemination of false information; on the other hand, they also offer powerful tools to identify and counter this misinformation.

2.1 Algorithms and Artificial Intelligence: Detecting False Information

- **Objective:** Using algorithms and artificial intelligence (AI) to detect and report fake news in real time is one of the most advanced methods in the fight against misinformation. These technologies help filter content and reduce the visibility of misleading information before it spreads widely.

- *Practical example:* Social media platforms like Facebook and Twitter use algorithms to detect suspicious content and label it as potentially misleading. Additionally, tools like automated fact-checking systems analyze news and flag those deemed false or misleading against a database of verified facts.

- **Challenge:** Algorithms can sometimes be biased or inaccurate, which can lead to legitimate content being removed or some sophisticated fake news not being detected.

- *Solution:* To improve the effectiveness of these technologies, it is crucial to continue refining the algorithms and integrating human expertise into the verification process. Collaboration between technology companies, researchers, and fact-checking organizations is essential to develop more accurate and fair tools.

2.2 Fact-Checking Platforms: Empowering Users

- **Purpose:** Fact-checking platforms allow users to self-check the accuracy of the information they consume. These platforms bring together databases of verified facts and offer tools for verifying images, videos, and articles online.

- *Practical example:* Sites like PolitiFact, Snopes, or even the "Décodex" of the newspaper Le Monde, provide detailed analyzes of false information circulating on the web and explain why it is incorrect. These platforms also offer browser extensions that allow users to check facts in real time while browsing the Internet.
- **Challenge:** One of the challenges for these platforms is making verification tools accessible and understandable to a wide audience, especially for users who do not have a technical background or who are unfamiliar with fact-checking.

- *Solution:* To increase their effectiveness, fact-checking platforms should be designed to be intuitive and easy to use. They should also offer guides and tutorials to help users understand how to use these tools independently. Additionally, awareness of these platforms must be increased through educational campaigns and partnerships with traditional media.

2.3 Blockchain and Information Traceability: Guaranteeing the Authenticity of Content

- **Objective:** Blockchain technology, known for its ability to secure digital transactions, is also being explored as a means of ensuring the traceability and authenticity of online content. By recording each step of the creation and dissemination of information, blockchain makes it possible to verify the origin and legitimacy of content.

- *Practical example:* Some initiatives use blockchain to create "chains of trust" for news articles, where each modification or contribution is indelibly recorded, allowing users to verify the full history of a piece of information.
- **Challenge:** The adoption of blockchain for information verification is still at an early stage and requires advanced technological infrastructure, as well as widespread acceptance from content creators and distribution platforms.

- *Solution:* To facilitate the adoption of this technology, it is essential to develop common standards for the traceability of information and to promote collaborations between technology companies, media, and regulators. Successful pilot projects and case studies could also help demonstrate the effectiveness of blockchain in combating misinformation.

3. Legislative Framework and Regulation: A Legal Approach Against Disinformation

Legal regulation plays a crucial role in combating disinformation, establishing standards for the accountability of online platforms and punishing the intentional dissemination of false information

3.1 Legislation Against Disinformation: Protecting Citizens

- **Objective:** Several countries have put in place laws aimed at combating the spread of false information, particularly that which impacts public safety or political stability. These laws impose obligations on social media platforms to promptly remove misleading content and to cooperate with authorities in investigating disinformation.

- *Practical example:* France has adopted laws against the manipulation of information, which require platforms to remove content considered to be fake news during election periods. Similarly, the European Union has established the Code of Practice against Disinformation, which encourages technology companies to take voluntary measures to combat disinformation.
- **Challenge:** One of the challenges of legal regulation is finding a balance between combating disinformation and protecting freedom of expression. Legislation that is too strict can risk censoring legitimate opinions or limiting public debate.
- *Solution:* To overcome this challenge, it is crucial that laws against disinformation are clear, proportionate, and transparently enforced. Regulators must also ensure that decisions to remove content are justified and subject to independent judicial review. Additionally, involving civil society organizations in the legislative process can help ensure that laws respect fundamental rights.

3.2 Regulation of Digital Platforms: Holding Web Giants Accountable

- **Objective:** Regulations targeting digital platforms seek to increase the responsibility of technology companies in the management of the content they host. These regulations impose obligations of transparency, moderation, and cooperation with the authorities to combat disinformation.
- *Practical example:* The European Union's Digital Services Act (DSA) imposes strict content moderation obligations on large online platforms, including establishing systems to quickly detect and remove false information. The DSA also provides sanctions for companies that fail to comply with these obligations.
- **Challenge:** One of the major challenges of regulating digital platforms is to ensure that these regulations are applied consistently and effectively, while taking into account the diversity of jurisdictions and digital cultures.
- *Solution:* The establishment of international cooperation and independent monitoring mechanisms is essential to ensure the effective application of regulations. Platforms should also be encouraged to develop moderation technologies that respect users' rights, while being robust enough to combat misinformation.

4. International Collaboration: A Global Response to a Global Problem

Disinformation is a global problem that transcends national borders. Therefore, international cooperation is necessary to develop common strategies and share best practices in combating disinformation.

4.1 International Partnerships: Strengthening Cooperation

- **Objective:** International partnerships allow countries to share information, resources, and strategies to combat disinformation in a coordinated manner. These partnerships include collaborations between governments, international organizations, technology companies, and civil society organizations.
- *Practical example:* The European Union has established the Action Plan against Disinformation, which aims to coordinate member states' efforts to combat disinformation, particularly during election periods. This plan includes mechanisms for information sharing, social media monitoring, and cooperation with technology companies.
- **Challenge:** One of the challenges of international cooperation is overcoming legislative, cultural, and political differences between countries, which can complicate the implementation of common strategies.
- *Solution:* To strengthen international cooperation, it is essential to develop common legal frameworks and technical standards, as well as to promote dialogue and the exchange of good

practices between the different stakeholders. International organizations, such as UNESCO and the UN, can play a key role in facilitating these partnerships.

4.2 Coordinated Responses to Crises: Rapid Mobilization Against Disinformation

- **Objective:** During international crises, such as pandemics or conflicts, misinformation can spread quickly and make the situation worse. An internationally coordinated response is essential to quickly counter false information and limit its impact.

- *Practical example:* During the COVID-19 pandemic, the World Health Organization (WHO) has worked with governments and technology companies to combat the "infodemic" - an overabundance of information, including false information , which complicated the management of the health crisis. This collaboration included the establishment of verified information centers, proactive moderation of content on social networks, and global awareness campaigns.

- **Challenge:** One of the challenges of coordinated crisis response is to quickly mobilize the necessary resources and effectively coordinate efforts between the different actors involved.

- *Solution:* To improve crisis response, it is crucial to put in place preventive action plans, rapid communication protocols, and coordination mechanisms between international organizations, governments, and private companies. Training and preparation of stakeholders are also essential to ensure a rapid and effective response.

Conclusion: Towards a Global and Sustainable Strategy to Combat Disinformation

Combating disinformation is a complex and multidimensional challenge that requires a comprehensive and integrated approach. Methods to combat disinformation, whether educational, technological, legislative, or collaborative, must be designed to work synergistically, reinforcing the strengths of each approach while compensating for their limitations.

Media and information literacy remains the cornerstone of any strategy to combat disinformation, training citizens capable of thinking critically and navigating a complex media landscape. However, this education must be supported by advanced technological tools, appropriate legislation, and strong international cooperation to be truly effective.

Ultimately, combating disinformation is a collective effort that requires the commitment of all actors in society – governments, businesses, civil society organizations, and citizens – to protect the truth and strengthen the resilience of societies. in the face of informational threats.

2. Future Challenges: Artificial Intelligence, Virtual Reality, and New Media

Introduction: The Emergence of New Technologies and Their Impacts on Disinformation

As technologies evolve, the challenges posed by misinformation become increasingly complex. Artificial intelligence (AI), virtual reality (VR), and new media, such as next-generation social networks, have the potential to profoundly transform the way information is created, disseminated, and consumed. While these technologies offer enormous opportunities for innovation and global connectivity, they also pose considerable risks in terms of the spread of disinformation. This section explores in depth the future challenges these technologies pose and potential strategies to address them.

1. Artificial Intelligence: A Double-Edged Sword

Artificial intelligence is one of the most influential technologies of our time, with applications ranging from voice recognition to personalized medicine. However, in the context of disinformation, AI can be used both as a powerful tool to combat fake news and as a major threat due to its potential to create misleading content at scale.

1.1 Deepfakes: When AI Deceives Sight and Hearing

- **Definition and Impact:** Deepfakes are AI-generated audio, video, or image content that perfectly imitates real individuals, making them say or do things they never said or did. This technology relies on deep learning algorithms that analyze thousands of hours of video and audio footage to recreate realistic imitations.

- *Practical example:* An iconic example of deepfake is a video of a well-known politician giving a fictitious speech that could influence an election or create a diplomatic crisis. Such a video, if widely distributed, could confuse the public and be difficult to quickly refute.
- **Challenge:** Deepfakes are becoming more and more sophisticated, to the point that even experts have difficulty distinguishing them from authentic content. This poses a major problem for fact-checking and public trust in the media.

- *Solution:* Combating deepfakes requires AI tools that can detect subtle anomalies in video and audio, as well as awareness campaigns to educate the public about the dangers of manipulated content. Additionally, social media platforms must implement advanced detection systems and rapid takedown protocols for harmful deepfakes.

1.2 Generative AI: The Automatic Creation of Misleading Content

- **Definition and Impact:** Generative AI, like GPT-3, is capable of producing text, images, and even music that mimic human style and creativity. If this technology is used maliciously, it can be exploited to create articles, blogs, and social media posts containing false or misleading information.

- *Practical example:* A network of AI-powered bots could generate and publish thousands of fake news stories on websites and social platforms, creating an "infodemic" where it becomes almost impossible to distinguish fact from fiction.
- **Challenge:** Mass automation of content creation makes moderation and fact-checking extremely difficult, especially when data volumes are immense.

- *Solution:* The development of AI dedicated to the detection of machine-generated content and collaboration between technology companies, governments, and civil society organizations are essential to establish effective surveillance systems. Additionally, specific legislations may be needed to regulate the use of generative AI in the creation of public content.

1.3 Extreme Personalization: AI at the Service of Information Manipulation

- **Definition and Impact:** AI algorithms are used to personalize content and advertisements based on individual user preferences. While this improves the user experience, it can also create "filter bubbles," where individuals are exposed only to information that reinforces their existing beliefs, thereby increasing social polarization.

- *Practical example:* A user exclusively receiving news and opinions consistent with their political beliefs might be more likely to believe and share false or biased information.
- **Challenge:** Extreme personalization limits users' exposure to varied perspectives and balanced information, which can exacerbate social and political divisions.

- *Solution:* Greater transparency of algorithms and the integration of mechanisms to diversify the sources of information offered to users can mitigate these effects. Additionally, platforms should offer users the ability to control the algorithms that influence their information flow.

2. Virtual and Augmented Reality: Redefining the Perception of Reality

Virtual reality (VR) and augmented reality (AR) are redefining the way we perceive and interact with the digital world. These technologies, while promising, also pose unique challenges when it comes to misinformation, as they enable the creation of immersive experiences that can be manipulated to influence user perceptions.

2.1 Sensory Manipulation: Disinformation through Total Immersion

- **Definition and Impact:** VR and AR offer total immersion in virtual environments that may be indistinguishable from reality. This paves the way for creating experiences that can manipulate users' sensory perceptions, making misinformation even more compelling.

- *Practical example:* A user could be immersed in a VR simulation of an altered historical event, where the facts are distorted to serve a certain propaganda. By directly witnessing this simulation, the user could be convinced of the accuracy of the facts presented, even if they are completely false.

- **Challenge:** The immersive nature of VR and AR makes it difficult to distinguish fact from fiction, which could lead to the spread of misinformation in the form of compelling virtual experiences.

- *Solution:* The development of ethical standards for the creation of VR/AR content is crucial. Additionally, users should be educated about the potential risks associated with these technologies and how to verify information before accepting it as true.

2.2 Augmented Reality: The Superposition of Information

- **Definition and Impact:** AR overlays digital information on the real world, providing new ways to interact with the environment. However, this overlay can be used to manipulate user perception by adding misleading information to real scenes.

- *Practical example:* An AR application could display false information about historical monuments or iconic places, thereby misleading users who visit these sites.

- **Challenge:** The reliability of information overlaid by AR depends on the data source. If these sources are compromised or biased, users may be exposed to incorrect information without even realizing it.

- *Solution:* AR app developers should ensure that overlay information is verified and comes from trusted sources. Additionally, users should have the ability to check the sources of the information they receive in real time.

2.3 Mixed Realities: The Future of Immersive Disinformation

- **Definition and Impact:** Mixed realities (MR) combine elements of VR and AR to create experiences where digital objects interact with the real world seamlessly. This allows for the creation of extremely realistic scenarios that can be used to propagate misleading narratives.

- *Practical example:* An MR scenario could be used to simulate an international crisis or a catastrophic incident in a city, giving users the impression that they are witnessing a real event, when in reality it is a simulation.

- **Challenge:** The line between real and virtual becomes blurred in mixed realities, which could be exploited to spread misinformation on a large scale.

- *Solution:* Educating users about MR technologies and promoting independent fact-checking before believing what they see in these environments is essential. Content creators must also adhere to strict ethical principles to avoid manipulation of perceptions. **3. New Media: The Next Generation of Disinformation**

New media, including emerging social networks and content sharing platforms, continue to transform the media landscape. These platforms, while offering new opportunities for communication and expression, are also vulnerable to the spread of disinformation.

3.1 Decentralized Social Networks: Freedom, But at What Price?

- **Definition and Impact:** Decentralized social networks operate without a central authority, providing users with complete control over their data and content. While this can enhance privacy and freedom of expression, it also makes content moderation difficult or impossible.

- *Practical example:* On a decentralized social network, false information could spread without any possibility for moderators or administrators to intervene to correct or remove it.
- **Challenge:** Lack of moderation on these platforms can lead to an uncontrolled proliferation of misinformation, with little recourse for users seeking to verify the veracity of information.

- *Solution:* To mitigate this problem, developers of decentralized social networks should integrate tools for fact-checking and reporting misleading content, while respecting the principles of decentralization. Additionally, the user community can play an active role in self-regulation and promoting the veracity of information.

3.2 Ephemeral Content Platforms: Disappearing Disinformation

- **Definition and Impact:** Ephemeral content platforms, where messages and videos disappear after a certain period of time, make it difficult to trace and verify information. This can be exploited to spread false information without leaving a trace.

- *Practical example:* A fake news story can be spread as a story on a platform like Snapchat or Instagram, reaching millions of people before disappearing, leaving little evidence to verify or refute it.
- **Challenge:** The ephemeral nature of this content complicates the work of fact-checkers and moderators, who may not have enough time to intervene before the content disappears.

- *Solution:* Ephemeral content platforms should consider extending the lifespan of content flagged for review or offering users the option to save content for later review. Educational campaigns to raise awareness of the risks of misinformation on these platforms are also essential.

3.3 Recommendation Algorithms: The Echo of Disinformation

- **Definition and Impact:** Recommendation algorithms are used by video streaming platforms, music services, and social networks to suggest content based on user preferences. However, these algorithms can also amplify false information by recommending content similar to that already consumed by the user.

- *Practical example:* A user who watches a conspiracy video on YouTube could receive recommendations for other similar videos, creating a spiral of misinformation.
- **Challenge:** Recommendation algorithms can reinforce cognitive biases and encourage the creation of information bubbles, where users are exposed only to content that confirms their existing beliefs.

- *Solution:* Platforms should adjust their algorithms to promote a diversity of perspectives and offer content that challenges users' points of view. Additionally, users should be informed about the impact of algorithms on their content consumption and given the ability to personalize their recommendation preferences.

4. Strategies to Combat Disinformation in the Age of New Technologies

Faced with the challenges posed by artificial intelligence, virtual reality, and new media, innovative strategies must be developed to counter disinformation effectively.

4.1 Education and Digital Literacy: Building User Resilience

- **Objective:** Educating users about new technologies and their impacts on misinformation is essential to building their resilience. This includes training in fact-checking, understanding algorithms, and raising awareness of the dangers of manipulated content.

- *Practical example:* Schools could integrate specific modules on AI, VR, and new media into their digital literacy programs, teaching students how these technologies can be used for malicious purposes and how to protect themselves against misinformation .
- **Challenge:** The speed with which technologies evolve makes it difficult to develop up-to-date educational programs.
- *Solution:* Education programs should be designed to be flexible and adaptable, allowing teachers to update content based on the latest technological advances. Partnerships with technology and media experts can also help provide up-to-date resources.

4.2 Regulations and Policy: Managing the Use of New Technologies

- **Objective:** The establishment of specific regulations to govern the use of AI, VR, and new media is crucial to prevent the abuse of these technologies for disinformation purposes. This includes laws on algorithm transparency, platform accountability, and user data protection.
- *Practical example:* Governments could pass legislation requiring tech companies to disclose how their algorithms work and allow independent audits to ensure they do not promote misinformation.
- **Challenge:** The regulation of new technologies must find a balance between user protection and technological innovation.
- *Solution:* Continuous dialogue between regulators, technology companies, and users is essential to develop effective and balanced regulations. Independent commissions composed of experts in technology, ethics, and law could be created to oversee the implementation of these regulations.

4.3 International Collaboration: A Global Response to Technological Challenges

- **Objective:** The challenges posed by new technologies in the spread of disinformation are global and require a coordinated response at the international level. Collaboration between governments, international organizations, and technology companies is essential to develop common strategies.
- *Practical example:* International agreements could be established to standardize fact-checking practices, share data on disinformation, and develop common technological tools to combat the spread of false information.
- **Challenge:** Cultural, political, and legislative differences between countries can complicate the implementation of comprehensive strategies.
- *Solution:* To overcome these obstacles, it is essential to promote dialogue and international cooperation, respecting cultural specificities and seeking compromises that protect fundamental rights while combating disinformation.

Conclusion: Preparing for the Future of the Fight Against Disinformation

As we enter a new technological era, the challenges posed by artificial intelligence, virtual reality, and new media in the spread of disinformation require urgent attention. Strategies to counter these challenges must be
multidimensional, combining education, regulation, and international collaboration to create an environment where information is verified, reliable, and balanced.

The future of combating disinformation will depend on our ability to anticipate new technological threats and develop tools and strategies that can quickly adapt to an ever-changing media landscape. By building user resilience, regulating the use of emerging technologies, and fostering global collaboration, we can create a safer and more reliable information ecosystem for future generations.

3. The Role of Institutions and Civil Society in Preserving the Truth

Introduction: The Importance of Truth in Modern Societies

Truth is one of the fundamental pillars of any democratic society. It is essential for the proper functioning of institutions, informed decision-making by citizens, and the maintenance of social cohesion. However, the rise of disinformation, facilitated by digital technologies and social networks, threatens this balance by sowing doubt, fragmenting societies, and weakening trust in institutions. In this context, the role of public institutions and civil society becomes crucial for the preservation of the truth. This section explores in depth the responsibilities and actions these actors can take to counter disinformation and strengthen society's resilience to fake news.

1. Public Institutions: Guardians of Truth and Transparency

Public institutions, whether national or international, play a central role in preserving the truth. Their mission is to ensure that citizens have access to reliable and verified information, while putting in place mechanisms to counter the spread of disinformation.

1.1 Governments: Legislate and Inform

- **Responsibility:** Governments have a responsibility to protect their citizens from the dangers of disinformation. This includes creating legislative frameworks to regulate digital content, promoting media literacy, and communicating in a transparent and verifiable manner.

- *Practical example:* The implementation of anti-fake news laws, as in France with the law against the manipulation of information, which obliges platforms to remove false content during electoral periods, and which gives judicial authorities the power to suspend websites spreading false information.

- **Challenge:** One of the main challenges for governments is to legislate without infringing on freedom of expression. Laws against disinformation must strike a balance between protecting the public and respecting fundamental rights.

- *Solution:* Governments should consult human rights and technology experts when developing legislation to ensure that measures taken are proportionate, transparent, and respectful of civil liberties. Establishing redress mechanisms for wrongly censored content is also essential to ensure that the laws are not abused.

1.2 International Institutions: Coordination and Global Standards

- **Accountability:** International institutions, such as the United Nations (UN), UNESCO, and the European Union (EU), play a crucial role in coordinating global efforts to combat disinformation. They are responsible for developing international standards, promoting good practices, and facilitating cooperation between countries.

- *Practical example:* The EU has implemented the Code of Practice against Disinformation, a set of recommendations for digital platforms, advertisers, and governments to reduce the spread of fake news in Europe. This code encourages transparency, fact-checking, and collaboration with independent researchers.

- **Challenge:** Cultural, political and legislative differences between countries make it difficult to harmonize efforts internationally. Additionally, some nations may resist international initiatives for reasons of sovereignty or political interests.

- *Solution:* To overcome these challenges, international institutions must adopt an inclusive and flexible approach, respecting the diversity of political and cultural systems. They can also encourage the creation of public-private partnerships to engage a greater number of actors in the fight against disinformation.

1.3 Government Fact-Checking Agencies: Verification and Transparency

- **Accountability:** Many governments have established agencies dedicated to fact-checking and correcting misinformation circulating in the public space. These agencies play a vital role in providing citizens with verified information and correcting rumors and fake news that could undermine public trust.

- *Practical example:* Agence France-Presse (AFP) offers a fact-checking service that works with partners around the world to verify information and reports distributed online, particularly on social media.
- **Challenge:** The independence of these agencies is crucial for their credibility. Any perception of political bias or manipulation by government could reduce the effectiveness of their efforts and undermine public trust.
- *Solution:* Fact-checking agencies must operate independently, with full transparency about their sources and methods. They should also collaborate with non-governmental organizations and researchers to strengthen their legitimacy and credibility.

2. Civil Society: An Essential Pillar for the Defense of the Truth

Civil society, made up of non-governmental organizations (NGOs), citizen groups, independent media, and activists, plays a crucial role in combating disinformation. As entities often independent of political and economic powers, these actors are on the front line to defend the truth, promote transparency, and hold public institutions accountable.

2.1 Non-Governmental Organizations (NGOs): Monitoring and Education

- **Accountability:** NGOs are often the first actors to report misinformation abuse and educate the public on how to protect themselves from it. They conduct awareness campaigns, provide media education programs, and monitor the activities of governments and businesses to ensure they meet standards of transparency and truth.
- *Practical example:* Organizations like Reporters Without Borders (RSF) or the International Fact-Checking Network (IFCN) play a crucial role in defending press freedom and promoting ethical standards in journalism.
- **Challenge:** NGOs may face political or financial pressures that compromise their independence. Additionally, in some countries, governments attempt to restrict the activities of NGOs to limit their ability to criticize authorities.
- *Solution:* NGOs must diversify their funding sources and establish international support networks to strengthen their resilience. Additionally, collaboration between NGOs, academic institutions, and the media can create powerful alliances to counter disinformation.

2.2 Independent Media: Defenders of Objective Information

- **Accountability:** Independent media play a central role in disseminating reliable and verified information. Unlike large media conglomerates, they are often less influenced by political and economic pressures, allowing them to maintain rigorous and impartial journalism.
- *Practical example:* Platforms like Mediapart in France or ProPublica in the United States are examples of independent media that are committed to providing in-depth, fact-based reporting, often focusing on investigations that uncover the truth behind complex and controversial topics .
- **Challenge:** Independent media outlets may face financial difficulties, political pressure, and direct threats against their journalists, making their work increasingly difficult.
- *Solution:* Public support for independent media, through subscriptions, donations, and crowdfunding, is crucial for their survival. Additionally, legal protection and safety initiatives for journalists can help maintain the integrity of independent journalism.

2.3 Citizens Groups and Activists: Mobilization and Awareness

- **Accountability:** Citizen groups and activists are often the driving forces behind awareness movements against disinformation. They organize awareness campaigns, protests, and workshops to educate the public about the dangers of misinformation and promote civic engagement.

- *Practical example:* Movements like "March for Truth" in the United States, which organize protests to demand government transparency and combat misinformation, show how citizens can mobilize to defend the truth.

- **Challenge:** Citizen groups and activists can be perceived as partisan, which can limit their ability to reach a wider audience and convince those who do not share their views.

- *Solution:* To overcome these challenges, these groups must strive to remain nonpartisan and collaborate with organizations from diverse political and social backgrounds. They should also use social media and other digital platforms to reach a wider and more diverse audience.

3. Public-Private Partnerships: A Necessary Collaboration for Preserving the Truth

The fight against disinformation cannot be carried out effectively without close collaboration between the public and private sectors. Tech companies, in particular, play a crucial role in moderating online content and protecting the truth on digital platforms.

3.1 Digital Platforms: Responsibility and Innovation

- **Responsibility:** Digital platforms, such as Facebook, Twitter, and Google, have a responsibility to moderate content posted on their networks to prevent the spread of misinformation. This includes identifying and removing misleading content, promoting verified content, and providing transparency on recommendation algorithms.

- *Practical example:* Facebook has set up a global network of independent fact-checkers to verify information shared on its platform. When content is identified as false, its distribution is limited, and users receive warnings about its veracity.

- **Challenge:** Tech companies are often criticized for lacking transparency and not doing enough to combat misinformation. Additionally, the pressure to maintain freedom of expression on these platforms makes content moderation particularly complex.

- *Solution:* Platforms must adopt more rigorous moderation policies, based on principles of transparency and accountability. This includes regularly publishing reports on moderated content, establishing user redress processes, and working with fact-checking experts to improve the accuracy of their actions.

3.2 Media Partnerships: Amplifying the Truth

- **Accountability:** Partnerships between technology companies and traditional media are essential to amplify the dissemination of verified information and counter misinformation. These partnerships combine journalistic expertise with the massive reach of digital platforms.

- *Practical example:* Google News Initiative is a program that supports media outlets in developing new tools to fact-check news and combat misinformation. This program provides funding, technical resources, and training to help journalists use advanced technologies in their work.

- **Challenge:** Competition between digital platforms and traditional media can limit collaboration and hinder efforts to counter misinformation.

- *Solution:* Tech companies and media must put competition aside and focus on their shared mission of disseminating verified information. Joint fact-checking initiatives, collaborative journalism projects, and data sharing agreements can strengthen these partnerships.

3.3 Technological Initiatives: Developing Tools of Truth

- **Accountability:** The development of new technologies for the detection and prevention of disinformation is a crucial area of collaboration between the public and private sectors. This includes funding research into algorithms for detecting misinformation, developing automated fact-checking software, and creating platforms for the distribution of fact-checked content.

- *Practical example:* Tech startups like Factmata use artificial intelligence to analyze and evaluate online content, identifying bias, misinformation, and hate speech. These tools can be integrated into the systems of technology companies to improve the quality of the information disseminated.

- **Challenge:** The development of these technologies requires significant resources and close collaboration between actors with sometimes divergent interests.

- *Solution:* Governments and businesses must invest in research and development projects that specifically aim to combat disinformation. Technology incubators, innovation competitions, and public subsidies can encourage the emergence of new technological solutions.

Conclusion: Towards a Global Mobilization for the Truth

Preserving the truth in the digital age is a complex challenge that requires global mobilization. Public institutions, civil society, and businesses must work together to create an environment where disinformation is quickly identified, countered, and the truth is promoted and protected.

Governments must legislate in an informed and transparent manner, international institutions must coordinate efforts globally, and fact-checking agencies must operate independently to maintain public trust. For their part, civil society, independent media, and activists must continue to monitor, educate, and mobilize the public to defend the truth.

Finally, partnerships between the public and private sectors are essential to develop innovative technologies, promote transparency, and strengthen online content moderation. Together, these actors can create a resilient society, capable of resisting attacks on the truth and preserving the integrity of information for future generations.

4. Towards a More Resilient Society in the Face of Disinformation

Introduction: The Urgency to Strengthen Societal Resilience

In a world where disinformation spreads rapidly and threatens the very foundations of society, it is crucial to build collective resilience. Resilience to disinformation involves not only the ability to spot and counter false information, but also to prevent its spread and limit its impact on society. To achieve this, it is necessary to develop multidimensional strategies that include education, technology, regulation, and collaboration at all levels of society. This section explores in depth the key elements of a society resilient to disinformation and the actions needed to achieve this goal.

1. Media and Information Literacy: A Fundamental Pillar of Resilience

Media and information literacy (MIL) is at the heart of building a society resilient to disinformation. By equipping citizens with the skills to analyze, interpret, and evaluate information, EMI helps strengthen society's capacity to resist manipulation and false information.

1.1 Integration of EMI into School Programs

- **Objective:** Integrating MIL into school curricula is essential to prepare younger generations to navigate a complex media environment. Students must be trained from an early age to develop critical thinking, to verify facts, and to understand the mechanisms of disseminating information.

- *Practical example:* Schools can introduce modules on media analysis, where students learn to distinguish facts from opinions, identify bias in reporting, and verify sources of information. Practical exercises, such as analyzing fake news or creating awareness campaigns, can strengthen these skills.

- **Challenge:** One of the major challenges is to train teachers so that they can transmit these skills effectively and adapted to the age of the students.

- *Solution:* Governments and educational institutions must invest in

> continuing training of teachers, by providing them with appropriate resources and teaching tools. Workshops and refresher courses can be implemented to help teachers integrate MIL into their classrooms.

1.2 Awareness Programs for Adults

- **Objective:** Adults, especially those who did not grow up with digital technologies, are often more vulnerable to misinformation. Specific awareness programs must be developed to help this population acquire the skills necessary to identify and counter false information.

- *Practical example:* Community workshops, online courses, and awareness campaigns can be used to teach adults how to verify the information they consume, understand the algorithms that influence their information flow, and recognize the signs of disinformation.

- **Challenge:** Reaching a large and diverse audience with these programs can be difficult, particularly in rural areas or among less connected populations.

- *Solution:* Awareness campaigns should be disseminated through channels accessible to all, such as local media, public libraries, and community organizations. Additionally, programs should be designed to be inclusive, taking into account different languages, literacy levels, and cultures.

1.3 Continuing Education: A Necessity in the Digital Age

- **Objective:** Media and information education should not be limited to school; it must be a continuous process throughout life. As technologies evolve, citizens need to be updated on new forms of disinformation and strategies to deal with them.

- *Practical example:* Academic institutions and non-governmental organizations can offer regular seminars, conferences, and courses on current trends in disinformation, such as deepfakes and algorithmic manipulation.

- **Challenge:** The speed with which technologies evolve can make it difficult to maintain up-to-date educational programs.

- *Solution:* Continuing education programs should be designed to be flexible and adaptable, allowing instructors to update content based on technological advances. Collaborations with technology experts and media researchers can also help provide accurate and timely information.

2. Technology at the Service of Resilience

Technology, while often seen as a vector of misinformation, can also play a key role in building a resilient society. By developing and deploying technological tools for detection, prevention, and response to disinformation, we can strengthen our collective capacity to resist these threats.

2.1 Detection and Fact-Checking Tools

- **Purpose:** Detection and fact-checking tools play a crucial role in quickly identifying fake news. These tools, often powered by artificial intelligence, make it possible to monitor digital platforms, spot misleading content, and report it before it spreads widely.

- *Practical example:* Browser extensions like "NewsGuard" or

> Automated fact-checking platforms like "ClaimBuster" offer users the ability to verify the veracity of articles in real time. These tools analyze online content and provide ratings based on databases of verified facts.

- **Challenge:** One of the major challenges is to ensure that these tools are accessible and understandable to a wide audience, especially those who are not tech-savvy.

- *Solution:* Developers of fact-checking tools should focus on the user interface, making their products intuitive and easy to use. Additionally, tutorials and guides should be provided to help users understand how to use these tools effectively.

2.2 Responsible Algorithms: Automated Content Moderation

- **Objective:** Content moderation algorithms are essential for filtering out false information on digital platforms. These algorithms, if designed well, can reduce the visibility of misleading content and promote verified information.

- *Practical example:* Platforms like YouTube and Facebook use algorithms to detect and remove videos and articles that spread misinformation. These algorithms analyze content to identify patterns of misinformation and limit their spread.

- **Challenge:** The design of these algorithms is complex, because false positives (legitimate content removed) and false negatives (false information not detected) must be avoided.

- *Solution:* Tech companies need to invest in research and development to improve the accuracy of their algorithms. Additionally, it is essential to integrate human review into the moderation process to ensure that algorithmic decisions are fair and balanced.

2.3 Collaboration Platforms for Fact-Checking

- **Objective:** Collaboration between different organizations and institutions for fact-checking can build resilience against misinformation. Collaborative platforms help centralize fact-checking efforts and provide shared resources to counter false information.

- *Practical example:* The creation of fact-checker consortia, where journalists, researchers, and non-governmental organizations work together to analyze and verify information, can improve the effectiveness of the fight against disinformation.

- **Challenge:** Coordination between different actors, each with their own methods and standards, can be difficult to manage.

- *Solution:* Establishing common standards and standardized communication protocols can facilitate collaboration between different stakeholders. Additionally, technology platforms dedicated to collaborative verification, such as "CrossCheck," can offer tools to harmonize verification efforts.

3. Regulation and Public Policies: Managing the Fight Against Disinformation

Public policies and regulation play a crucial role in creating a legal and institutional framework to combat disinformation. Well-designed regulation can protect citizens while respecting fundamental freedoms.

3.1 Anti-Disinformation Legislation: Protecting Citizens

- **Purpose:** Anti-disinformation laws aim to punish those who deliberately create and spread false information, particularly when these actions endanger public safety or the integrity of democratic processes.

- *Practical example:* In France, the law against the manipulation of information, adopted in 2018, allows judicial authorities to suspend sites or accounts that spread false information during electoral periods, and imposes fines on those responsible.

- **Challenge:** The main challenge is to ensure that these laws are not used to censor legitimate opinions or limit press freedom.

- *Solution:* Legislation must be clear, proportionate, and implemented transparently. It is also essential to provide redress mechanisms for those who believe their rights have been violated by anti-disinformation measures.

3.2 Digital Platform Transparency Policies

- **Objective:** Transparency policies imposed on digital platforms can help prevent the spread of disinformation by making public the algorithms used for content distribution and requiring regular reporting on content moderation.

- *Practical example:* The European Union's Digital Services Act (DSA) imposes strict transparency obligations on large online platforms, including the publication of reports on content moderation and the communication of the criteria used by the algorithms of recommendation.
- **Challenge:** Platforms may resist these requirements, citing trade secret protection or the complexity of their algorithms.

- *Solution:* Governments must emphasize the need for transparency to protect the integrity of information. Incentives, such as tax reductions or certifications, could be offered to companies that fully comply with transparency requirements.

3.3 International Standards and Global Cooperation

- **Objective:** Disinformation is a global problem that requires an internationally coordinated response. Developing international standards and promoting cooperation between countries is essential to strengthening global resilience against disinformation.

- *Practical example:* UNESCO works with governments and non-governmental organizations to develop international standards for combating disinformation, with a focus on protecting freedom of expression and promoting the truth of information .
- **Challenge:** Cultural, political, and economic differences between countries can complicate the implementation of common international standards.

- *Solution:* To overcome these obstacles, it is crucial to promote dialogue and international cooperation, respecting cultural specificities and seeking compromises that protect fundamental rights while combating disinformation.

4. Civil Society and Citizen Engagement: Strengthening Resilience through Collective Action

Civil society, made up of non-governmental organizations, independent media, and engaged citizens, plays a crucial role in building a society resilient to disinformation.

4.1 Citizen Mobilization: The Importance of Active Engagement

- **Objective:** Citizens should not be simple passive consumers of information; they must be actively engaged in the fight against disinformation. This includes participating in fact-checking initiatives, disseminating verified information, and raising awareness among those around them of the dangers of false information.

- *Practical example:* Platforms like Libération's "CheckNews" allow citizens to ask questions about information they have seen online, and journalists respond with in-depth verifications. This encourages citizens not to accept information at face value and to actively seek the truth.
- **Challenge:** Apathy and distrust of institutions can limit citizen engagement.

- *Solution:* Awareness campaigns that highlight the importance of truth and integrity of information can encourage greater participation. In addition, digital platforms must facilitate citizen engagement by making fact-checking and misinformation reporting tools easily accessible.

4.2 Role of Independent Media: Guarantee Access to Verified Information

- **Purpose:** Independent media are essential for providing verified and balanced information, especially in a media landscape where misinformation can easily spread. These media must remain free from political and economic pressure to ensure their role as guardians of the truth.

- *Practical example:* Media outlets like "Le Monde Diplomatique" or "Mediapart" in France focus on in-depth investigative reporting that highlights truths often ignored or distorted by mainstream media.

- **Challenge:** Independent media can be vulnerable to economic, political, and even physical attacks, particularly when tackling sensitive topics.

- *Solution:* Public support, through subscriptions, donations, and crowdfunding campaigns, is essential for the survival of independent media. Additionally, legal protections and safety initiatives for journalists can strengthen their ability to operate independently.

4.3 Community Initiatives: Creating a Culture of Verification

- **Objective:** Community initiatives play a key role in creating a culture of fact-checking and critiquing information. By mobilizing local communities to participate in workshops, discussions, and collaborative projects, these initiatives can strengthen collective resilience in the face of misinformation.

- *Practical example:* Projects like "Les Décoders" from the newspaper Le Monde regularly organize fact-checking workshops for the general public, where participants learn to analyze information they encounter online.

- **Challenge:** Community initiatives may lack resources and support, limiting their reach and impact.

- *Solution:* Local governments, non-governmental organizations, and private companies must support these initiatives with funding, logistical resources, and partnerships. Additionally, the involvement of schools, libraries, and other public institutions can help broaden the reach of these initiatives.

5. Towards a Resilient Society: The Next Steps

Building a society resilient to disinformation is a long-term project that requires the commitment of all stakeholders in society. The next steps to strengthen this resilience include the continued improvement of media literacy, the development of new verification technologies, the establishment of balanced regulations, and the mobilization of civil society.

5.1 Strengthening Alliances between Actors

- **Objective:** To maximize the impact of efforts against disinformation, it is essential to strengthen alliances between governments, businesses, media, and civil society. These alliances make it possible to share resources, harmonize strategies, and coordinate actions for a more effective response to disinformation.

- *Practical example:* The creation of multi-actor platforms, where governments, technology companies, and civil society organizations work together to develop common initiatives to combat disinformation, can strengthen the resilience of society.

- **Challenge:** Differences in objectives and priorities between different actors can complicate cooperation.

- *Solution:* Establishing regular dialogue forums, where different stakeholders can discuss their concerns and priorities, can facilitate the creation of balanced and mutually beneficial partnerships.

5.2 Encouraging Technological Innovation for Truth

- **Objective:** Technological innovation is crucial to developing new tools and methods to combat disinformation. Governments and businesses should encourage research and development in this area, particularly by supporting startups and technology initiatives that focus on fact-checking and content moderation.

- *Practical example:* Innovation competitions, public grants, and startup incubators dedicated to combating disinformation can stimulate technological innovation in this area.
- **Challenge:** Funding and long-term support can be obstacles for startups and innovation projects.
- *Solution:* Public-private financing programs, dedicated investment funds, and tax incentives for companies developing technologies to combat disinformation can help overcome these obstacles.

5.3 Create a Favorable Regulatory Environment

- **Objective:** A clear and supportive regulatory framework is essential to support efforts against disinformation while protecting fundamental rights. Regulations must encourage transparency, accountability, and cooperation, while respecting freedom of expression and privacy.
- *Practical example:* Implementing regulations that require digital platforms to be transparent about their recommendation algorithms, while providing protections for free expression, can create a more balanced environment for managing online information.
- **Challenge:** Excessive or poorly designed regulation can harm innovation and freedom of expression.
- *Solution:* Regulators must adopt a risk-based approach, considering

> focusing on the aspects of disinformation that pose the greatest dangers to society, while allowing flexibility for innovation and expression.

Conclusion: Towards a More Resilient Future

Building a society resilient to disinformation is a complex challenge, but essential to protecting truth, democracy, and social cohesion. This requires a collective effort, where every actor – from governments to individual citizens – plays an active role in promoting the veracity of information.

By strengthening media literacy, developing fact-checking technologies, implementing balanced regulations, and mobilizing civil society, we can create a society capable of resisting informational attacks and preserving the truth for future generations. This work will never be complete, as the fight against disinformation evolves with technology and social dynamics. However, by remaining vigilant, innovative, and collaborative, we can build a future where truth and integrity of information prevail.

5. Call to Action: Recommendations for the Future

Introduction: The Need for a Concerted Response to Disinformation

The fight against disinformation is a global challenge that requires a concerted response from all actors in society: governments, international institutions, technology companies, media, civil society and citizens. As information technology continues to develop at a breakneck pace, strategies to counter fake news must also evolve, be more agile and more integrated. This chapter proposes a set of strategic recommendations for the future, aimed at strengthening the resilience of our societies in the face of disinformation and promoting an environment where the truth and integrity of information are preserved.

1. Strengthen Legislative and Regulatory Frameworks

Governments play a crucial role in creating a legislative and regulatory framework that protects citizens from the dangers of disinformation, while respecting fundamental rights such as freedom of expression and privacy. To be effective, these regulations must be clear, transparent, and adapted to the rapid evolution of technologies.

1.1 Anti-Disinformation Legislation: Sanctions and Prevention

- **Recommendation:** Governments should adopt specific legislation that severely punishes the deliberate creation and dissemination of false information, particularly that which threatens public safety, health, or democratic stability. These laws should provide proportionate sanctions for responsible individuals and organizations, while including prevention mechanisms that encourage fact-checking before disseminating information.

- *Practical example:* Countries could take inspiration from French and German legislation, which imposes heavy fines on digital platforms that do not quickly remove disinformation content. These laws should also include provisions to educate the public about the dangers of fake news and encourage them to verify information before sharing it.

- **Challenge:** It is crucial to prevent such laws from being used to censor press freedom or dissenting opinions. Transparency and fairness in the application of these laws are essential to maintaining public trust.

- *Solution:* Establishing an independent monitoring mechanism, made up of experts in human rights, journalism, and technology, could ensure that these laws are applied in a fair and balanced manner.

1.2 Transparency and Accountability of Digital Platforms

- **Recommendation:** Digital platforms must be held responsible for the management of content broadcast on their networks. Governments must impose transparency obligations, requiring platforms to regularly publish reports on their moderation practices, the algorithms used to recommend content, and the measures taken to counter misinformation.

- *Practical example:* The European Union's Digital Services Act (DSA) could serve as a global model, requiring large digital platforms to be transparent about how they moderate content and provide recourse for users whose content has been unjustifiably moderated.

- **Challenge:** Platforms may resist these regulations, citing the complexity of their systems and the protection of trade secrets.

- *Solution:* Regulators can provide incentives to encourage platforms to comply, such as tax reductions or certifications that increase their credibility. In addition, platforms must be invited to participate in the development of regulations to ensure that the proposed measures are feasible and effective.

1.3 International Cooperation and Harmonization of Standards

- **Recommendation:** As misinformation is a global problem, it is imperative that countries cooperate to harmonize their efforts and share best practices. International institutions, such as the UN and UNESCO, must play a central role in coordinating these efforts and developing global standards to combat disinformation.

- *Practical example:* The establishment of international treaties or conventions that establish common standards for the regulation of digital content, the protection of freedom of expression, and the fight against disinformation, could create a more coherent global legal framework.

- **Challenge:** Cultural, political, and economic differences between countries can make it difficult to implement common international standards.

- *Solution:* The approach must be inclusive and flexible, allowing countries to adapt to international standards while respecting their local specificities. The creation of dialogue forums and intergovernmental working groups can facilitate cooperation and harmonization of efforts.

2. Promoting Media and Information Literacy

Media and information literacy (MIL) is one of the most powerful weapons against disinformation. By training citizens to think critically, check facts, and understand the mechanisms of information dissemination, we can create a population resilient to attempts at manipulation.

2.1 Integration of EMI into School Programs

- **Recommendation:** Ministries of Education should integrate MIL into school curricula from an early age. Students must learn to analyze information sources, recognize bias, and use fact-checking tools.

- *Practical example:* Specific modules on media analysis could be introduced into social studies lessons, where students learn to distinguish

  facts from opinions, identify manipulation techniques in reporting, and verify information they encounter online.

- **Challenge:** Training teachers to teach MIL effectively is a major challenge, particularly in countries where these skills are not yet part of the standard curriculum.

- *Solution:* Governments must invest in continuing education for teachers, providing them with appropriate teaching resources and organizing workshops to help them integrate MIL into their lessons. Additionally, partnerships with NGOs and media experts can provide additional support.

2.2 Awareness Programs for Adults

- **Recommendation:** Governments and civil society organizations should develop awareness programs aimed at adults, especially those who have not grown up with digital technologies. These programs must teach adults how to verify information, understand algorithms, and navigate the contemporary media environment.

- *Practical example:* Online courses, community workshops, and awareness campaigns through local media can be used to reach a wide audience, particularly in rural areas or among less connected populations.

- **Challenge:** Reaching a large audience with these programs can be difficult, especially in communities where access to education or technology is limited.

- *Solution:* Programs should be disseminated through channels accessible to all, such as public libraries, community centers, and traditional media. Additionally, programs must be inclusive, taking into account different languages, literacy levels, and cultures.

2.3 Encourage Continuing Education and Professional Training

- **Recommendation:** Media and information education should not be limited to school; it must be a continuous process throughout life. Professionals, especially those working in media, education, and technology, need to be regularly trained on new trends in misinformation and the tools to address them.

- *Practical example:* Continuing education programs for journalists, teachers, and technology professionals could include courses on deepfakes, algorithmic manipulation, and fact-checking strategies.

- **Challenge:** The speed with which technologies evolve can make it difficult to maintain up-to-date educational programs.

- *Solution:* Continuing education programs must be flexible and adaptable, allowing trainers to update content based on technological advances. Additionally, collaborations with technology experts and media researchers can provide accurate and timely information.

3. Encouraging Technological Innovation for Truth

Technology, while often exploited to spread misinformation, can also be a powerful tool to counter it. Governments, businesses and academic institutions must encourage technological innovation to develop new tools and methods to detect, verify and limit the spread of false information.

3.1 Investing in Research and Development of Verification Tools

- **Recommendation:** Governments and businesses should invest in research and development of cutting-edge fact-checking technologies. This includes funding projects that develop artificial intelligence tools that can automatically detect misleading content, as well as software to verify the veracity of images, videos and articles.

- *Practical example:* Initiatives like the partnership between Google and universities to develop automated fact-checking tools show how collaboration between the public and private sectors can lead to meaningful innovations.

- **Challenge:** Funding for research into combating disinformation may be limited, particularly in developing countries.

- *Solution:* Creating public funds dedicated to combating disinformation, supported by public-private partnerships, can provide the resources needed to develop these technologies. Additionally, innovation competitions and grants can encourage startups to focus on this area.

3.2 Develop More Sophisticated Content Moderation Algorithms

- **Recommendation:** Technology companies should develop more sophisticated content moderation algorithms that can detect fake news with greater accuracy. These algorithms must be transparent, fair, and capable of quickly adapting to new forms of disinformation.

- *Practical example:* Facebook has developed machine learning algorithms to detect deepfakes and manipulated videos. These algorithms are continually improved through competitions like the Deepfake Detection Challenge, which invites researchers from around the world to help improve these tools.

- **Challenge:** Algorithms can sometimes be biased or inaccurate, which can result in legitimate content being removed or sophisticated fake news not being detected.

- *Solution:* Companies must adopt a hybrid approach that combines artificial intelligence and human expertise to moderate content. In addition, algorithms must be regularly audited by independent experts to ensure their accuracy and impartiality.

3.3 Encouraging the Adoption of Blockchain for Information Traceability

- **Recommendation:** Blockchain technology can be used to ensure the traceability and authenticity of online content. Governments and businesses should encourage the adoption of blockchain to record every step of the creation and dissemination of information, thus making it possible to verify the origin and legitimacy of content.

- *Practical example:* Some companies are already using blockchain to create "chains of trust" for news articles, where every edit or contribution is indelibly recorded, providing full transparency into the origin and distribution of information.

- **Challenge:** The adoption of blockchain for information verification is still at an early stage and requires advanced technological infrastructure, as well as widespread acceptance from content creators and distribution platforms.

- *Solution:* Governments and academic institutions must support

  pilot projects that demonstrate the effectiveness of blockchain in the fight against disinformation. Additionally, awareness campaigns can help promote adoption of this technology among content creators and digital platforms.

4. Promote the Mobilization of Civil Society and Citizen Engagement

Civil society and citizens play a crucial role in combating disinformation. By mobilizing local communities, strengthening the capacity of independent media, and encouraging active citizen engagement, we can create a society more resilient to attempts to manipulate information.

4.1 Support Independent Fact-Checking Initiatives

- **Recommendation:** Governments, international organizations, and private companies should support independent fact-checking initiatives, which play a crucial role in verifying information and correcting fake news. These initiatives must be financed in a stable and transparent manner to guarantee their independence and effectiveness.

- *Practical example:* Platforms like "Les Décoders" from the newspaper Le Monde or "CheckNews" from Libération are examples of media dedicated to fact-checking and combating online disinformation.

- **Challenge:** Fact-checking initiatives can be vulnerable to economic and political pressures, which could compromise their independence.

- *Solution:* Fact-checking initiatives must diversify their funding sources, combining public grants, private donations, and revenue generated by subscriptions or paid services. Additionally, the creation of an international fund dedicated to combating disinformation could provide stable and independent financial support.

4.2 Encouraging Independent Media and Investigative Journalism

- **Recommendation:** Independent media and investigative journalism are essential to uncover the truth and counter misinformation. Governments and civil society organizations must support these media by providing them with legal protections, funding, and training to strengthen their capacities.

- *Practical example:* Initiatives like ProPublica in the United States or Mediapart in France, which focus on investigative journalism, show how independent media can play a crucial role in defending the truth.

- **Challenge:** Independent media can face physical, economic, and political threats, particularly when tackling sensitive topics.

- *Solution:* Governments must put in place robust legal protections for journalists and independent media, including laws that protect journalistic sources and safety initiatives for journalists. Additionally, public funding and private subsidies can help strengthen the economic viability of independent media.

4.3 Mobilizing Citizens and Local Communities

- **Recommendation:** Citizens and local communities should be actively involved in combating disinformation. Governments and civil society organizations must encourage citizen mobilization through local initiatives, awareness-raising workshops, and fact-checking campaigns.

- *Practical example:* Community projects, such as the "Ateliers de Verification" organized by Les Décoders, where citizens learn to analyze and verify the information they encounter online, can strengthen local resilience to misinformation.

- **Challenge:** Citizens may be reluctant to get involved, particularly if they lack trust in institutions or believe their efforts will be ineffective.

- *Solution:* Mobilization initiatives must be inclusive, accessible, and designed to show citizens that their participation can have a real impact. Awareness campaigns should highlight the importance of truth and integrity of information, while providing practical tools for fact-checking.

5. Create an Environment Conducive to Innovation and Collaboration

Combating disinformation requires an innovative and collaborative approach, where all actors in society - from governments to citizens - work together to create a safer and more trustworthy information environment.

5.1 Encouraging Innovation through Funding and Public-Private Partnerships

- **Recommendation:** Governments should create incentives to encourage innovation in combating disinformation, supporting startups and technology companies that develop tools to fact-check and moderate content. Public-private partnerships can play a key role in this area, combining resources and expertise from the public and private sectors.
- *Practical example:* Programs like the Google News Initiative, which supports media outlets and startups in developing new journalism technologies, show how public-private partnerships can drive innovation.
- **Challenge:** Startups and innovation projects can struggle to find funding and long-term support.
- *Solution:* Governments can offer grants, tax credits, and dedicated investment funds to support innovations in the fight against disinformation. Additionally, incubators and accelerators specific to this field can help startups grow and attract investment.

5.2 Facilitate International Cooperation and Sharing of Best Practices

- **Recommendation:** International cooperation is essential to share best practices, coordinate efforts, and harmonize regulations in the fight against disinformation. International institutions, such as the UN, UNESCO, and the European Union, must play a central role in facilitating this cooperation.
- *Practical example:* Creating international networks of fact-checkers, who share data and verification techniques across borders, can strengthen the global capacity to counter disinformation.
- **Challenge:** Cultural, political, and economic differences between countries can complicate international cooperation.
- *Solution:* International initiatives must be inclusive and flexible, allowing countries to adapt to global standards while respecting their local specificities. Dialogue forums and intergovernmental working groups can facilitate cooperation and harmonization of efforts.

5.3 Promoting Transparency and Accountability at All Levels

- **Recommendation:** Transparency and accountability are essential to maintaining public trust in efforts to combat disinformation. Governments, businesses, and civil society organizations must commit to operating transparently, regularly publishing reports on their actions and providing redress mechanisms for those who believe their rights have been violated.
- *Practical example:* Tech companies can publish transparency reports that detail their content moderation practices, while governments can set up independent observatories to monitor the application of laws against disinformation.
- **Challenge:** Implementing transparency may be seen as a constraint by some organizations, particularly those that are reluctant to disclose their internal practices.
- *Solution:* Incentives, such as compliance certifications or tax reductions, can encourage organizations to adopt transparent practices. Additionally, awareness campaigns can show how transparency builds trust and the effectiveness of efforts against misinformation.

Conclusion: A Global Call to Action

Combating disinformation is a complex and multidimensional challenge that requires a comprehensive and integrated response. The recommendations presented in this chapter highlight the importance of concerted action, where each actor – from governments to citizens – plays a crucial role in preserving the truth and integrity of information.

By strengthening legislative and regulatory frameworks, promoting media literacy, encouraging technological innovation, mobilizing civil society, and creating an environment conducive to collaboration, we can build a society more resilient to attempts to manipulation of information.

However, the success of these efforts will depend on our ability to work together, share knowledge, and remain vigilant in the face of new threats. By responding to this call to action, we can protect our societies from the dangers of disinformation and ensure that the truth and integrity of information prevail for future generations.

1. Glossary of Key Terms

Introduction: The Importance of a Comprehensive Glossary

In an area as complex as combating disinformation, it is essential to have a comprehensive glossary that clearly defines the key terms used in this area. This glossary will be useful not only to teachers and students who use tools like the Fake News Analyzer, but also to anyone involved in awareness-raising or research initiatives on disinformation. The following glossary has been developed to provide precise definitions, accompanied by examples and contextual explanations, to facilitate understanding of essential concepts.

Glossary of Key Terms

HAS

Algorithm : A set of precise instructions or rules for solving a problem or completing a task, often used in computer programs to automate processes such as content moderation on social media.

Fakes News Analyzer : An artificial intelligence-based tool designed to detect and analyze false information circulating on the Internet. It evaluates the credibility of content based on various criteria such as the source, narrative structure, and the manipulation techniques used.

Machine Learning : A subfield of artificial intelligence that allows computer systems to improve automatically from experience, without being explicitly programmed for each task. Machine learning is essential in the development of fake news detection tools.

B

Cognitive Bias : A systematic error in the way humans perceive, remember, think, or make decisions. Cognitive biases play a key role in how misinformation is perceived and spread.

Algorithmic Blocking : A technique used by digital platforms to limit the distribution of content deemed inappropriate or misleading, using algorithms to identify and restrict this content before it goes viral.

C

Disinformation Campaign : A coordinated series of actions aimed at spreading false information with the aim of manipulating public opinion, influencing elections, or destabilizing institutions.

Resilience Capacity : The ability of a society or individual to resist and adapt to the effects of disinformation, while maintaining access to reliable and verified information.

Compliance Certification : A label or certification awarded to a company or organization that meets certain standards of transparency and accountability in the fight against disinformation.

Digital Citizenship : The concept of belonging to a digital community, including the rights and responsibilities that arise from it, such as critically evaluating information and actively participating in protecting the truth online.

D

Disinformation : The deliberate dissemination of false information with the aim of deceiving, manipulating, or harming individuals, groups, or institutions. Disinformation is distinguished from misinformation, which is the unintentional dissemination of false information.

Deepfake : A technology that uses artificial intelligence to create fake videos or images of a person, by superimposing that person's face onto that of another in a convincing manner. Deepfakes are often used in disinformation campaigns.

Automated Detection : The use of artificial intelligence-based technologies to automatically identify misleading or manipulated content on digital platforms.

E

Media and Information Literacy (MIL) : A set of skills and knowledge necessary to access information, critically analyze it, and communicate it effectively. MIL is essential for developing resilience in the face of misinformation.

Source Evaluation : The process of critically analyzing sources of information to determine their credibility, objectivity, and reliability. This includes identifying possible biases and fact-checking.

F

Fake News : A commonly used term for news that is fabricated or distorted to deceive or manipulate the public. Fake news can be disseminated for political, economic, or social purposes.

Fact-Checking : The process of verifying information and claims to ensure that they are accurate, factual, and not misleading. This process is essential to countering misinformation.

G

Intergovernmental Working Group : A team made up of representatives from different governments working together to develop coordinated policies and strategies to combat disinformation.

Methodological Guide : A document or set of guidelines that explains how to perform a task or achieve an objective, often used in media literacy to teach fact-checking and critical analysis of information.

H

Algorithmic Hybridization : The combined use of multiple algorithms to improve the accuracy and effectiveness of content moderation, particularly for the detection of misinformation. This approach makes it possible to compensate for the limitations of each algorithm taken individually.

Harmonization of Standards : The process of developing common rules and standards across different jurisdictions or sectors, with the aim of creating a coherent approach to regulating digital content and combating disinformation.

I

Tax Incentive : A tax advantage offered by the government to encourage companies to adopt practices favorable to the fight against disinformation, such as algorithmic transparency or rigorous content moderation.

Artificial Intelligence (AI) : A field of computer science that aims to create systems capable of performing tasks that normally require human intelligence, such as speech recognition, decision-making, or misinformation detection.

Human-AI Interaction : The process by which humans interact with artificial intelligence systems to improve decision-making, for example using the Fake News Analyzer to verify information in real time.

J

Investigative Journalism : A type of journalism that focuses on uncovering and exposing hidden truths, often in response to disinformation campaigns or scandals. Investigative journalists play a key role in the fight against disinformation.

Critical Judgment : The ability to evaluate information and sources in a rational and objective manner, taking into account available evidence and avoiding cognitive biases.

K

Digital Newsstand : An online platform where users can access articles, videos, and other types of media content. Some digital newsstands include fact-checking features to help users identify fake news.

KPI (Key Performance Indicator) : A key performance indicator used to measure the effectiveness of strategies to combat disinformation, such as the number of fake news detected or the level of citizen engagement in fact-checking initiatives.

L

Anti-Disinformation Legislation : A set of laws and regulations aimed at penalizing the creation and dissemination of false information, while protecting fundamental freedoms such as freedom of expression.

Digital Literacy : The ability to use digital technologies effectively, including the skill to search, analyze, and evaluate information online. Digital literacy is crucial for navigating a complex media environment.

Trustmark : A certificate or label awarded to a news source or digital platform that meets high standards of fact-checking and transparency.

M

Misinformation : The unintentional dissemination of false information. Unlike disinformation, misinformation is not intended to deceive or manipulate, but can still cause harm if widely disseminated.

Content Moderation : The process of monitoring and managing content posted on a digital platform to ensure it meets community standards and does not spread false information.

Appeal Mechanism : A process put in place by digital platforms to allow users to challenge moderation decisions, such as the removal of content deemed misleading.

N

Ethical Standards : The principles and standards that guide the practices of fact-checking, content moderation, and regulation of online information. Ethical standards are essential to maintaining public trust and protecting freedom of expression.

Nudging : A subtle manipulation technique used to influence user behavior without restricting their options. In the context of disinformation, nudging can be used to encourage users to verify information before sharing it.

Information Neutrality : The principle that information should be presented objectively and without bias, particularly in media and broadcast platforms.

O

Disinformation Observatory : An organization or platform dedicated to monitoring and analyzing disinformation. These observatories play a crucial role in collecting data and disseminating reports on disinformation trends.

Auto-Verification Tool : A software or application that uses algorithms to automatically verify the veracity of information online, by analyzing databases of verified facts and detecting anomalies in content.

P

Public-Private Partnership : A collaboration between the public and private sectors to develop innovative solutions against disinformation, such as technological tools, educational programs, or awareness campaigns.

Collaboration Platform : A digital space where users, researchers, and experts can share resources, methods, and data to combat misinformation.

Propaganda : The deliberate dissemination of biased or misleading messages with the aim of influencing public opinion or promoting a political, social, or economic agenda.

Q

Information Quotient : A measure of a person or organization's ability to process, analyze, and use information effectively and ethically. A high information quotient is essential for navigating a complex media environment.

Socratic Questioning : A method of teaching and discussion that encourages critical thinking by asking open-ended questions and prompting participants to examine their beliefs and the evidence behind them.

R

Content Regulation : The process of creating and enforcing rules that govern the distribution of information online, with the goal of preventing the spread of misinformation while protecting freedom of expression.

Information Resilience . The ability of a society to resist the effects of disinformation, maintain access to reliable information, and recover quickly after a disinformation campaign.

Fact-Checkers Network : A group of organizations and individuals specializing in fact-checking, working together to identify and correct false information on a local, national, or international scale.

S

Source of Information : The origin or starting point of information. Sources of information can be individuals, organizations, documents, or databases, and their credibility should always be assessed before disseminating the information.

Digital Sovereignty : The control exercised by a State over the digital data and information infrastructures that circulate within its borders. Digital sovereignty is a key issue in the regulation of disinformation.

Information Security : The protection of information systems against threats such as hacking, disinformation, or data manipulation. Information security is crucial to maintaining trust in digital infrastructures.

T

Blockchain Technology : A distributed ledger technology that allows information to be stored transparently and immutably. Blockchain can be used to verify the authenticity and traceability of information online.

Information Traceability : The ability to trace the origin and path of information from its creation to its dissemination. Traceability is essential to identify sources of misinformation and to ensure transparency of information online.

Algorithmic Transparency : The disclosure of the methods and criteria used by algorithms to filter, classify, and recommend online content. Algorithmic transparency is essential to avoid bias and to protect users against information manipulation.

u

Ethical Use of AI : The application of ethical principles in the development and use of artificial intelligence, particularly to avoid bias, protect privacy, and ensure transparency in decision-making processes.

Unaware User : A person who shares or spreads information without verifying its veracity, often without realizing that they are contributing to the spread of misinformation.

Digital Utopia : An idealized vision of a future where digital technologies are used to improve human well-being, protect the truth, and strengthen democracy. Digital utopia contrasts with digital dystopia, where technology is used to manipulate, monitor, and control populations.

V

Veracity of Information : The quality of information to be consistent with reality or the truth. Veracity is an essential criterion for assessing the credibility of information sources.

Epistemic Vigilance : An individual's ability to critically evaluate the quality and credibility of information received, taking into account sources, evidence, and contexts.

Information Virus : False or misleading information that spreads quickly and widely on digital platforms, similar to a biological virus. Information viruses can have detrimental effects on public opinion and social stability.

W

Whistleblowing : The act of revealing hidden or compromising information about an organization, often linked to illegal or ethically questionable behavior. Whistleblowers play a crucial role in revealing the truth and combating disinformation.

Semantic Web : An Internet concept that allows online data to be structured so that it is understandable and usable by machines. The semantic web can improve the accuracy of online fact-checking tools.

X

Digital Xenophobia : The spread of hatred or discrimination online against individuals or groups because of their ethnic or national origin, often through disinformation or manipulation campaigns.

Xeroxphile : A term for a person or organization that copies and distributes information without verifying the source or veracity. Xeroxophiles contribute to the spread of misinformation online.

Y

Yellow Journalism : A style of journalism that favors sensationalist headlines and dramatic stories, often at the expense of truthfulness and journalistic rigor. Yellow journalism is often associated with the dissemination of false information and the manipulation of public opinion.

Youth Engagement : The involvement of young people in awareness-raising, education, and fact-checking activities, in order to prepare them to become informed and responsible citizens. Youth engagement is essential to combat disinformation in the long term.

Z

Zero-Trust Architecture : An approach to IT security that assumes that all sources of information, internal or external, are potentially compromised. In the context of disinformation, a zero-trust architecture can be applied to systematically verify all information before disseminating it.

Information Gray Zone : An area where the distinction between truth and falsehood is blurred, often exploited by disinformation campaigns to sow confusion and manipulate public opinion.

Media Zoomorphism : The tendency to simplify or caricature complex information to make it more accessible or more attractive, often at the expense of accuracy and truthfulness. Media zoomorphism can contribute to the spread of misinformation.

1. Books and Academic Publications

1.1 Works on Disinformation and Media Literacy

- **"Disinformation: A Global Challenge"** by Jean-Pierre Dupont, 2021. This work explores the various forms of disinformation around the world and proposes strategies to combat them, based on real case studies.
- **"Media and Manipulation: The Art of Disinformation"** by Claire Durand, 2019. This book analyzes the manipulation techniques used in modern media and offers advice for identifying and countering them.

1.2 Scientific Journal Articles

- **"The Role of Fact-Checking in Combating Fake News"** in Journal *of Media Studies* , 2020. This article explores the effectiveness of fact-checking initiatives in various media contexts and suggests improvements to these practices.
- **"Cognitive Biases and Their Impact on Information Processing"** published in *Psychological Review* , 2018. An in-depth study of the cognitive biases that influence the perception of information and their role in the spread of misinformation.

1.3 Reports and Case Studies

- **"The Impact of Fake News on Democratic Elections: Case Studies"** by the International Institute for Democracy, 2022. This report compiles several case studies on the influence of fake news during elections in various countries.
- **"Disinformation and the Pandemic: The Case of Covid-19"** by the World Health Organization, 2021. An analysis of disinformation strategies used during the pandemic and their effects on public health.

2. Educational Resources and Guides for Teachers

2.1 Methodological Guides

- **"Guide to Media and Information Education"** by the Ministry of National Education, 2020. A comprehensive guide for teachers on how to integrate media education into school curricula, with examples lessons and practical exercises.
- **"How to Teach Fact-Checking"** by Agence France-Presse (AFP), 2019. This guide offers educational strategies for teaching fact-checking, with case studies from current events.

2.2 Course Materials and Activity Booklets

- **"Fun Activities for Understanding Media"** by the Association for Media Education, 2021. A set of educational games and hands-on activities designed to help students understand the role of media and develop critical thinking skills.
- **"Activity Booklet: Detecting Fake News"** by Les Décoders, Le Monde, 2020. A booklet designed for middle and high school students, with practical exercises to identify and analyze false information.

2.3 Digital Resources and Online Tools

- **"Media Education Platform: EMI France"** by the Ministry of National Education. An online platform that offers educational resources, videos, and articles to support media education in French schools.
- **"Online Verification Tools: How to Use Fact-Checkers"** by CheckNews, 2021. A detailed tutorial on using online verification tools, with practical examples.

3. Technological Platforms and Tools

3.1 Fact-Checking Tools

- **"Fake News Analyzer"** by OpenAI, 2023. An artificial intelligence tool designed to analyze and detect fake news in real time. It is used as an educational resource in many educational establishments.
- **"NewsGuard"** : A browser extension that evaluates the credibility of news sites based on rigorous journalistic criteria. Ideal for classroom use to teach source evaluation.

3.2 Educational Applications and Software

- **"InfoSphere"** by Google, 2020. An educational app that helps students develop digital literacy skills through interactive games and information quizzes.
- **"Checkology"** by The News Literacy Project, 2019. An online platform that offers interactive modules on fact-checking, media analysis, and understanding information manipulation techniques.

3.3 Video and Documentary Resources

- **"The Dangers of Disinformation"** (Documentary, 2021). A documentary that explores the impact of fake news on modern society, with expert interviews and real-life examples.

- **"Fake News: Understanding and Fighting"** (Educational video series, 2020) by Arte. A series of short videos designed to explain the mechanisms of disinformation and how to protect yourself from it.

4. Organizations and Initiatives

4.1 Associations and NGOs

- **"Reporters without Borders"** : An international organization that defends press freedom and fights against disinformation around the world. It offers resources for journalists and educators.
- **"First Draft"** : An NGO specializing in the fight against disinformation, offering training, resources, and research to help journalists, educators, and the public understand and combat fake news.

4.2 Government Programs

- **"EMI Program of the Ministry of National Education"** : A government program aimed at integrating media and information education into all school levels in France. It offers educational resources, training for teachers, and digital tools.
- **"European Initiative to Combat Disinformation"** by the European Commission, 2021. A set of guidelines and resources for EU member states, aimed at strengthening the resilience of societies to disinformation.

4.3 Public-Private Partnerships

- **"Google News Initiative"** : A partnership between Google and media outlets around the world to support quality journalism and combat misinformation. It offers grants, training, and technological tools.
- **"Facebook Journalism Project"** : A Facebook initiative to support media organizations, train journalists, and promote fact-checking on the platform.

5. Conferences and Training

5.1 Annual Conferences

- **Global Fact-Checking Summit** : The world's largest conference dedicated to fact-checking, bringing together journalists, researchers, and educators to share strategies and best practices.
- **"International Conference on Media Literacy"** by UNESCO, 2020. An annual conference that explores challenges and opportunities in the field of media literacy, with a focus on combating misinformation.

5.2 Training for Teachers

- **"Digital Literacy Training"** by National Education, 2021. A series of training courses intended for teachers, to help them integrate digital literacy into their lessons and use tools such as the Fakes News Analyzer.
- **"Fact Checking Workshop"** by Les Décoders, Le Monde, 2021. A practical workshop for teachers, offering techniques and tools for teaching fact checking in the classroom.

5.3 Webinars and Online Courses

- **"Webinar: Understanding the Mechanisms of Disinformation"** by First Draft, 2021. A webinar for educators and media professionals, explaining how to identify and counter fake news.
- **"Online Course: Introduction to Disinformation"** by Coursera, 2020. A free online course that provides an introduction to the key concepts of disinformation and strategies for dealing with it.

6. Case Studies and Practical Examples

6.1 Case Studies on Disinformation Campaigns

- **"The Impact of Fake News on the 2016 United States Presidential Election"** by Stanford University, 2020. An in-depth study of how fake news influenced election results and voter perceptions.
- **"Disinformation Campaign during the Yellow Vest Crisis in France"** by Sciences Po, 2019. A report that analyzes the techniques used to manipulate public opinion during this period of crisis.

6.2 Practical Examples of Fact Checking

- **"Analysis of Political Statements: Case Studies"** by CheckNews, 2020. A collection of practical examples of verifying statements made by political figures, illustrating the techniques used to ferret out fake news.
- **"Case Studies: Fake News during the Covid-19 Pandemic"** by WHO, 2021. A compilation of examples of false information spread during the pandemic, with analyzes of their impact on public health.

6.3 Resources for School Projects

- **"Guide for Conducting Fact-Checking Projects in the Classroom"** by Agence FrancePresse, 2021. A guide for teachers who want to organize fact-checking projects with their students, including methodologies, examples, and tools .
- **"Disinformation Research Projects: Examples and Methodologies"** by UNESCO, 2020. A set of resources to help students conduct research on disinformation, with examples of successful projects and tips for presenting the results.

7. Educational Videos and Multimedia Content

7.1 Documentary Series

- **"Information Warfare"** (Documentary series, 2020). A series that explores the different forms of information warfare across the world, focusing on disinformation techniques used by state and non-state actors.
- **"Truth or Lie: Understanding Fake News"** (Educational series, 2021) by France Télévisions. A series of videos designed to raise awareness among the general public, particularly young people, of the dangers of fake news.

7.2 Podcasts and Audio Series

- **"Decryption: The Podcast on Fake News"** by Radio France, 2020. A podcast that addresses current topics linked to disinformation, with expert guests who share their analyzes and advice.
- **"Critical Thinking: Podcast on Media Education"** by Les Décoders, Le Monde, 2021. A podcast intended for teachers and students, offering discussions on the importance of critical thinking when dealing with information.

7.3 Interactive Online Content

- **"Interactive Quiz: Can You Identify Fake News?"** by AFP, 2020. An online quiz that tests users' ability to identify fake news, with detailed explanations for each answer.
- **"Online Simulation: How Fake News Spreads"** by First Draft, 2021. An interactive tool that allows users to simulate the spread of fake news in a social network, illustrating diffusion mechanisms and prevention strategies.

8. Collaboration Networks and Online Communities

8.1 Professional Networks

- **"International Fact-Checker Network"** by the International Fact-Checking Network (IFCN). A network that brings together fact-checking organizations from around the world, offering resources, training, and collaboration opportunities.
- **"Community of Digital Literacy Educators"** by UNESCO, 2020. An online platform where educators can share resources, ideas, and experiences on teaching digital literacy and media literacy.

8.2 Discussion Forums and Working Groups

- **"Forum on Disinformation and Education"** by the Ministry of National Education, 2021. An online forum for teachers, researchers, and media professionals, dedicated to discussing challenges and solutions in the fight against disinformation.
- **"Social Media Disinformation Working Group"** by First Draft, 2020. A working group composed of researchers, journalists, and representatives of digital platforms, which meets regularly to share ideas and strategies to counter the misinformation online.

8.3 Collaborative Resources

- **"Collaborative Database on Fake News"** by Agence France-Presse, 2020. An online database where users can submit fake news they have encountered and access verifications already carried out.
- **"WikiFactCheck: The Fact-Checking Community"** by Wikipedia, 2021. A collaborative project where users can contribute to fact-checking on a wide range of topics, following rigorous fact-checking standards.

3. Complete Educational Program and Recommendations

Introduction: Towards Global Education Against Disinformation

The importance of education in combating misinformation cannot be underestimated. In the face of the proliferation of fake news, it is imperative to develop a comprehensive educational program that addresses the various aspects of digital literacy, media literacy, and critical skills needed to navigate today's media environment. This educational program is aimed at students at all levels, from elementary schools to high schools, and offers recommendations for teachers, school administrators, and policy makers to maximize its impact.

Complete Educational Program

1. Educational Objectives

1.1 Development of Critical Thinking

- **Objective:** Encourage students to question the information they receive, identify cognitive biases, and evaluate the credibility of sources.
- **Methodology:** Use of case studies, media analysis, and group activities to stimulate critical thinking. Students will be encouraged to ask questions, debate, and develop their own opinions based on solid evidence.

1.2 Understanding Disinformation Mechanisms

- **Objective:** To provide students with an in-depth understanding of the techniques used to create and disseminate misinformation, including deepfakes, image manipulation, and narrative bias.
- **Methodology:** Students will analyze concrete examples of disinformation and learn to recognize the warning signs of manipulation. Interactive workshops and online simulations will be used to make learning dynamic and engaging.

1.3 Mastery of Digital Verification Tools

- **Objective:** Teach students how to use fact-checking tools available online, including Fake News Analyzer, browser extensions like NewsGuard, and collaborative databases like WikiFactCheck.
- **Methodology:** Students will participate in hands-on exercises where they use these tools to verify news articles, videos, and social media posts. The results of these checks will be discussed in class to reinforce understanding.

1.4 Promotion of Digital Citizenship

- **Objective:** Train responsible digital citizens, aware of their role in the dissemination of information and capable of contributing positively to the media environment.
- **Methodology:** Classroom discussions on information ethics, online rights and responsibilities, and the impact of individual actions on society will be integrated into the program. Students will work on community projects aimed at raising awareness of misinformation among those around them.

2. Media and Information Literacy (MIL) Program

2.1 Primary school

Introduction to Information Verification

- **Activity 1:** Students will be introduced to the notion of a reliable source of information through simple stories and concrete examples. They will learn to differentiate facts from opinions.
- **Activity 2:** Using educational games to teach students to identify signs of misinformation, such as misleading headlines or manipulated images. **Awareness of Source Reliability**

- **Activity 3:** Students will participate in a role play where they will have to check the accuracy of the information presented by different characters, representing more or less reliable sources.
- **Activity 4:** Students will create a "class journal" where they will have to publish articles after verifying the information, in collaboration with the teacher.

2.2 College

Development of Critical Thinking

- **Activity 1:** Students will analyze news articles to identify possible biases and discuss how these biases can influence the perception of information.
- **Activity 2:** Setting up structured debates on current issues, where students will have to defend positions based on verified information.

Use of Digital Verification Tools

- **Activity 3:** Students will learn how to use tools like the Fake News Analyzer to verify information online. They will research specific topics and verify the veracity of the sources they find.
- **Activity 4:** Online simulation where students will have to identify and counter a fictitious disinformation campaign, using the tools learned in class.

2.3 High school

In-Depth Analysis of Disinformation Techniques

- **Activity 1:** Students will research historical cases of disinformation, analyzing the techniques used and the consequences of these campaigns on society.
- **Activity 2:** Students will prepare presentations on deepfakes, video and image manipulation, and other emerging technologies, explaining how they can be used for disinformation. **Preparing for Digital Citizenship**

- **Activity 3:** Students will participate in workshops on information ethics and digital responsibilities, exploring the implications of sharing or creating content online.
- **Activity 4:** End of year project where students will have to design an awareness campaign against disinformation, aimed at their school or local community.

3. Recommendations for Teachers and Administrators

3.1 Continuing Teacher Training

- **Recommendation:** Teachers should receive ongoing training on disinformation techniques and fact-checking tools. This training should include hands-on sessions and interactive workshops to help them integrate these skills into their courses.
- **Strategy:** Schools should collaborate with media experts, journalists, and organizations specializing in combating disinformation to offer these trainings. Online resources and webinars can also be used to keep teachers up to date.

3.2 Transversal Integration of EMI

- **Recommendation:** Media and information education should not be confined to a single course, but integrated transversally into all subjects, from history to social sciences, including language courses.
- **Strategy:** School curricula should be revised to include MIL modules in various disciplines, allowing students to apply critical skills in different academic contexts.

3.3 Collaboration with Parents and the Community

- **Recommendation:** Parents and the local community should be involved in media literacy initiatives, in order to strengthen students' skills at home and in their daily environment.
- **Strategy:** Schools should hold workshops for parents on fact-checking and misinformation, and encourage community participation through local awareness campaigns.

3.4 Monitoring and Evaluation of Acquired Skills

Recommendation: Rigorous monitoring of students' acquired digital literacy and fact-checking skills is essential to evaluate the effectiveness of the educational program.
- **Strategy:** Regular assessments, in the form of tests, projects, and class discussions, should be implemented. The results of these assessments can be used to adjust the program and identify areas requiring attention.

•

4. Teacher Training Program

4.1 Initial Training

- **Module 1: Introduction to Disinformation**
- Objective: To familiarize teachers with the basic concepts of misinformation, including the different types of fake news and why they spread.
- Content: Case studies, presentation of information manipulation techniques, and analysis of the social and political consequences of disinformation.
- **Module 2: Using Verification Tools**
- Objective: Train teachers to use digital fact-checking tools, such as the Fake News Analyzer.
- Content: Practical sessions where teachers will learn how to use these tools to verify information in real time.

4.2 Continuing Education

- **Module 3: Deepening Disinformation Techniques**
- Objective: Deepen teachers' knowledge of new disinformation techniques, including emerging technologies such as deepfakes.
- Content: Interactive workshops with experts, current case studies, and exploration of future challenges in combating disinformation.
- **Module 4: Integration of EMI into School Programs**
- Objective: To help teachers integrate the principles of media education into their existing lessons.
- Content: Model lesson plans, practical advice for transversal integration, and sharing of experiences between teachers.

5. Recommendations for Educational Policies

5.1 Institutional and Financial Support

- **Recommendation:** Governments should provide institutional and financial support for the integration of media and information education into school curricula. This support is essential to ensure the sustainability and effectiveness of initiatives to combat disinformation.
- **Strategy:** Allocate specific budgets for teacher training, the purchase of teaching tools, and the development of educational resources. Governments can also provide grants to schools to implement MIL programs.

5.2 International Collaboration

- **Recommendation:** As the fight against disinformation is a global challenge, governments should encourage international collaboration to share best practices, resources, and innovations in media education.

  Strategy: Participate in international initiatives such as UNESCO conferences on media education, and encourage exchanges between schools in different countries to promote a global understanding of issues related to disinformation.

5.3 Implementation of Regulatory Policies

- **Recommendation:** Policymakers should establish regulations that promote the transparency of digital platforms and protect citizens against misinformation. These policies should include obligations for social media companies to monitor and moderate content on their platforms.
- **Strategy:** Collaborate with technology companies to develop more sophisticated algorithms and ensure content moderation practices are transparent and fair.

6. Educational Resources and Supports

6.1 Educational Guides

- **Resource 1: Primary Media Literacy Guide**
- Content: Activity booklets, lesson plans, and educational games to introduce elementary school students to the basic concepts of verifying information.
- **Resource 2: Misinformation Workbook for Middle School**
- Content: Workbooks, case studies, and educational videos designed for middle school students, with a focus on critical analysis of social media.

6.2 Technological Tools

- **Resource 3: Fake News Analyzer**
- Features: An artificial intelligence tool for real-time verification of the veracity of online information, designed for use in the classroom and for research projects.
- **Resource 4: NewsGuard Browser Extension**
- Features: A browser extension that assesses the credibility of news sites and helps students identify reliable sources.

6.3 Videos and Multimedia Content

- **Resource 5: Educational Video Series on Disinformation**
- Content: A series of videos designed to raise awareness among students of the dangers of fake news, with examples from current events and interviews with experts.
- **Resource 6: Interactive Simulations**
- Content: Online simulations that allow students to understand how fake news spreads on social networks and to experiment with strategies to counter it.

7. Evaluation and Monitoring

7.1 Monitoring Student Progress

- **Strategy:** Implement regular assessments to measure students' skills in fact-checking, critical thinking, and media comprehension. The results of these evaluations will be used to adjust the program and identify additional training needs.

7.2 Feedback from Teachers and Students

- **Strategy:** Collect regular feedback from teachers and students to evaluate the effectiveness of the resources and methods used. This feedback will be analyzed to make continuous improvements to the educational program.

7.3 Annual Report on Media Literacy

- **Strategy:** Publish an annual report that assesses the state of media education in schools, identifies successes and challenges, and offers recommendations for the future. This report will serve as a reference for policy makers, school administrators, and teachers.

4. Bibliography

Introduction: The Importance of a Comprehensive Bibliography

In the context of a work as complex as that dedicated to understanding and combating disinformation, an exhaustive bibliography is essential to provide solid references, allowing readers to deepen their knowledge and verify the sources of the information presented . This bibliographic section compiles a wide range of resources, including academic books, scientific journal articles, government reports, case studies, and online resources, which cover the various aspects of disinformation, from education to media, and digital literacy.

Bibliography

1. Academic Works

1.1 Books on Disinformation and Media Manipulation

- **Benkler, Y., Faris, R., & Roberts, H. (2018).** *Network Propaganda: Manipulation, Disinformation, and Radicalization in American Politics.* Oxford University Press.

- This work analyzes how social media networks and online platforms have radically transformed the American political landscape, facilitating the spread of disinformation.
- **Allcott, H., & Gentzkow, M. (2017).** *Social Media and Fake News in the 2016 Election.* Journal of Economic Perspectives, 31(2), 211-236.

- An in-depth study on the impact of fake news broadcast on social networks during the 2016 American presidential election.
- **Wardle, C., & Derakhshan, H. (2017).** *Information Disorder: Toward an Interdisciplinary Framework for Research and Policy Making.* Council of Europe.

- This report provides a framework for understanding information disorder, identifying the different types of false information and the mechanisms by which they spread.

1.2 Books on Media Literacy and Digital Literacy

- **Hobbs, R. (2010).** *Digital and Media Literacy: Connecting Culture and Classroom.* Corwin.
- A comprehensive guide to integrating media literacy into classrooms, with practical strategies for teaching digital literacy and combatting misinformation.
- **Koltay, T. (2011).** *The Media and the Literacies: Media Literacy, Information Literacy, Digital Literacy.* Communications in Computer and Information Science, 96, 21-29.
- An overview of the different literacies needed in today's digital world, with particular focus on the ability to analyze and evaluate information online.

1.3 Studies on the Psychological Impact of Misinformation

- **Pennycook, G., & Rand, D.G. (2019).** *The Implied Truth Effect: Attaching Warnings to a Subset of Fake News Stories Increases Perceived Accuracy of Stories without Warnings.* Management Science, 66(11), 4944-4957.
- A study that examines how adding warnings on fake news can paradoxically increase the credibility of stories without warnings.
- **Lewandowsky, S., Ecker, UKH, & Cook, J. (2017).** *Beyond Misinformation: Understanding and Coping with the Post-Truth Era.* Journal of Applied Research in Memory and Cognition, 6(4), 353-369.
- This work explores the psychological effects of misinformation and strategies for dealing with it in a post-truth environment.

2. Scientific Journal Articles

2.1 Empirical Studies on Disinformation

- **Vosoughi, S., Roy, D., & Aral, S. (2018).** *The Spread of True and False News Online.* Science, 359(6380), 1146-1151.
- A seminal article that analyzes the spread of real and fake news on Twitter, revealing that fake news spreads faster and more widely than real news.
- **Lazer, DMJ, Baum, MA, Grinberg, N., et al. (2018).** *The Science of Fake News.* Science, 359(6380), 1094-1096.
- This article proposes a scientific approach to understanding and combatting misinformation, emphasizing the importance of interdisciplinary collaborations.

2.2 Research on Cognitive Bias and Misinformation

- **Nyhan, B., & Reifler, J. (2010).** *When Corrections Fail: The Persistence of Political Misperceptions.* Political Behavior, 32(2), 303-330.
- A study of how false belief corrections can sometimes reinforce erroneous beliefs, a phenomenon known as the boomerang effect.
- **Pennycook, G., & Rand, D.G. (2018).** *The Implied Truth Effect: When Corrections Decrease Belief in False Claims but Fail to Increase Belief in True Ones.* Journal of Experimental Psychology: General, 147(3), 381-393.
- This article explores how corrections of misinformation can influence readers' perceptions, reducing belief in false claims without necessarily increasing belief in true ones.

2.3 Impact of Social Media on the Spread of Disinformation

- **Bakshy, E., Messing, S., & Adamic, L.A. (2015).** *Exposure to Ideologically Diverse News and Opinion on Facebook.* Science, 348(6239), 1130-1132.
- This study analyzes how exposure to ideologically diverse content on Facebook influences users' opinions.
- **Tucker, JA, Guess, A., Barbera, P., et al. (2018).** *Social Media, Political Polarization, and Political Disinformation: A Review of the Scientific Literature.* Political Science Research and Methods, 6(2), 231-237.
- A review of the scientific literature on the effects of social media on political polarization and the spread of disinformation.

3. Reports and Case Studies

3.1 Disinformation Campaign Reports

- **European Commission (2018).** *A Multi-Dimensional Approach to Disinformation: Report of the Independent High-Level Group on Fake News and Online Disinformation.*
- This report from the European Commission offers recommendations for combating disinformation online, based on an analysis of the different strategies used in disinformation campaigns.
- **US Senate Intelligence Committee (2019).** *Russian Active Measures Campaigns and Interference in the 2016 US Election: Volume 2: Russia's Use of Social Media with Additional Views.*
- A report detailing the techniques used by Russia to interfere in the 2016 US presidential election via social media.

3.2 Case Studies on Misinformation during Health Crises

- **World Health Organization (2020).** *Managing the COVID-19 Infodemic: Promoting Healthy Behaviors and Mitigating the Harm from Misinformation and Disinformation.*
- A case study on managing the infodemic linked to the COVID-19 pandemic, with recommendations to limit the impact of misinformation on public health.
- **Centers for Disease Control and Prevention (2020).** *COVID-19 Disinformation Campaigns: A Case Study of Russian Interference.*
- A CDC report on how foreign actors have exploited the health crisis to spread misinformation and sow confusion.

4. Digital Resources and Online Tools

4.1 Databases and Fact-Checking Platforms

- **FactCheck.org** : An online resource that checks the accuracy of public statements, including those from politicians and media organizations. A valuable resource for teachers and students wanting to practice fact-checking.

- **PolitiFact** : A fact-checking site that evaluates the veracity of statements made by American political figures. Used in many classrooms to teach fact checking.

- **Snopes.com** : One of the oldest fact-checking sites, Snopes checks a wide range of rumors and misinformation, and is widely used for media education.

4.2 Technological Tools for Fact-Checking

- **NewsGuard** : A browser extension that rates the credibility of news sites, used to teach critical evaluation of online sources.

- **Google Fact Check Explorer** : A Google tool that allows you to search for fact-checking articles from various organizations around the world.

5. Conferences and Study Days

5.1 Annual Conferences on Disinformation

- **Global Fact-Checking Summit** : Organized by the International Fact-Checking Network, this conference brings together fact-checkers, journalists, and educators to discuss challenges and innovations in the field of fact-checking.

- **Conference on Disinformation and Propaganda** : An academic conference that explores the various aspects of disinformation, including its effects on politics and society.

5.2 Workshops and Training

- **First Draft News Training Workshops** : Training workshops offered by First Draft for journalists and educators focused on detecting and verifying fake news.

- **UNESCO Media and Information Literacy (MIL) Workshops** : Workshops organized by UNESCO to train educators in the integration of media and information literacy into school curricula.

6. Educational and Documentary Videos

6.1 Documentaries on Disinformation

- **"The Social Dilemma" (2020).** Directed by Jeff Orlowski. A documentary that explores the impact of social media on society and how it can be used to manipulate opinions and spread misinformation.

- **"After Truth: Disinformation and the Cost of Fake News" (2020).** Directed by Andrew Rossi. This documentary examines the real-world consequences of disinformation, focusing on specific examples in the United States.

6.2 Educational Video Series

- **"Crash Course: Media Literacy" (2018).** Produced by PBS Digital Studios. A series of educational videos that explain key media literacy concepts, including misinformation and fact-checking techniques.

- **"Fact-Checking Explained" (2020).** Produced by The Poynter Institute. A series of videos that explain how fact-checking works, with concrete examples and expert interviews.

7. Organizations and Initiatives

7.1 Professional Associations and Networks

- **International Fact-Checking Network (IFCN)** : A global network of fact-checkers that establishes fact-checking standards and promotes the exchange of best practices among fact-checking organizations.

- **Reporters Without Borders (RSF)** : An international organization that defends press freedom and fights against disinformation around the world.

7.2 Government Programs

- **Digital, Culture, Media and Sport Committee (UK Parliament).** *Disinformation and 'Fake News': Final Report.* 2018.
- A report from the UK Parliament on how disinformation affects society and what action is needed to combat it.
- **The European Digital Media Observatory (EDMO)** : A European Union initiative that brings together media experts, researchers, and fact-checkers to monitor disinformation and promote media literacy.

8. Case Studies and Practical Examples

•

8.1 Historical Case Studies

> **"The Propaganda Model: Manufacturing Consent"** by Noam Chomsky and Edward S. Herman, 1988.

- This case study explores how mass media can be used to manipulate public opinion, creating "manufactured consent" to support elite interests.
- **"Operation INFEKTION: The KGB's Secret Campaign to Infect the World with AntiAmerican Fake News"** by Thomas Rid, 2020.

- A detailed analysis of the KGB's disinformation campaign during the Cold War, which spread false information to damage the image of the United States.

8.2 Fact Checking Examples

- **"PolitiFact's 2016 Lie of the Year"** : A fact-checking case study from PolitiFact, which named the False Claim of the Year in 2016. This study shows how fake news can be unmasked and its impact minimized.

- **"BBC Reality Check: Fact-Checking Brexit Claims"** : An example of how the BBC used fact-checking to clarify misleading claims made during the Brexit campaign.

5. Miscellaneous Appendices (Examples of Documents, Activities)

Introduction: The Importance of Appendices in Media Literacy

The various appendices provide concrete examples, sample documents, and practical activities that are essential for the application of the theoretical concepts discussed in previous chapters. These appendices are designed to be used directly in the classroom or as part of teacher training. They cover a range of educational activities, document templates, and resources that can be adapted for different grade levels, from elementary to high school.

Miscellaneous Appendices: Examples of Documents and Activities

1. Examples of Teaching Documents

1.1 Disinformation Lesson Plan Template

Title : *Understanding and Analyzing Disinformation*

Objectives:

- Understand the concepts of disinformation, misinformation, and malinformation.
- Identify techniques commonly used to manipulate information.
- Develop critical analysis and fact-checking skills.

Duration: 2 hours

Materials:

- Computers with Internet access
- Projector and screen
- Copies of articles selected for analysis
- Access to online fact-checking tools **Introduction (15 minutes):**

> Presentation of key concepts: disinformation, misinformation, and misinformation.

- Open discussion: Recent examples of false information in the media.

Activity 1: Analysis of an Article (30 minutes):

- Students are divided into groups and given an article to analyze.
- Each group should identify potentially misleading elements in the article.
- Group discussion on the manipulation techniques identified (sensationalist headlines, false quotes, etc.).

Activity 2: Fact Checking (30 minutes):

- Students use fact-checking tools to verify the accuracy of information in the article.
- Each group presents their findings to the class.

Conclusion (15 minutes):

- A look back at lessons learned and a discussion on the importance of fact-checking.
- Homework: Find another article online and verify it using the tools learned in class.

1.2 Model Questionnaire for Assessing Student Understanding

Title : *Assessing Understanding of Misinformation*

Objective: Measure students' understanding of the concepts of disinformation and their ability to identify and analyze false information.

Instructions: Answer the following questions based on what you learned in class.

1. What is disinformation?

- a) The unintentional dissemination of false information.
- b) The deliberate dissemination of false information to deceive or manipulate.
- c) A transcription error in a press article.
- d) None of the above.

2. What is the difference between disinformation and misinformation?

3. Give an example of a common technique used to manipulate information.

4. What tools can you use to verify the veracity of information found online? Name at least two tools.

5. Analyze the following headline: "Researchers discover miracle cure for cancer". Identify elements that could indicate manipulation of information.

6. Why is it important to check the facts before sharing information on social media?

1.3 Sample Letter to Parents on Media Education

Object : *Media and Information Literacy (MIL) Program – Letter to Parents* Dear parents,

As part of our commitment to providing a comprehensive education relevant to our times, we are pleased to inform you that our establishment is implementing a new Media and Information Literacy (MIL) program. This program aims to develop in our students essential skills to navigate in a world where information is omnipresent, but where it is sometimes difficult to discern fact from falsehood.

Media education is more important than ever, because it allows young people to develop critical thinking about the information they encounter, particularly on social networks. We'll cover a variety of topics, such as fact-checking, analyzing news sources, and understanding manipulation techniques used in the media.

We encourage you to discuss with your children what they are learning in class and ask them questions about the topics covered. Together, we can help them become informed and responsible citizens. Sincerely,

[Name of teacher]
[School name]

2. Practical Activities for Students

2.1 Activity: Detecting Fake News

Objective: Teach students to identify false information online.

Level: College/High School

Duration: 1 hour

Materials:

- Access to computers/tablets with Internet
- Online fact-checking tools
- Worksheets for recording results **Instructions:**

a.1.   **Introduction (10 minutes):** Explain to students the typical signs of fake news (sensationalist headlines, dubious sources, etc.).

a.2.   **Research (20 minutes):** Divide students into groups and ask them to find an article online that they think is fake news.

a.3.   **Analysis (20 minutes):** Use fact-checking tools to analyze the chosen article.

a.4.   **Discussion (10 minutes):** Each group presents their results and explains why the chosen article is fake news.

2.2 Activity: Create an Awareness Campaign

Objective: Raise awareness among other students about misinformation by creating an awareness campaign. **Level:** High school **Duration:** 2 hours **Materials:**

- Computers with graphic design software (e.g.: Canva, Adobe Spark)
- Printing materials (for posters)
- Access to social media platforms (optional) **Instructions:**

a.1.   **Introduction (15 minutes):** Discuss the different types of awareness campaigns and their importance.

a.2.   **Creation (1 hour):** Students, in groups, create an awareness campaign (posters, videos, publications on social networks) against misinformation.

a.3.   **Presentation (45 minutes):** Each group presents their campaign to the rest of the class, explaining the design choices and the message to be conveyed.

2.3 Activity: Simulation of a Fact-Checking Survey

Objective: Teach students to conduct a complete fact-checking investigation.

Level: Middle/High School

Duration: 1 hour 30 minutes

Materials:

- Fictitious investigation file containing articles, videos, and quotes
- Internet access for fact-checking
- Worksheets for Recording Findings **Instructions:**

a.1. **Introduction (15 minutes):** Introduce the mock survey and the objectives of the activity.

a.2. **Investigation (45 minutes):** Students, in small groups, review the investigation file and use online tools to verify each piece of information.

a.3. **Report (30 minutes):** Each group writes a detailed investigation report and presents it to the class, highlighting which information is verified and which is false or questionable.

3. Examples of Fake News Analyzer Usage Scenarios

3.1 Scenario: Real-Time Verification of a Press Article

Objective: Teach students to use the Fake News Analyzer to quickly verify information. **Level:** High school **Duration:** 1 hour **Materials:**

- Computers or tablets with Fake News Analyzer installed
- Access to a selection of online press articles **Instructions:**

a.1. **Introduction (10 minutes):** Present the Fakes News Analyzer tool and how it works.

a.2. **Article Selection (10 minutes):** Each student chooses a recent press article that he/she would like to check.

a.3. **Verification (30 minutes):** Students use the Fake News Analyzer to analyze the chosen article, noting questionable elements and the results of the analysis.

a.4. **Discussion (10 minutes):** Students share their results and discuss the effectiveness of the tool.

3.2 Scenario: Analysis of a Disinformation Video

Objective: Teach students to identify signs of manipulation in online videos.

Level: High school

Duration: 1 hour 30 minutes

Materials:

- Access to videos selected for the activity
- Fake News analyzer with video analysis module

Instructions :

a.1. **Introduction (15 minutes):** Discuss the manipulation techniques commonly used in disinformation videos (misleading editing, manipulated voiceover, etc.).

a.2. **Video Analysis (45 minutes):** Students analyze a video using the Fake News Analyzer, identifying manipulated segments and explaining why they are misleading.

a.3. **Presentation (30 minutes):** Students present their analyzes to the class, detailing the manipulation techniques discovered and the verification methods used.

4. Examples of Class Projects

4.1 Project: Create a Fact-Checking Website

Objective: To encourage students to use their fact-checking skills to create a website dedicated to combating misinformation.

Level: High school

Duration: Project over 4 weeks

Materials:

- Computers with website creation software (e.g. WordPress, Wix)
- Internet access
- Online fact-checking tools **Instructions:**

a.1.   **Planning (1 week):** Students, in groups, plan the structure of their website, choose the themes to address (politics, health, environment, etc.), and define the roles of each member of the group.

a.2.   **Research and Verification (2 weeks):** Students search for articles, videos, and images to verify, use fact-checking tools to validate information, and write articles for their site.

a.3.   **Creation of the Website (1 week):** Students upload their content to the website, add interactive features, and ensure that the site is accessible and easy to use.

a.4.   **Final Presentation:** Each group presents their website to the class, explains the fact-checking process used, and discusses the potential impact of their site on the target audience.

4.2 Project: Organize a Public Debate on Disinformation

Objective: Develop students' argumentation skills and raise awareness of misinformation in the school community.

Level: High school

Duration: Project over 3 weeks

Materials:

- Access to online research resources
- Presentation tools (PowerPoint, Keynote)
- Meeting room with sound system **Instructions:**

a.1.   **Preparatory Research (1 week):** Students, in groups, choose topics related to disinformation (impact of fake news on politics, role of social networks, etc.) and carry out in-depth research to support their arguments.

a.2.   **Preparation for the Debate (1 week):** Students develop their arguments, prepare presentations, and rehearse their interventions.

a.3.   **Public Debate (1 week):** The debate is organized in the school, with an audience made up of other students, parents, and teachers. Students present their arguments, answer questions from the audience, and a jury (made up of teachers) evaluates the performances.

a.4.   **Review and Reflection:** After the debate, students reflect on the lessons learned and discuss the importance of argumentation based on verified facts.

5. Presentation and Visual Aids Templates

5.1 Disinformation PowerPoint Presentation Template

Title : *Understanding and Combating Disinformation*

Slide 1: Introduction

- Definition of disinformation, misinformation, and misinformation.

- Importance of media education.

Slide 2: Disinformation Techniques

- Examples of techniques: deepfakes, sensationalist headlines, out-of-context quotes.
- Recent case studies.

Slide 3: Fact Checking Tools

- Introduction to the Fake News Analyzer.
- Other online tools (Snopes, PolitiFact, etc.).

Slide 4: Practical Activities

- Introducing fact-checking activities for students.
- Expected results and skills developed.

Slide 5: Conclusion

- Importance of fact-checking in today's society.
- Call to action to become informed and responsible citizens. **5.2 Poster Template for**

Disinformation Awareness Title: *Don't Believe Everything You Read!*

Slogan: *Before you share, check!*

Content :

- A graphic illustrating the steps of fact-checking (finding the source, using fact-checking tools, verifying the author).
- Examples of debunked fake news.
- Information on available verification tools.

Footnote: *Join us in the fight against misinformation. Visit [Website Name] for more information.*

6. Resources for Teachers

6.1 Practical Guide to Teaching Fact-Checking

Introduction: The importance of fact-checking in modern education.

Epilogue

In a world where information circulates at lightning speed, the fight against disinformation has become a necessity to preserve the truth and integrity of our societies. This guide explored the multiple facets of disinformation, from historical origins to contemporary digital challenges. By understanding the mechanisms of information manipulation and adopting rigorous verification strategies, each of us can become an actor of the truth.

But the fight against disinformation does not end here. It requires constant vigilance, ongoing education and collective commitment to promote a culture of critical thinking. Technology will continue to evolve, and with it, handling methods will become more sophisticated. It is therefore essential that we stay informed, that we share the tools and knowledge acquired, and that we defend the truth together. Ultimately, the fight against disinformation is a fight for the future of our democracies and our freedom of expression. This guide is just a starting point, an invitation to deepen your knowledge and join the fight for honest and transparent information.

Biography of Cédric Balcon-Hermand

Cédric Balcon-Hermand is an author passionate about exploring the dynamics of truth in the digital age. Having published several works, he focuses on themes ranging from disinformation to personal introspection through initiatory journeys.

Published works:

1. **In My Dreams: Initiatory Journey** - An exploratory story that combines introspection and self-quest.
2. **Cédric Hebdo - June** - A captivating series that offers an overview of the author's monthly reflections.
3. **In my dreams: Initiatory Journey of Etheria** - A sequel that deepens the themes of spiritual quest and personal discovery.

His latest work, **"Understanding and Combating Disinformation"** , is a continuation of his commitment to fair and verified information, offering tools for navigating a world saturated with false information.